New Orleans

Bethany Ewald Bultman
Photography by Richard Sexton
and Syndey Byrd

COMPASS AMERICAN GUIDES
An Imprint of Fodor's Travel Publications, Inc.

New Orleans

Copyright © 1998 Fodor's Travel Publications, Inc.
Maps Copyright © 1998 Fodor's Travel Publications, Inc.

LIBRARY OF CONGRESS CATALOGING-IN-PUBLICATION DATA
Bultman, Bethany Ewald
New Orleans/Bethany Ewald Bultman; photography by Richard Sexton and
    Syndey Byrd—3rd Ed.
    p. cm. – (Compass American Guides)
    Includes bibliographical references and index
    ISBN 0-679-03597-4
    1. New Orleans (La.) — Guidebooks. I. Sexton, Richard.
    II. Byrd, Syndey III. Title. IV. Series: Compass American Guides (series)
    F379.N53B85   1997   97-33361
    917.63'350463—dc21   CIP

Editors: Kit Duane, Julia Dillon, Jessica Fisher   Designers: Christopher Burt, David Hurst
Managing Editor: Kit Duane   Map Design: Eureka Cartography
Photo Editor: Christopher Burt
Compass American Guides, 5332 College Avenue, Suite 201, Oakland, CA 94618
Production house: Twin Age Ltd., Hong Kong   Printed in China

10 9 8 7 6 5 4 3 2 1

COMPASS AMERICAN GUIDES gratefully acknowledges the following institutions and individuals: Photographs ©Richard Sexton, except as noted. ©Syndey Byrd, cover, pp. 18, 19, 107, 110-111, 112, 120, 159, 163, 166, 167, 170, 171, 175, 177, 180, 181, 196, 197, 200, 208, 212, 213 (both), 238; Michael P. Smith, pp. 67, 83, 145, 183, 194, 201-207, 210-212, 219, 231, 246; Historic New Orleans Collection, pp. 11, 27, 30-31, 32, 35, 40, 41, 45, 46, 48, 49, 51, 58, 61, 62, 69-71, 77, 89, 104, 121, 139, 141, 144, 149, 150, 153, 174, 223, 224; New Orleans Museum of Art, musem purchase, p. 155; Porché West, p. 23; Underwood Archives, pp. 53, 55; The Louisiana State Museum, p. 65; Hogan Jazz Archive, Tulane University, pp. 73, 189, 191, 192, 198; Sharon Dinkins Collection, Inc., 59462 Neslo Rd., Slidell, LA 70460, pp. 78, 221, 234; Eric Lassing, Art Resource/NY, p. 106; The Maryland Historical Society, p. 186. All hotel and plantation pictures courtesy of institutions covered. Thanks also to Dan Duane for his piece on Audubon; Bernard Guste of Antoine's for his alligator story; Sara Deseran, Debi Dunn, and Julie Searle for her meticulous fact-checking; Kelly Mays for line editing; Howard Tilton Memorial Library at Tulane University for access to Helen d'Aquin Allain's memoirs; Kit Duane for Louis Henderson's memoirs; Alice Dillon for help on voodoo and Mardi Gras Indian sections.

To my parents, who first shared New Orleans with me.
To my husband and sons who make living here such a joy.

C O N T E N T S

Maps

Getting into the spirit of New Orleans. (Syndey Byrd)

ACKNOWLEDGMENTS

MY HEARTFELT THANKS to Kit Duane, Julia Dillon, and Tobias Steed of Compass for making the research, writing, and editing of this book such a pleasurable process; to photographers and friends, Syndey Byrd and Richard Sexton; to my assistant, Evelyn Feagin for the stacks of notes she had to decipher; and to my son Gwyther for logging information. Thanks also to my patient agent John Ware, my versatile husband, Johann, my clever little chef Tristan and the hours and hours that Zachary Richard, Maria Maldaur, and The Neville Brothers spent singing to keep me awake and working.

I'm also grateful for the invaluable support and assistance of Jason Berry, Inez Douglas, Gwen Carter, Chief Larry Bannock, Charmaine Neville, Vaughn Banting, Lucy Burnett, Julie Smith, Dorian and Kell Bennett, Marguerite Oestricher, Leah Chase, Miki DeJean, Chef Kevin Graham, Michael Llewelyn, Bernard Guste, Macon Riddle, Roxy Wright, Mari Kornhauser, Bess Carrick, Andrea Hanson and Bill Carr, Alexandra Stafford Rathle, Brian Savagar, and Nita Wilson.

To those gracious guardians of New Orleans's historic treasures and present resources, I owe my deep appreciation. They are: Dr. Alfred Lemmon, John Magill, Elsa Schneider, and Pamela Arceneaux at the Historic New Orleans Collection; the Special Collections at Tulane University; Dr. Fred Steilow and the late Ulysses Ricard at the Amistad Research Center; Beverly Gianna and Anthony Leggio, Jr. of the Greater New Orleans Tourist and Convention Commission; Simone Rathle-Enlow; Britton Trice of the Garden District Bookshop; Marsha Underwood of the New Orleans Jazz & Heritage Foundation; and Nancy Marinovic, President of Enplanar, Inc.

Many thanks to those who helped in the fact-checking process, especially Dr. Bruce Boyd Raeburn of the Hogan Jazz Archives, Lucy Core, the staff of the Louisiana Collection of the New Orleans Public Library, the Louisiana Landmarks Society, the Preservation Resource Center, David Johnson of the Louisiana Endowment for the Humanities.

Thanks also to Rob Boyd and Kevin Woo, Eddie Breaux, Mark Cooper and Hilary Ivin at the Vieux Carré Commission, Louis Edwards at the New Orleans Jazz & Heritage Festival, Deb Wehmeyer at Garden District Books.

Eating beignets at Café du Monde in the 1940s. (Historic New Orleans Collection)

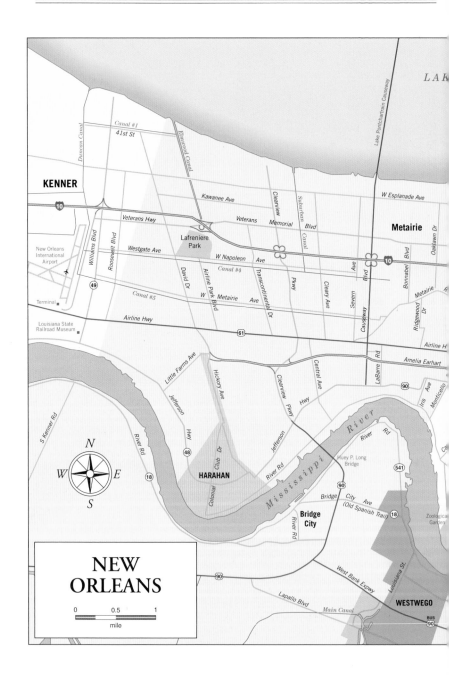

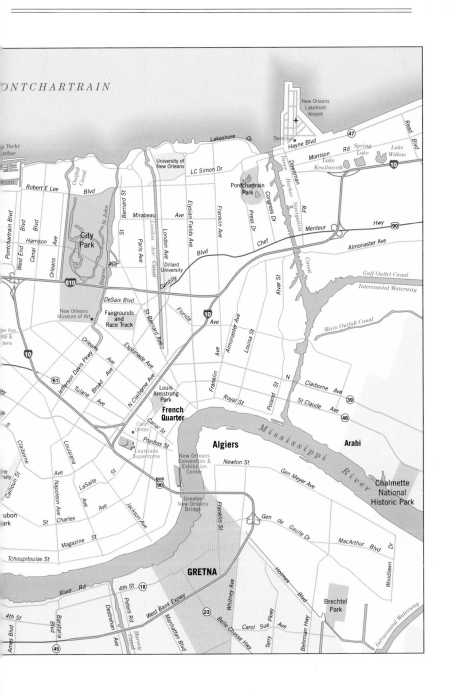

PONTCHARTRAIN

New Orleans Lakefront Airport

Lakeshore Dr

Terminal

Hayne Blvd

47

Read Blvd

University of New Orleans

LC Simon Dr

Morrison Rd

Spring Lake

Lake Willow

Inner Harbor Navigation

Downman Rd

Lake Kenilworth

10

Pontchartrain Park

Congress Dr

Press Dr

Robert E Lee Blvd

Outfall Canal

Bernard St

Mirabeau

London Ave

Ave

Elysian Fields Ave

Franklin Ave

Chef

Menteur

Hwy

90

Pontchartrain Blvd

West End Blvd

Canal Blvd

Orleans Ave

Harrison Ave

City Park

St John

Paris Ave

London Ave Canal

Blvd

Almonaster Ave

y Yacht rbor

610

Dillard University

Gentilly

Canal

Gulf Outlet Canal

Intercoastal Waterway

DeSaix Blvd

Alvar St

New Orleans Museum of Art

Fairgrounds and Race Track

St Bernard Ave

Florida

10

Ave

Almonaster Ave

Louisa St

Main Outfall Canal

e Vue se & dens

10

Orleans

Ave

Esplanade Ave

N Claiborne Ave

Franklin

Ave

N St

Claiborne Ave

39

61

Jefferson Davis Pkwy

Tulane

Broad

Ave

Ave

Louis Armstrong Park

Royal St

Poland St

St Claude Ave

46

French Quarter

Civic Center

Canal St

Poydras St

Louisiana Superdome

New Orleans Convention & Exhibition Center

Algiers

Newton St

Mississippi River

Arabi

Chalmette National Historic Park

Claiborne St

Louisiana

Ave

Calhoun St

LaSalle Ave

Ave

Jackson Ave

BUS 90

Greater New Orleans Bridge

Gen Meyer Ave

ne sity

Napoleon Ave

St Charles Ave

Franklin St

Gen de Gaulle Dr

MacArthur Blvd

Woodlawn Dr

ubon ark

Magazine St

Tchoupitoulas St

GRETNA

River Rd

4th St

18

West Bank Expwy

Whitney Ave

Holmes Blvd

Brechtel Park

Intracoastal Waterway

4th St

Ames Blvd

Barataria Blvd

Destrehan Ave

Peters Rd

Harvey Canal

Manhattan Blvd

45

23

Belle Chasse Hwy

Carol Sue Ave

Terry Pkwy

Behrman Hwy

O V E R V I E W

HISTORY
New Orleans has a history as rich as crawfish bisque. Its sovereignty passed through the hands of the French and Spanish, then escaped the British before being secured by the Yankees (who briefly lost it to Dixie). Far from being a typical Southern city, New Orleans boasts a one-of-a-kind society, where Old World aristocracy meets New World grit, and an exuberant culture percolates on every street corner.

THE FRENCH QUARTER
The heart and soul of the city may be found along the streets of the Vieux Carré, New Orleans oldest and most intriguing neighborhood. Bourbon Street, Jackson Square, Preservation Hall, and block after block of cast-iron balconies, brick cottages, and music clubs conspire to make this the city's most visited area.

THE GARDEN DISTRICT
In the mid-19th century, New Orleans' American citizens—many newly rich from sugar and cotton—called this area their home. Take a ride on the St. Charles Avenue streetcar or a walk through the Lower Garden District to see the innovative work of architects who incorporated wrought iron, columns, Mediterranean pastels, and all manner of eclectic design elements into these Greek Revival mansions.

CARNIVAL & MARDI GRAS

To anyone who loves a good time, New Orleans and Mardi Gras are synonymous. Carnival, the festive season preceding Mardi Gras—literally Fat Tuesday, the last gasp before Lent—culminates in a raucous four-day weekend of costume parties, society balls, and dozens of float-filled parades. The entire city and countless visitors participate in this centuries-old tradition of no-holds-barred revelry and masquerade.

BIRTHPLACE OF JAZZ

Since the invention of ragtime and Dixieland, New Orleans has been America's music hotspot. Natives like Jelly Roll Morton, Louis Armstrong, Mahalia Jackson, Fats Domino, and the Neville and the Marsalis brothers made jazz, blues, gospel, and R&B *happen*. Cajun and zydeco music made their national debuts here, too. Today, rhythms spill from clubs at all hours, and Jazz Fest—a 10-day showcase in late April—is almost as popular as Mardi Gras.

UNPARALLELED CUISINE

New Orleans' truly distinct cuisine interweaves two unique cooking traditions: Creole and Cajun. Born of many traditions —classic French, West African, Spanish, Italian, German, Indian—savory Creole dishes include crawfish etouffée and jambalaya. Cajun cooks add fire to the mix with dishes like blackened fish and peppery gumbo. Breakfast here means café au lait with chicory and sugary beignets.

Citizens' Bank of **Louisiana**

Will pay **TEN DOLLARS** to the bearer
on demand New Orleans,   186

CASHIER.   PRESIDENT.

INTRODUCTION

THE NAME NEW ORLEANS invariably conjures up the succulent aroma of sweet olive, the syncopation of jazz and ceiling fans, and the vision of black-haired, magnolia-fleshed damsels fanning themselves as they sit in white wicker chairs on lacy wrought-iron verandas. La Nouvelle Orleans was the original Dixie, named in the mid-19th century by the hell-raising Kentucky flatboatmen who traded their merchandise in the city for the *dix* or $10 paper tender minted in New Orleans. Though geographically Southern (Rhett Butler brought Scarlett O'Hara to New Orleans for their honeymoon), it is not a garden-variety Southern city in the sense of Richmond, Memphis, Savannah, or Montgomery. It is more of a Caribbean port city, anchored in the continental United States by what often seems a mere socio-geographical accident.

An hour before dawn, the French Quarter becomes mantled in timelessness. The shimmer of streetlights is reflected on cobbled sidewalks dampened by gentle mist. The cries of a trumpet commingle with a few bluesy chords from Luther Kent's finale in the dying hours. On the swollen Mississippi, giant tankers quietly slip down the river towards the open mouth of the Gulf. For a few moments the dull roar of their engines is drowned out by the clanging bell of the riverfront street-car, which beckons a handful of the night shift from a late-night restaurant. They have stopped to savor conversation, thick chicory-laced coffee, and *beignets* (New Orleans' famous doughnuts) en route to their beds Uptown. A few blocks down-river, at the 200-year-old French Market, the produce vendors lean against the dull green fender of a Ford pick-up as they sing along with Fats Domino on the radio.

New Orleans is an archipelago of ethnicity. Tuning in to WWOZ, the New Orleans Jazz & Heritage Foundation jazz station; sucking the spicy juice from the head of a crawfish at an open-air seafood joint; taking a ride on the Algiers ferry at dawn: these are a few of the things that locals and visitors savor as they enjoy this twinkle in the eye of the old Protestant American South. The sensuous and exotic street names of Elysian Fields, Bourbon, Erato, and Desire bespeak a society that is not unsympathetic to the weaknesses of the flesh. William Faulkner once said of the city that it is "a place created for and by voluptuousness, the abashness and un-abashed senses."

The term "Dixie" originated from the "dix" note ($10) minted in New Orleans.

Culture in New Orleans spews from the ground up and is carried away to intoxicate the rest of the world. The city's sultry environs have served as the fertile foundation for the backstreet movers and shakers whose thunder is heard in the worlds of music and food. It is the hometown of a potpourri of celebrities whose talents were fostered in any number of the city's ethno-cultural enclaves: from the queen of gospel Mahalia Jackson, to the darling of New York cafe society, Harry Connick, Jr.; from international opera star Marguerite Piazza to diet guru Richard Simmons; from R&B legend Fats Domino to Emmy Award–winning actor John Larroquette; from renowned musician Wynton Marsalis to writer Anne Rice.

New Orleanians prefer to see themselves as part of a festival of cultures. There are more facets to the city's multi-culturalism than there are varieties of hot sauce in a local grocery store. New Orleans is a place where people from all walks of life smile or nod when they pass strangers on the street. People encountering each other on a public bus or streetcar more than three times may feel like they're close enough friends to share a grandmother's recipe for bread pudding.

The ambiance and magic of New Orleans is impossible to appreciate at a fast clip. It is a city that gladly relinquishes its secrets to those who take the time to

Fats Domino (above) and Kid Thomas Valentine (right), legendary New Orleans musicians. (Syndey Byrd)

wander. For those who have only a short time between meetings, parades, concerts, or meals, the best thing to do would be to see one area thoroughly, preferably on foot. New Orleans is a loosely connected amalgam of neighborhoods, many of which still have their own curbside vegetable wagons, at least three snowball stands, 10 or so corner bars, a half-dozen combination po-boy sandwich/grocery stores, and a smattering of folks who pass the day stoop-sitting and visitin' with all those who pass and savor the aroma that drifts out of their kitchens.

In the older residential districts from Faubourg Marigny to the Irish Channel, each street is a visual delight as one shotgun-style house gives way to another. Some are weathered down to the bare cypress boards, others shine with color as vividly as Easter eggs. Houses that are essentially wood-frame shoeboxes have been tarted up with ornamental scrolls, brackets, shutters, hanging ferns, the occasional balustrade, and porch swings whose creaking chains and rusty springs attest to three generations of "swingers."

It's possible to spend an entire week in the French Quarter, another wandering through the Garden District and browsing through the antique and junk shops along Magazine Street, and a third enjoying the Uptown area, Audubon Park, and the zoo. The problem is that stepping into any of these areas is much like falling into visual quicksand for the aficionado of architecture and local culture. New Orleans is a city that never quite gives up all of her mysteries. Each trip to a certain street provides just one more layer in a multifaceted and often contradictory paradise of funk and splendor.

New Orleans is fueled by diversity. Its neighborhoods are a Crayola box of bright, intense, ethnic influences. On any Friday, old-line businessmen gather at noon at Galatoire's to dip their crusty French bread in the butter sauce just as their grandfathers once did. The people who live in the mansions on St. Charles Avenue are just as likely as those in half of a shotgun-style house in Gert Town to tune in to WWOZ as they drive to work, or to take their kids to watch the bonfires on the levee Christmas Eve. On Monday nights, historically wash day, most families from the Garden District to Chalmette will sit down to a supper of red beans and rice, just as their ancestors did. All households want to own their own shopping cart for household chores. A little girl might make her First Communion at the same church and in the same dress as her great grandmother. It's tradition, and until something a lot better comes along, it will continue to be passed from generation to generation.

■ TALK OF THE TOWN

The name New Orleans is sort of a linguistic rite of passage between the initiated and the outsider. Locals say "Or-leens" Avenue and "Or-leens" Parish, but the minute that the adjective "new" is added in front it must be pronounced in an entirely different way. The only exception is when it is used to add rhythm to a song such as "Way Down Yonder in New Or-leens" or "Do You Know What it Means to Miss New Or-leens?"

Pronunciation of the city's name varies depending on which part of town a person comes from, but it is almost always linguistic sacrilege to call the city "New Or-leens." "N'Awlins" is the funky way to say it; local old-timers say New "Oy-uns." The very name La Nouvelle Orleans has gotten a few students of French history and language to cock an eyebrow: They ask why in French the masculine "Orleans" is preceded by the feminine "La Nouvelle." Local historians go to great pains to set the rumor to rest that the city was named for Louis XIV's brother, Philippe, Duc d'Orleans, noted for wearing women's clothes to court. The city, they stress, was actually named for the second Philippe, Duc d'Orleans, the Sun King's nephew and son-in-law who became the regent of France after Louis XIV's death on September 8, 1716. This Duke of Orleans's favorite three activities seem to have been womanizing, power-mongering, and murder.

The French names of the streets in the French Quarter, or Vieux Carré ("Voo-Car-Ray"), can also be a trifle confusing. Burgundy is not pronounced like the wine or the province in France, but as "Burr-GUN-dee." Conti is "Con-TEE," Chartres is "Charters," Decatur is "D-cate-ur," and Esplanade is "S-plaine-ADE." Other street names that may cause linguistic distress are Carondelet ("Care-on-da-LET"), Tchoupitoulas ("Chop-a-tool-us"), Melpomene ("Mel-po-mean"), Milan ("My-lan"), and Terpsichore ("Turp-sick-ory"). Finally, because of the oversight of a dotted *i* on the street signs, Clio is known by some as "C-L-ten."

New Orleansese is a local version of the American language spoken on the streets, the buses, by the lady who serves boiled ("burled") crabs at Gee and Lil's, or the guy who sells Lucky Dogs at the airport. This accent sounds Brooklynese, sort of the "dem, dat, and dose" way in which Archie Bunker spoke, but with a few anglicized French idioms thrown in. Vowels undergo a metamorphosis on the tongues of the Irish Channel and St. Bernard Parish natives. A chicken drumstick becomes a "laig." Algiers Point is "The Pernt." Words ending with "st" lose the last "t" to an "ez" when they are made plural: more than one post be-comes "po-sez."

Those educated in the city's private schools have their own subtle accent, though theirs is closer to that of the Piedmont country of Virginia, with a sprinkle of Charleston and a dash of the British Royal Family. They do not speak street slang. About the only words that call attention to the breeding of old-liners is the pronunciation of mayonnaise ("my-nez") and room ("rum"). They also prefer old family names for their children: during Carnival season, old-line krewes are easy to detect when court participants have first names such as Marigny, Mathilde, Dun-bar, Eugenie, Corinne, Angele, and Delphine.

■ N E W   O R L E A N S E S E   M A D E   E A S Y

Aw-right. A universally accepted greeting or acclamation of working folk. People encountering one another getting on and off a bus may say, "Aw-right."

Banquette. ("Ban-ket") Creole term for sidewalk. The term comes from the origi-nal raised wooden sidewalks.

Bayou. ("By-you") A creek or waterway.

Cajun. ("Kay-jun") The descendants of the distinctive 17th-century, dialect-using Acadian settlers to the remote, swampy region of rural southwestern Louisiana near Lafayette, three hours away from New Orleans.

Dressin' room. The polite working-class term for the bathroom.

Heart. ("hawt") A favorite endearment from waitresses and clerks.

French Quarter. Pronounced by local working men "Da Franch Kwatas."

K&B. A New Orleans–based regional drugstore chain, sold in 1997 to Rite Aid Corp. It is commonly called "Kay Bee," and is a popular navigational point in directions, e.g., "You get off the streetcar at the second 'Kay Bee' and go three blocks…" Woolworth's ("Woolz-woit") on Canal Street is similarly used.

Lagniappe. ("Lan-yap") A baker's dozen, a little something extra.

Mista. A title used exclusively during Carnival season and only for parading male krewes, as in "Throw me sumtin', Mista!"

Mo bettah. Literally, the best there is, e.g., "mo bettah blues" or "mo bettah trout."

Whereyat and **Whereyat ya mother**. A greeting that originated on the streets of New Orleans. The racial epithet "yat" used to describe white working-class lo-cals comes from this expression.

Yeah, you right. Pleasant affirmation.

A girl dresses for a Mardi Gras ball under the watchful eye of her mother.
(Porché West, from the collection of the Amistad Research Center)

FAMOUS WRITERS ON NEW ORLEANS

MARK TWAIN, a.k.a. Samuel Clemens, 1835-1910
Noted Titles: *Huckleberry Finn; Life on the Mississippi*

Though known for writing of his travels all over the United States, Twain is probably best known for the stories he wrote about the southern Mississippi River region. He visited New Orleans several times, and loved its people, as well as its cultural mix.

The old French part of New Orleans—anciently the Spanish part—bears no resemblance to the American end of the city: the American end which lies beyond the intervening brick business center. The houses are massed in blocks; are austerely plain and dignified; uniform of pattern, with here and there a departure from it with pleasant effect; all are plastered on the outside, and nearly all have long, iron-railed verandas running along the several stories. Their chief beauty is the deep, warm, varicolored stain with which time and the weather have enriched the plaster. It harmonizes with all the surroundings, and has as natural a look of belonging there as has the flush upon sunset clouds. This charming decoration cannot be successfully imitated; neither is it to be found elsewhere in America.

—Life on the Mississippi, 1874

GEORGE WASHINGTON CABLE, 1844-1925
Noted Titles: *Old Creole Days; Strange True Stories of Louisiana*

Born and raised in New Orleans, Cable met success with his first work, Old Creole Days, *a controversial collection of stories set in his hometown. He went on to write many other stories and novels with an ironic and humorous twist on the city's local color.*

In the heart of New Orleans stands a large four-story brick building, that has so stood for about three-quarters of a century. Its rooms are rented to a class of persons occupying them simply for lack of activity to find better and cheaper quarters elsewhere. With its gray stucco peeling off in broad patches, it has a solemn look of gentility in rags, and stands, or, as it were, hangs, about the corner of two ancient streets, like a faded fop who pretends to be looking for employment.

— "'Sieur George," Old Creole Days, 1879

KATE CHOPIN, 1851-1904
Noted Title: *The Awakening*

Born Kate O'Flaherty to an upper middle class family, she moved in 1870 to New Orleans after her marriage to a French-born cotton merchant (their house is now 1413-1415 Louisiana Avenue). His business failed in 1879, and the couple moved with their six children to the bayous of northern Louisiana. Her husband died of "swamp fever" in 1882; Chopin later returned to St. Louis and embarked on a literary career writing about the people and places of Creole country.

The Pontelliers possessed a very charming home on Esplanade Street in New Orleans. It was a large, double cottage, with a broad front veranda, whose round, fluted columns supported the sloping roof. The house was painted a dazzling white; the outside shutters, or jalousies, were green. In the yard, which was kept scrupulously neat, were flowers and plants of every description which flourishes in South Louisiana.

—*The Awakening,* 1899

SHERWOOD ANDERSON, 1876-1941
Noted Titles: *Winesburg, Ohio; Beyond Desire*

After meeting with great success for his collection of stories, Winesburg, Ohio, *Anderson settled in New Orleans's Pontalba Apartments. For the next few years he was the leading light of the New Orleans literary world, acting as an editor on the* Double Dealer, *a literary magazine, where he wrote a column and was partly responsible for publishing some of the first work of both William Faulkner and Ernest Hemingway.*

We walked slowly, on account of his bad leg, through many streets of the Old Town, Negro women laughing all around us in the dusk, shadows playing over old buildings, children with their shrill cries dodging in and out of old hallways. The old city was once almost altogether French, but now it is becoming more and more Italian. It, however, remains Latin. People live out of doors. Families were sitting down to dinner within full sight of the street—all doors and windows open. A man and his wife quarreled in Italian. In a patio back of an old building a Negress sang a French song.

—"Death in the Woods," 1921

WILLIAM FAULKNER, 1879-1962
Noted Titles: *As I Lay Dying; Absalom, Absalom*

In 1925 William Faulkner spent six months in the French Quarter (living in what is now 624 Pirates Alley) where he wrote his first short stories, some of which were published by the Times-Picayune. *He also worked on his first novel,* Soldier's Pay, *which was published thanks largely to Faulkner's friend Sherwood Anderson.*

The violet dusk held in soft suspension lights slow as bellstrokes, Jackson square was now a green and quiet lake in which abode lights round as jellyfish, feathering with silver mimosa and pomegranate and hibiscus beneath which lantana and cannas bled and bled. Pontalba and cathedral were cut from black paper and pasted flat on a green sky; above them taller palms were fixed in black and soundless explosions. The street was empty, but from Royal street there came the hum of a trolley that rose to a staggering clatter, passed on and away leaving an interval filled with the gracious sound of inflated rubber on asphalt, like a tearing of endless silk. Clasping his accursed bottle, feeling like a criminal, Mr. Talliaferro hurried on.

—Mosquitoes, 1927

LILLIAN HELLMAN, 1905-1984
Noted Titles: *The Little Foxes; The Children's Hour*

Born in New Orleans, Hellman wrote plays known for their exploration of conventional mores, and later became prominent for her leftist leanings. She also published three volumes of memoirs, including An Unfinished Woman *and* Pentimento, *the latter describing a brief return to New Orleans.*

Hammett was drinking heavily, dangerously. I was sick of him and myself and so one weekend I took off to see my aunts in New Orleans. I would not have liked to live with them for very long, but for a few days I always liked their modest, disciplined life in the shabby little house that was all they could afford since each had stopped working. It was nice, after the plush of Hollywood, to sleep on a cot in the ugly living room, crowded with stuff that poor people can't bring themselves to throw away, nice to talk about what we would have for the good dinner to which one of many old ladies would be invited to show off my aunts' quiet pride in me. Nicest of all was to take a small piece of all the Hollywood money and buy them new winter coats and dresses at Maison Blanche, to be delivered after I left for fear that they'd make me return them if I were there, and then to go along to Solari's, the fine grocers, and load a taxi with delicacies they liked and would never buy. . . .

—*Pentimento*, 1973

TENNESSEE WILLIAMS, 1911-1983
Noted Titles: *A Streetcar Named Desire; Cat on a Hot Tin Roof*

Williams lived in New Orleans throughout the 1940s, often as a houseguest at 1525 Louisiana Avenue. Over the next years, he would set many of his plays in New Orleans.

"Don't you just love those long rainy afternoons in New Orleans when an hour isn't just an hour—but a little piece of eternity dropped into your hands—and who knows what to do with it?"

—*A Streetcar Named Desire*, 1947

The streetcar named Desire no longer services the street by that name.
(Historic New Orleans Collection)

TRUMAN CAPOTE, 1924-1984
Noted Titles: *In Cold Blood; Breakfast at Tiffany's*

Born and raised in New Orleans, Capote wrote many stories set in his hometown, several of which can be found in Music for Chameleons. *Also known as a consummate socialite, Capote is often credited with the pioneering of the "non-fiction novel" genre.*

. . . Big Junebug's is a popular hangout, if little known beyond the waterfront and that area's denizens. It contains three rooms—the big barroom itself with its mammoth zinc-topped bar, a second chamber furnished with three busy pool tables, and an alcove with a jukebox for dancing. It's open right around the clock, and is as crowded at dawn as it is at twilight. Of course, sailors and dockworkers go there, and the truck farmers who bring their produce to the French Market from outlying parishes, cops and firemen and hard-eyed gamblers and harder-eyed floozies, and around sunrise the place overflows with entertainers from the Bourbon Street tourist traps. Topless dancers, strippers, drag queens, B-girls, waiters, bartenders, and the hoarse-voiced doormen-barkers who so stridently labor to lure yokels into *vieux-carré* sucker dives.

—*Music for Chameleons,* 1975

ANNE RICE, 1941-
Noted Titles: *Interview with the Vampire; Feast of All Saints; The Witching Hour*

Born in New Orleans, Rice has written well over a dozen novels, several of which have been set in her native city. After living in San Francisco for 28 years, she returned to New Orleans, where she currently resides.

So walking up the Rue Dumaine in the twilight, he felt an awful apprehension, redolent with memories of his own sister, and knew from much past experience that he was all the more susceptible to it at this time of day, this quiet dreary sensual time between the sun and the moon when the Saturday night excitement of the Quarter had not yet begun though the business was all but concluded and the lamps were lit beneath a sky the color of blood.

It was deepening to purple over the river, descending in layers of violent gold and red clouds behind the masts of the ships; and cicadas sang in the dense foliage of walled courtyards, while from open windows came occasional billowing curtains, and the sounds of supper, tinkling, the scrape of a knife.

Without realizing it, he turned his eyes to everyday things, a horse and cart passing, a woman on an upstairs gallery who stopped beating the dust from a small Turkey rug long enough for him to pass.

—*Feast of All Saints,* 1979

H I S T O R Y

IF THE TRUTH BE TOLD, THE EARLY FRENCH COLONISTS did not come to this verminous swamp to set about building any high-minded utopian communities. Those first seventeenth-century colonists must have been brave though, for their maps warned them that this part of the world was inhabited by "savage man eaters." Apparently, they were risking their lives in an effort to cozy up to Spain's golden kingdom in Mexico.

The first French colonists came to Louisiana at a time when France was the most powerful nation in Europe, and their liege, King Louis XIV, its most illustrious personage. Louis was heir to the Bourbon dynasty, which had ruled France for 128 years before the king embarked on his own lengthy 72-year reign. More importantly, he was married to Marie-Therese, Infanta of Spain, the half-sister of King Charles II of Spain—the man who controlled most of the New World's wealthiest colonies.

The colonists were, of course, preceded by explorers. In 1682, the French explorer René-Robert Cavalier Sieur de la Salle came down the Mississippi River and arrived at a site about 90 miles (145 km) below New Orleans and proclaimed the area drained by the river a possession of the French king. La Salle was followed by two French Quebec-born brothers, Sieur d'Iberville (Pierre le Moyne) and Sieur de Bienville (Jean Baptiste le Moyne), who sailed into the Caribbean and landed at what is now Ocean Springs, Mississippi. On March 2, 1699, they sailed to the mouth of the Mississippi and landed at a point near a tiny bayou. They named it Pointe du Mardi Gras, as the Catholic holiday ("Fat Tuesday") was to fall on March 3 that year. In the autumn of 1699, two British ships also found the mouth of the river, but the two brothers from Quebec were able to convince them that they were in the wrong pew. To commemorate the event, the spot in the river where the Brits turned back is still called English Turn. (Today, English Turn is the name of one of the city's finest golf courses.)

Exploring, conquering, and dominating the world was an expensive proposition, however, and the Bourbons and France were flat broke. Enter a dapper Scottish financier, John Law, with his "Law System." In 1716, he explained to the powerful nobles of France that there was a simple solution to their problem: the creation of a New World development company in which the French could invest and from

(following pages) Explorer La Salle claims the Louisiana Territory for the French crown after sailing down the Mississippi River. He planted a cross inscribed "Louis the Great, King of France and Navarre, reigns, April 9, 1682." (Historic New Orleans Collection)

which investors would prosper. His Company of the West, which sought to settle the Lower Mississippi Valley, was a colossal land-speculation scheme that involved bilking money from investors in return for selling them a piece of paradise, i.e., Louisiana. Then in 1719, Law was given a monopoly on trade in much of France's New World land by his pal Philippe Duc d'Orleans, regent to the child-king Louis XV. Law's Company of the West merged with all other French trading and colonizing companies, and became the Company of the Indies. Even though Law's investment company would ultimately be revealed as a pyramid scheme—bursting the "Mississippi Bubble"—enough of the people who had come to the Louisiana territory were willing to stay and create a land of opportunity in this semi-tropical outback.

John Law, the Scottish financier who master-minded the French colonization of Louisiana. (Historic New Orleans Collection)

During the first year of the company's operation, Law had decided that a town should be founded at a spot which could be reached from both Lake Pontchartrain and the Mississippi. So in 1718, the town of La Nouvelle Orleans was founded on the company's behalf by the younger French-Canadian le Moyne brother, Jean Baptiste, Sieur de Bienville, who'd accompanied his brother to Pointe du Mardi Gras in 1699. This time he came commanding a six-vessel flotilla that included six carpenters and 30 convict laborers. Bienville landed at a strategic crescent on the Mississippi River, 30 leagues (about 90 miles) upriver from the Gulf of Mexico on land of the Muskhogean tribes and began building a city. Shortly thereafter, he became the city's first governor. Nobody in Europe paid much attention to this French attempt to create a great city in the New

World. Peter the Great of Russia was having his son and heir Alexis murdered; Voltaire was imprisoned in the Bastille for sowing the seeds of revolution in France; and England had declared war on Spain. A thousand or so miles to the northeast of New Orleans, in the British colonies, the Collegiate School of America was being renamed Yale University.

■ FRENCH PERIOD

Development of the new city began in earnest in 1718, but work was slow and arduous. Father Charlevoix, a French priest, commented on New Orleans in 1720, "The town is the first that one of the world's greatest rivers has seen rise on its banks." When a huge flood hit shortly after construction had begun on the new

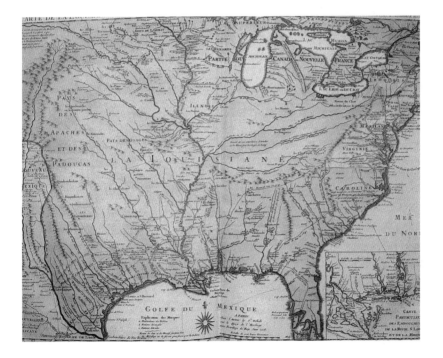

This map executed by Guillaume de l'Isle in 1718 was the first to accurately chart the course of the lower Mississippi. The river delta and site of New Orleans is shown in the inset.

town, there was talk of moving the city. Among those accompanying Bienville on his maiden voyage to New Orleans had been an engineer, Pierre Blond de la Tour, who'd never been that keen on the site chosen for New Orleans. Indeed, he had earlier warned Bienville that the Mississippi could overflow the city whenever it felt like it. Realizing that Bienville had no intention of moving, Blond de la Tour started constructing levees. As the city and nearby plantations spread out, so did their protective levees. By 1735, the levee lines on both sides of the river extended from 30 miles above the city to about 12 miles below.

Construction of the city, meanwhile, became more organized. Father Charlevoix had also written of New Orleans, "There are only about a hundred huts placed without much order." In 1721, shortly after a major flood, Blond de la Tour sent for an engineer named Adrien de Pauger, and, with the help of 10 men, cleared a large swath close to the river and laid out a grid pattern of streets. Soon after, a hurricane blew down almost every one of the original buildings, but the basic plan of the city was established, and the settlers rebuilt their quarters in the same pattern. Despite his many accomplishments, Bienville, New Orleans' first governor, was often at odds with other administrators in the colony, and was recalled to France in 1725.

At the same time, Scottish financier John Law was hard at work trying to satisfy a charter in which he and his Company of the Indies had promised investors that 6,000 settlers and 3,000 slaves would inhabit the Louisiana colony by 1727. One of the stumbling blocks in population expansion seems to have been the lack of women: "The white men," Governor Bienville declared in a letter to John Law, "are running in the woods after the Indian girls."

The lack of suitable nurses and teachers in La Nouvelle Orleans had earlier prompted then-governor Bienville to coax the good Sisters of the Ursuline to come from France and assist him in setting things right. The first Ursulines arrived in 1727, and set immediately to work. They cared for orphans, conducted a free school, operated a hospital, and instructed slaves for baptism. They also provided a safe haven for the upstanding, middle-class *filles à la cassette,* or "casket girls" (so named—depending on whose history you read—for either the style of hats they wore or their government-issued trousseau chests of clothes and linen). First arriving in 1728, these young women would continue to come until 1751, marrying those single male colonists unable to snare one of the "professional girls" who'd been sent from Parisian jails prior to 1720.

Les filles à la cassette were sent to establish good French families in the colony.
(Historic New Orleans Collection)

But the young city's problems were far from over. The lower valley of the Mississippi where the fledgling colony began had for centuries been the kingdom of the Chickasaw Indians, part of North America's Muskhogean civilization. In 1700, the Muskhogean tribes lived in over 50 villages and numbered between 3,000 and 4,000 people. During his first term as governor, Bienville had eventually managed to gain the respect of the Indians for the French. But after Bienville was recalled, this relationship went downhill. In 1729, the Natchez Indians, allies of the Chickasaw, attacked Fort Rosalie at Natchez, killing about 250 and kidnapping another 450 women, children, and slaves.

By 1731, in light of the Natchez Indian raid and political disorder, investors in the Company of the Indies petitioned the King of France to rid them of unprofitable Louisiana once and for all. The Bourbon monarch complied, and Bienville was called out of retirement to govern for the crown. John Law had already endowed New Orleans with a tenacious breed of colonists, and by the time the company gave up on the city, La Nouvelle Orleans had a population of 7,000 with thriving businesses that supplied lumber, bricks, tar, meat, and hides to the Indies, and sugar and rum to France. Their ships returned with silk, cocoa, tanned leather, spices, silver, and porcelain from Europe. As for Bienville, the reinstalled governor launched two campaigns against the Chickasaw in 1736 and 1739, the first ending in an Indian victory, and the second in a close French win in 1740. With his spirit crushed by his inability to gain a decisive victory over the Native Americans, Bienville resigned permanently in 1743.

■ SPANISH PERIOD

In 1762, France slipped ownership of New Orleans to Spain by the secret Treaty of Fontainebleu. In the same year, Spain entered the Seven Years War—the European arm of the French and Indian War—just in time to share in the French defeat. As part of the terms of the Treaty of Paris ending the war, France had to agree to give up all of its territory in North America to the British. "Not so fast," said the French King Louis XV. "I gave Louisiana to my cousin Carlos III of Spain last year."

Nobody in Louisiana knew anything about this for many months, when the colonists suddenly found themselves under the control of the unpopular Spanish Governor Don Antonio de Ulloa for whom they immediately formed an intense dislike. They also found that their trading partners in the West Indies no longer wanted to do business with them, deeming the colony too financially risky since it was unclear whether Louisiana was governed by French or Spanish laws of trade.

In 1768, six hundred courageous New Orleans citizens led by Nicolas Chauvin de Lafreniere mounted the first revolutionary movement of American colonists against a European power. The ranks of this troop were made up of Acadians (French-speaking immigrants from Canada), who had been told that they were going to be sold into slavery by the Spanish, and German immigrants, who thought that the Spanish were going to default on money that they were owed by John Law's Company of the Indies. By November 1, the Spanish governor Ulloa had escaped to Havana, and his three top aides were held by the rebels loyal to France.

His Majesty Carlos of Spain was not amused, and just to make sure his other colonial subjects didn't get any ideas, he sent a 2,600-man mercenary force to New Orleans. The force was larger than the entire male population of the city, and was led by Don Alexander O'Reilly, an Irishman in the service of Spain. Subsequently, he earned the sobriquet "Bloody O'Reilly" after he sent all of the revolutionaries before the firing squad. Local legend holds that the leader of the firing squad later married the widow of one of his victims. But as severe as their government could be, the Spanish did preserve French culture and language in New Orleans.

Louisiana passed out of Spanish hands just as surreptitiously as it had entered them, when the citizens of New Orleans discovered that their city had been retro-ceded to Napoleon in 1800 as the result of the secret Treaty of San Ildefonso. But Napoleon was busy that year conquering the Turks, the Austrians, and the Italians, and quelling the slave uprising in Saint-Domingue. And since New Orleans was struck with a particularly vicious yellow fever epidemic, Napoleon let the Spanish continue to govern his Louisiana colonists.

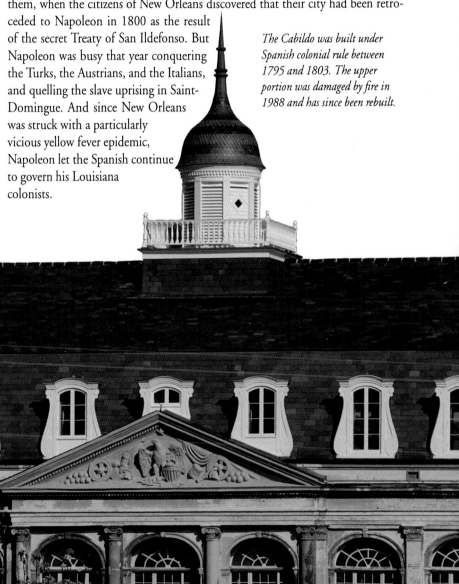

The Cabildo was built under Spanish colonial rule between 1795 and 1803. The upper portion was damaged by fire in 1988 and has since been rebuilt.

Napoleon may have stayed away, but the "Kaintocks," the buckskin-clad American frontiersmen, weren't about to. Within five years, a total of 5,000 keelboats (40–80 feet long had floated down to New Orleans. This heavy traffic from the hill country lasted until steamboats claimed the river for their own.

Spanish control of New Orleans only lasted for a third of a century, but by the time they left in 1803 the city had come into its own as a thriving port. Its population was estimated at 10,000 residents: 5,000 whites, 2,000 free people of color, and 3,000 slaves. As a slave-based economy, almost all of the physical work was done by enslaved blacks who made the bricks, cleared the land, forged the cast iron, planted and harvested the commercial crops, kept the house of the master, cooked his meals, reared his children, and, in some cases, bore his children.

■ LOUISIANA PURCHASE

At a dinner party in Paris on April 12, 1803, given to welcome the American emissary James Monroe, a French official announced that Napoleon wanted to sell a fan-shaped tract of land extending from New Orleans to the Rocky Mountains and Canada. Like President Jefferson, Monroe believed that the fledgling United States must protect itself from England, France, and Spain by controlling as much of the North American continent as possible. Jefferson had been extremely displeased when the Spanish government, the de facto governors of France's Louisiana, had closed the Mississippi River to American ships, and he hoped to prevent this from happening again. At the same time, Napoleon knew he could use American money to finance France's war with the British, and he must have reasoned that it was preferable to have Louisiana in the hands of one of Britain's enemies. Although the price came to less than five cents an acre, the frugal New Englanders in Congress tried to block the sale, as it seemed a dishonorable investment since the United States Treasury didn't contain the money to pay for it. It took all of Jefferson's statesmanlike skill to get the sale approved. After two weeks of negotiations, the Americans had finessed the greatest real estate deal in history, acquiring over 900,000 square miles—600 million acres—for about $15 million.

By mid-August word reached New Orleans that the city would soon pass out of the jewel-encrusted fingers of the Catholic European powers into those mud-

JEFFERSON ON THE FRENCH IN NEW ORLEANS

*T*he cession of Louisiana and the Floridas by Spain to France works most sorely on the United States. On this subject the secretary of state has written to you fully, yet I cannot forbear recurring to it personally, so deep is the impression it makes on my mind. It completely reverses all the political relations of the United States and will form a new epoch in our political course. Of all the nations of any consideration, France is the one which, hitherto, has offered the fewest points on which we could have any conflict of right and the most points of a communion of interests. From these causes, we have ever looked to her as our natural friend, as one with which we never could have an occasion of difference. Her growth, therefore, we viewed as our own, her misfortunes ours.

There is on the globe one single spot the possessor of which is our natural and habitual enemy. It is New Orleans, through which the produce of three-eighths of our territory must pass to market, and from its fertility it will ere long yield more than half of our whole produce and contain more than half of our inhabitants. France, placing herself in that door, assumes to us the attitude of defiance. Spain might have retained it quietly for years. Her pacific dispositions, her feeble state, would induce her to increase our facilities there, so that her possession of the place would be hardly felt by us, and it would not, perhaps, be very long before some circumstance might arise which might make the cession of it to us the price of something of more worth to her. Not so can it ever be in the hands of France; the impetuosity of her temper, the energy and restlessness of her character, placed in a point of eternal friction with us, and our character, which though quiet and loving peace and the pursuit of wealth, is high-minded, despising wealth in competition with insult or injury, enterprising and energetic as any nation on earth—these circumstances render it impossible that France and the United States can continue long friends when they meet in so irritable a position.

—President Thomas Jefferson,
letter to U.S. envoy Robert Livingston, 1802

under-the-fingernails hands of the Protestant rabble-rousing Americans. The Ursuline sisters were so frightened that they temporarily fled to Cuba.

For the transaction to be legal, the deed to Louisiana had first to be transferred from Spain to France. This transaction was accomplished in the Sala Capitular at the Cabildo in the French Quarter on November 30, 1803, and was accompanied by a flurry of salutes and flag waving in the Place d'Armes, later to become Jackson Square. On December 20, the Louisiana territory was transferred from France to the United States, and from that moment English became the official language in the French-speaking city.

■ AMERICAN PERIOD

With its mixture of French- and Spanish-speaking Creoles, Anglo-Americans, slaves, and free people of color (manumitted slaves, mixed-race legitimate heirs of white colonists, and/or their descendants), New Orleans in 1810 established itself as the largest city in the South and the fifth largest city in the United States. Louisiana became the nation's 18th state on April 30, 1812, and barely a month later, Congress declared war against Great Britain. A few weeks after Mardi Gras in 1814, rumors filled the city that the British were planning to attack New Orleans.

The citizens of New Orleans had a long history of being governed by the Catholic enemies of the Protestant British. Being attacked by the British was just the catalyst needed to harness the magnificent bravado of the New Orleanians.

New Orleans quickly developed into a major riverine port during the American period following the introduction of the steamboat in 1812. (Historic New Orleans Collection)

Andrew Jackson led a motley crew of soldiers, frontiersmen, Indians, and pirates to victory over the British during the Battle of New Orleans in 1814. (Historic New Orleans Collection)

Word reached Louisiana that the Capitol and the White House in Washington were in smoldering ruins, and that President James Madison was unable to raise an army because the United States Treasury was empty.

Andrew Jackson, then a 47-year-old major general, appeared to be the only hope for the new nation. Unfortunately, that December he was extremely ill and trying to block the British attack from his sickbed at 412-414 Royal Street (where the courthouse now stands) in the French Quarter. To accomplish a victory General Andrew Jackson needed every breathing human who could fire a gun. Not only did he impose martial law, but he readily accepted the assistance of the regiments of free people of color, Choctaw Indians, and the pirate Jean Lafitte.

On December 23, 1814, his health regained, General Jackson attacked the British troops as they were camped along the banks of the Mississippi. British forces led by General Pakenham, fresh from defeating Napoleon, suffered a severe blow. Throughout a bitterly cold week between Christmas and New Year's, the British continued to get reinforcements, attacking the Americans at daybreak on New Year's Day 1815. It was a prelude to the final confrontation which began on January 8 on the mist- and mud-covered Chalmette Plantation. Huddled behind the bales of straw and cotton, those along the American lines began to hear the

THE PIRATES LAFITTE

History often has the effect of sandblasting the misdeeds of its colorful characters and making them appear more intriguing than evil. Nowadays, visitors to New Orleans seeing the Lafitte name everywhere—there's even a national historic park named after Jean Lafitte—might think the Lafitte brothers were the French Quarter's first Royal Street antique dealers. In fact, they were pirates—responsible for attacks and plunder of many early Louisiana settlers and citizens, including children, who were aboard the ships these privateers boarded. One of the most profitable illegal cargoes which they traded was slaves, seized from masters and resold in the markets in New Orleans.

Jean and Pierre Lafitte were known to have been in New Orleans as early as 1805. Some say that they were natives of Marseilles, France, while others claim that they hailed from Port au Prince in Santo Domingo. Nineteenth-century author and historian George Washington Cable states that the brothers claimed the Bordeaux region of France as their birthplace circa 1780-85 in order to be entitled to French privateers' credentials. This may be true, since the eldest Lafitte brother, Alexandre, known as Dominique You, was the famed diminutive artillery officer of Napoleon.

Once in Louisiana, the pirates' base of operations was in Barataria Bay, near New Orleans, inland from Grand Isle, and within striking distance of the Gulf Coast, where trading ships made their entrances and exits from the Mississippi River. By 1811, Barataria was a thriving community with 32 armed warships, more ships than there were in the entire American navy at the start of the War of 1812.

Andrew Jackson enlisted the aid of Jean Lafitte and his brothers in fighting the British at the Battle of New Orleans, after which the men were pardoned of piracy charges. The Lafittes went right back to piracy. By 1818, they had established a colony of privateers off the coast of Galveston, where it is thought that Jean became a spy for Spain.

Theories regarding Jean Lafitte's final resting place flow as freely as beer on St. Patrick's Day. The latest theory, based on the recent discovery of a "diary," is that when the camp in Galveston was destroyed by a hurricane, Lafitte remarried and moved up to Alton, Illinois. There he became passionate about furthering the cause of the working man. He was even supposed to have contributed some of the money he had once robbed from the rich to aid the work of Karl Marx. All that is known for certain is that Lafitte's brother Pierre died in Missouri in 1844 and was buried in St. Louis. Pierre's children have been quoted as saying that their "esteemed" uncle changed his name to Jon Lafflin and dropped out of sight.

This information usually falls on deaf ears. Napoleonic groupies are convinced that the Emperor, John Paul Jones, and the pirates Lafitte are buried together in Lafitte Cemetery on Bayou Barataria. Another American historical group erected a monument to the pirate in 1976 at a grave-site at the village of Dzilam de Bravo, near Merida, on the Yucatan peninsula. They believe that Jean died of yellow fever off the coast of Yucatan in 1826.

Pirate Jean Lafitte (from an old print)

eerie cry of bagpipes and the cadence of the drums. Soon they could make out the vibrant color of the uniforms of the Duchess of York's Light Dragoons and the tartans of the 93rd Highlanders as they made a tightly formed, rapid frontal assault.

Jackson and his ragtag army of Kentuckian Long Rifles, ill-prepared militiamen, Indian braves, Creoles, free men of color, and pirates blasted the British lines with mercilessly accurate cannon fire and artillery. When it was over the Americans had lost about 15 men and had about 40 men wounded. The carnage on the British side was appalling, with 858 dead and about 2,500 men wounded. This turn of events left the defeated British nowhere to turn for medical attention but to the citizens of New Orleans. Legend has it that one place they turned for solace was the good Catholic Ursuline Sisters, back from Cuba, who sheltered some of the enemy troops within the walls of their convent.

January 8 became an official day of celebration in New Orleans, though the British didn't sail away until January 27. Soon afterwards news reached the city that the United States and Great Britain had signed a peace treaty at Ghent on Christmas Eve, two weeks before the famous Battle of New Orleans. Much to the chagrin of Governor Claiborne and the local citizenry, Lafitte and his pirates were offered full pardons for their service by the Americans. The battle continues to be re-enacted each year on its anniversary.

■ La Belle Epoque

The end of the war only served as the beginning of another siege, this one by the Protestant Americans who came to enjoy their new, French-speaking city. During this period, New Orleans was one of the most important cities in the South—a cosmopolitan port city and cotton market that seemed ripe with opportunity for shopkeepers, clerks, and bookkeepers. Sophisticated opportunists and hard-working middle-class people arrived in droves, as did buckskin-clad hill people who came pouring downriver to stay for good. Arriving on their flatboats and bringing with them brown crockery jugs of Monongahela whiskey, Protestantism, and rough ways, these "hillbillies" thoroughly offended the sensibilities of the Creole families of the Vieux Carré who slammed shut their wrought-iron gates, pursed their lips, and set about a tenacious protection of their culture from incursions by English-speakers. After the Louisiana Purchase, altercations between the Catholic

Creoles and the Protestant Americans became so frequent that a strip of land between the French Quarter and the American sector was designated as a "neutral ground" by Congress on March 3, 1807. It later became known as Canal Street.

In 1812, the steamboat *New Orleans* arrived in the port of New Orleans, heralding an age of prosperity for the United States' cosmopolitan new city. Textile mills in England and France seemed unable to get enough Southern cotton, the sugar industry was thriving, banks were strong, and the port was bustling. At the same time the city seemed like an oasis of sophistication among otherwise agrarian and puritanical adjacent Southern states. Within the homes of the gentry, French-style decorum and gallantry came into full bloom. The city's aristocrats filled their lavish mansions with the finest Aubusson carpets, Venetian crystal chandeliers, and treasures from the Orient, and they served the finest French wines on tables covered with immaculate damask and linens.

Luxuries aside, New Orleans was still not a place for the weak of spirit and the faint of heart. Located below sea level in a particularly wet climate, New Orleans was a city of oppressive humidity from June to October, and was infested with

Lafayette Square in 1858. (Historic New Orleans Collection)

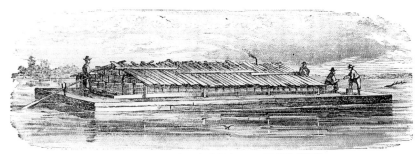

FLATBOAT FROM ST. LOUIS TO NEW ORLEANS, TIME FOUR MONTHS.

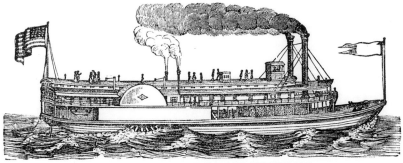

STEAMBOAT FROM NEW ORLEANS TO ST. LOUIS, TIME THREE DAYS.

(Historic New Orleans Collection)

swarms of mosquitoes. The city was swept by frightful cholera and tropical fever epidemics, and gained the reputation of being a damp grave. If that wasn't enough, the precious possessions of the wealthy were continually threatened by fierce hurricanes and torrential thunderstorms.

That the mighty Mississippi sometimes overflowed its banks—as the city's first engineer, Blond de la Tour, had predicted—was a fact that the citizenry had come to accept. Spring floods regularly poured two feet of muddy water and debris, not to mention snakes and rats, into the shops and homes of the city. Between 1800 and 1840, the Mississippi River changed its course, borrowing land from the west bank and depositing it on the east bank. Maps from 1810 show that Tchoupi-toulas Street hugged the edge of the river, but by 1840 it was five blocks inland. Even though the river's cycle had come to be anticipated, the great flood of 1849 caused amazing devastation, wiping out entire sugar plantations and vast tracts of farm land that provided much of the city's food. And just to prove its sovereignty, the Mississippi unleashed its power again the following year. New levees were constructed which held until the floods of 1858 and 1859, when the river again attacked New Orleans and its environs.

In 1832, the enemy was cholera; in addition, between 1817 and 1860, there were 23 visits of "Bronze John," as yellow fever was called. Yellow fever was spread by mosquitoes which bred in the household cisterns, and multiplied unchecked in mild winters. The most serious epidemic of yellow fever hit the city in the summer of 1853, sending those who could flee to the higher ground in surrounding cities such as Natchez or Mobile. Over 8,000 people died before the first cool air of October eased away the deadly visitor. For those who didn't die and had no clue as to what brought this plague, there were days of prayer accompanied by the constant blast of cannons as New Orleanians tried to break up the clouds, which they believed held the disease over the city.

■ CONFEDERACY, RECONSTRUCTION, AND AFTERMATH

In 1860 New Orleans had the largest cotton market in the world and was the wealthiest city per capita in the United States. It had been an American city just over 50 years when it found itself at war. On February 4, 1861, Senator Judah P. Benjamin announced to Congress that Louisiana had seceded from the Union. The state stood alone for three months until it joined the Confederate States of America.

The decision to secede was not unilaterally popular with the citizens of New Orleans, especially the merchants who depended on the North for their livelihood and recent European immigrants. The question of loyalty was also an issue with the free people of color (about 750 of whom were slave owners), now citizens of a country at war with the Union which proposed not only the abolition of slavery but giving the vote and public education to people of color. As for the roughly 12,000 slaves, most must have yearned for freedom. Despite these mixed emotions, it was a Louisiana regiment that initiated the opening salvo of America's Civil War when Pierre Gustave Toutant Beauregard and his Louisiana regiment opened fire on Fort Sumter on April 12, 1861.

The Union began its blockade of the Mississippi River on May 26, 1861, and

The cotton plantations upriver from New Orleans contributed greatly to the city's wealth. (Historic New Orleans Collection)

almost instantly cut New Orleans off from the imported supplies of flour, paper, and coffee it had come to depend on. By spring of the following year, the Union Navy began bombarding the well-fortified forts along the flooded Mississippi below the city from their position near Ship Island in the Gulf of Mexico. During the thunderous battle, cannon fire rained down on both sides for over four hours. In the end, Union troops passed the forts and headed upriver towards New Orleans. Immediately, the people of New Orleans were thrown into a panic. The hungry citizens had to watch as the warehouses of food, cotton, and lumber were burned to keep them out of the hands of the enemy. Mobs of looters raced through the streets trying to steal anything which might be bartered for food with their conquerors.

Major General Benjamin "Spoons" Butler of Massachusetts took control of the city and its citizens for the United States on May 1, 1862. The fall of New Orleans was catastrophic for the Confederacy, as the Union Army was thereby able to control much of the river and keep the South divided. This occupation was to last for 15 years until April 24, 1877, giving New Orleans the distinction of having suffered through a Reconstruction (a term that wasn't used until the war ended) government longer than any other Southern city.

An estate auction in the rotunda of the St. Louis Exchange, prior to the Civil War, included slaves along with personal possessions. (Historic New Orleans Collection)

RIOT OF 1866

The rights of emancipated slaves—specifically, suffrage and education—comprised a highly divisive issue for Louisiana's post-Civil War government. When legislators supporting those rights called a meeting at the Mechanics Institute in 1866 a mob incited a riot outside the building in angry protest to rights for freed slaves, ultimately killing many rights advocates. This unpublished diary recounts a meeting between a prominent New Orleans attorney (representing Myra Clark Gaines) and his brother, a plantation owner and ex-Confederate cavalry officer.

. . . I was reading in the law office of my father, when my uncle Elliot strode in. He stepped up to father, who rose from his desk, and they glared into one another's eyes, enemies though half brothers. "Are you going on with this foolish business, John, of educating the Negro, and trying to give him the vote?" said my uncle Elliot.

"I certainly am," said my father. "My back is to the wall, and my friends and I are going to fight for this object until it is forced upon the entire South."

"Then I want to tell you," said Elliot, "that if you ever try any such thing, you will be killed as sure as you are a foot high, and I know what I am talking about." Turning his back upon my father, he strode from the room, and the brothers never met again during their lives.

೧   ೧   ೧

A howling mob of many thousands had surrounded the Mechanic's Pavilion, the meeting had broken up in disorder, and most of the members had fled, some over adjoining roofs, and some by back stairs. My father, with about twenty of the members, stayed in the hall. When the mob had surrounded the building, some one or two of this band of twenty, crazed by fear, fired upon the mob below. This fire was returned until not a window was left whole in the building. When it had decreased somewhat, my father tied his white handkerchief to the end of his walking cane, and stuck it out of several of the windows of the building. Immediately, as if by a pre-concerted signal, the firing stopped, and a strong voice from the crowd yelled out:

"Come down the front steps, you fellows in there, and if you do not fire a shot, we will protect you." This, the band of twenty or more proceeded to do, when, just as they neared the last few stone steps, a tremendous fire from every kind of arm was poured into them. Most of them were at once killed, while a few, like my father, though he was the recipient of at least twenty shots, stabbings, and blows with clubs, lived through it, since the crowd thought them dead. Some of my father's friends, although Southern sympathizers, found him alive, and he was instantly placed in an ambulance and the driver was directed to go at full speed to the Marine Hospital. The driver had not gone very far before the mob, through what strange means I cannot tell, learned that Father was still alive. Immediately a howl went up and a dash was made for the ambulance.

"John Henderson is in that ambulance!" they cried, "Kill him!"

Instantly the crowd parted, and a man of iron-gray hair and beard forced his way to the ambulance, and with a spring he was up beside the driver. Drawing two huge pistols from his pockets, he addressed the crowd. "Boys, you all know me. I am Colonel _____ of the Louisiana _____ Regiment. I fought all through this war, and now we are licked. John Henderson was my enemy in politics, but in other ways my friend, as I have known him and esteemed him for years. Now, let me tell you, that if any man puts his hand on this ambulance, or stops one of these horses, I will shoot him like a dog! Now drive on," he said to the driver, and they proceeded to the hospital.

Unnecessary to recount the long weeks of suffering endured by my father before his end came . . .

—Louis Henderson, memoir describing events in 1866

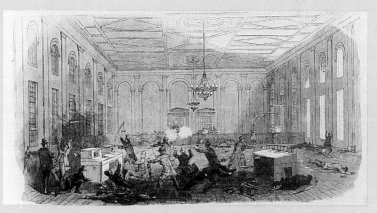

The Riot of 1866 at the Mechanics Institute. (Historic New Orleans Collection)

During those 15 years the major general's name was used as a verb by local people. To "Butlerize" meant to steal. With their wholesale scalawaggery, the Union troops did nothing to endear themselves to the locals. Proper Creole ladies allegedly hired artists to paint a likeness of Butler inside their porcelain chamber pots. Otherwise well-mannered ladies took pride in the dumping of their morning slops atop the Union troops' heads. When "Spoons" Butler's daughter was married, each of the local guests was said to have sent her a single silver spoon. Both Episcopalian and Catholic priests were called to task by Butler for refusing to conduct funerals and prayer services for his troops. One priest was said to have replied, "No, sir, I did not refuse to bury a member of your army. I'd like to bury all of them!"

One of Butler's first official acts was to carry out the Federal Confiscation Act, which allowed seizure of the private property of anyone who would not swear allegiance to the United States. If that outraged citizens, Butler's far greater crime in the eyes of the entire South was the ungentlemanly Order No. 28, in which he stated, " . . . any women (calling themselves ladies) who by word, gesture or movement, insult or show contempt for any officer of the United States, shall be regarded as a woman of the town plying her trade."

Congress re-admitted Louisiana to the Union in June of 1868. The period from the end of Reconstruction until the depression of the 1890s was marked by social and economic upheaval balanced by periods of prosperity and hopefulness. The mule-driven mass transit system was going full force by the 1880s. Perhaps the most famous of its drivers was Thomas Lipton, later to become a millionaire tea merchant as well as a knight, who came to New Orleans in the 1870s to make his fortune.

By the 1880s, the city had close to a quarter of a million inhabitants, most of whom were eager to see New Orleans return to its former glory. The port had still not regained the vitality lost during Reconstruction, and, unlike cities such as Atlanta and Baltimore, the city did not attract major manufacturing. Yet local cotton futures speculators, called factors, formed the Cotton Exchange in 1871, bankers established the Clearing House Association in 1872, and the Sugar Exchange began to function in 1883. Though New Orleans was trying to move ahead, her location and the effects of the Reconstruction kept her isolated and struggling with racial and labor strife. In addition, by the 1880s the debt of $24,000,000, accumulated under the carpetbag regimes had increased in subsequent administrations and needed to be paid.

It was World War I that finally revitalized the port. Imports and exports were under $300 million in 1914 and well over $500 million by 1918. The end of World War I brought great celebration, but soon afterward the city was hard hit by an influenza epidemic that killed 35,000 New Orleanians—a staggering number, considering that there had been 120,000 American deaths in the entire war.

■ HUEY LONG YEARS

Meanwhile the government of Louisiana had passed from the hands of the Reconstruction government, which had taken over the reigns from the plantation aristocracy, into the waiting pockets of out-of-state corporations who controlled most of the state's oil, lumber, shipping, and sugarcane. If there was a positive side to this state of affairs, it was that by the 1920s New Orleans no longer seemed

to be an Old World fiefdom controlled by a few families but had moved into the mainstream of commerce and development enjoyed by America's other major cities. Out-of-town corporations were coming in and spreading development dollars around. Skyscrapers were built in the downtown area, and a movement to restore the French Quarter (or "Vieux Carré") had begun. But the interests of an urban society and of powerful corporations were far removed from those of the provincial small farmers in the rest of the state.

Senator Huey P. Long joins in a football day parade. The "Kingfish" entertained the crowds with his "cakewalk and monkey-shine antics" according to the Associated Press byline of November 18, 1934. (Underwood Archives)

In 1929, the Great Depression hit, cutting a wide swath in the optimism of the city folk. Five major banks and many of the "homesteads" (S&Ls) failed. Hard on the heels of the economic catastrophe came the voice of change from a northern Louisiana, Bible-belt Protestant, the former patent medicine and shortening salesman, Huey Pierce Long. Huey "Everyman a King" Long ran for governor on the promise that he would break the big-city socio-political machine in New Orleans. His home base was a region of small farms worked by people who had been squeezed out of the other Southern states just prior to the Civil War by the plantation-based economic system.

In Louisiana, where just under 12 percent of the population was on federal relief, it was easy for a man who promised to redistribute wealth and power to find willing listeners and passionate supporters. From the day Long won office as a railroad commissioner at the age of 25, he set out to break the back of Standard Oil, the Rockefeller-owned corporation that was the major oil driller in the state. Long was a revolutionary; some said his breed of populism was simply socialism with an American accent.

After Long was elected governor in 1928, the state legislature in Baton Rouge soon came under his control and that of his populist cronies. Long used his power to revenge himself upon the New Orleans politicians and newspapers who had opposed him. After serving as governor, he ran for and won a seat in the U.S. Senate. Before leaving for Washington, Long fired the legally elected lieutenant governor and replaced him with two designated successors, thus cementing his control of Louisiana and New Orleans by taking power away from the local old-guard and out-of-town types. While serving as senator, he continued to control the state, convening 11 specially called sessions of the state legislature—which passed every bill that he proposed. It was on his way to the twelfth session on the night of September 8, 1935, that he was shot by a Baton Rouge physician, Dr. Carl Weiss. Weiss's motive has never been clear and is still much debated. Some scholars feel that Weiss killed Long to preserve his wife's family's honor, because Long had threatened to reveal that the prominent St. Landry Parish family had black blood. Weiss's family has maintained that Weiss, who was killed during the assassination, was not the assassin but was killed in the crossfire of an assassination plot by Long's bodyguards.

Canal Street in the 1920s. (Underwood Archives)

■ MODERN TIMES

World War II brought prosperity and prominence back to New Orleans. The local shipyards began to run full tilt, producing PT boats and landing craft for the U.S. Navy. German subs lurked off the mouth of the Mississippi in the Gulf and sank 13 ships within a year after Japan attacked Pearl Harbor.

Within a few years after the end of World War II, New Orleans reaped the benefits of the oil boom from offshore fields in the Gulf, but when the price of oil crashed in the 1980s, the city felt the loss not only in terms of jobs and general prosperity but because much of the base of philanthropy that had revitalized the arts community pulled up stakes and headed back to Texas. In recent years, a laissez-faire, "let the good times roll" attitude has fueled the tourist industry while fostering an indifference on the part of the better-off to the Third World–style living conditions of the less advantaged. Historically, the city has no industrial wage base, and its vast tourist industry is supported by a plethora of minimum wage jobs. Even the port is no longer an important employer.

The Greater New Orleans metropolitan area includes four parishes (or counties): Orleans, Jefferson, St. Bernard, and St. Tammany. Orleans, or New Orleans proper, is definitely the poorest. Statistics reveal that the median income in Orleans Parish is $16,465. Thirty-three percent of all New Orleans households have an income below $10,000, with the median being $8,164. Fifty percent of all children in New Orleans live in poverty. It is further estimated that 43 percent of the 7,000–10,000 homeless who live on the streets of New Orleans are under the age of 18. Perhaps it's not surprising that the city ranks in the top ten U.S. cities when it comes to the number of violent crimes committed annually. During the 1980s, New Orleans lost 26 percent of its middle income residents, thus decreasing the tax base. And with the shrinking population came the loss of one U.S. Congressional seat and significant federal funds. At the same time, demographers project that between 70,000 and 90,000 recent immigrants, mostly Hispanic and Asian, will settle in the New Orleans metropolitan area in the 1990s. Through it all, the soul and spirit of New Orleans remains resilient. The city seems to weather hardship well: economic depressions and geographic isolation have fostered a unique culture in which limited resources and preserved Old World traditions are reborn as distinctive and exuberant customs, music, and cuisines.

HISTORY TIMELINE

1704 *Pelican* arrives in Louisiana from France with soldiers, workmen, and marriageable women.

1717 Scottish financier John Law and his Company of the West (later, Company of the Indies) receive the charter for control of Louisiana for 25 years from the French government.

1718 Sieur de Bienville selects townsite on the Mississippi and names it New Orleans in honor of Philippe Duc d'Orléans, the regent of France. Population: 68.

1765 France asks Spain to assume control of Louisiana.

1777 Spanish governor Bernardo de Galvez demonstrates his partisanship for the American side of the revolution by seizing 11 richly laden English ships on the Mississippi.

1803 Colonial Prefect Pierre Laussat announces the transfer of Louisiana from Spain back to France. James Monroe, representing the United States, concludes the purchase of Louisiana from France for $15,000,000.

1812 Louisiana is admitted to the Union.

1813 U.S. dragoons capture the pirate Lafitte. Legal prosecution begins in the United States District Court in New Orleans but no conviction obtained.

1815 American troops and local supporters defeat British at Chalmette.

1834 Napoleon's death mask is presented in New Orleans by his former physician.

1861 Louisiana secedes from the United States.

1861 New Orleans blockaded by the Union Army.

1873 The first through train service to Chicago from New Orleans begins.

1896 Louisiana Supreme Court makes the first decision on "separate but equal doctrine" in "Plessy vs. Ferguson." They held for "separate."

1904 Fifty automobiles are in operation in New Orleans.

1909 The last epidemic of yellow fever.

1928 Inauguration of Huey P. Long as governor.

1930 Huey P. Long joins the U.S. Senate.

1956 Federal judge orders desegregation of public schools.

1969 The trial of New Orleans businessman Clay Shaw begins. He is charged by District Attorney Jim Garrison with being a conspirator in the assassination of President Kennedy. He is acquitted.

1977 First black mayor of New Orleans since the Reconstruction, Ernest N. "Dutch" Morial, is elected.

P E O P L E

THE TRADITIONAL CREOLE AND CAJUN CATHOLIC cultures of the southern part of Louisiana survived purely through the dogged chauvinism of their practitioners. Television delivers homogenized white-bread America to their doorsteps. They say "no thanks," continuing instead to revel in their brand of French heritage. That heritage is reflected in the names that they bear from birth, their special affinity for certain over-the-edge heroes such as the pirate Jean Lafitte, and the careful preservation of the social, culinary, and musical rituals of their ancestors.

While New Orleans maintains its traditional connections to the Old World, the greatest post–World War II migrations to the city have come from Cuba, Latin America, and Vietnam. Each of these new groups has brought along its native culture to a place that continues to nurture ethnic communities; and each new group has established its own native-language churches (usually Catholic),

Philippe, Duc d'Orleans, after whom the city of New Orleans was named. (Historic New Orleans Collection)

as well as its own festivals. While these immigrants have brought altogether new cultural riches, their arrival has also ensured that New Orleans remains what it has always been—a uniquely exciting, multi-cultural, multi-ethnic city, where a world of traditions are honored and preserved, yet intermingled with an unrivaled exuberance.

■ FRENCH AND CREOLES

In the early days of New Orleans, the French Company of the Indies needed to colonize the territory, so they accepted just about any able-bodied "volunteers." The combination of the violence of the elements and Louisiana's remoteness pretty much insured that few decent folk would want to get near New Orleans. Among the few eager French immigrants were those from debtors'

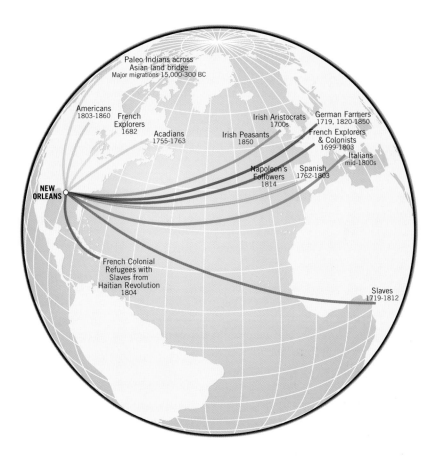

Paleo Indians across
Asian land bridge
Major migrations 15,000-300 BC

Americans
1803-1860 French
Explorers
1682

Irish Aristocrats
1700s

German Farmers
1719, 1820-1850

Acadians
1755-1763

Irish Peasants
1850

French Explorers
& Colonists
1699-1803

Italians
mid-1800s

Napoleon's
Followers
1814

Spanish
1762-1803

NEW
ORLEANS

French Colonial
Refugees with
Slaves from
Haitian Revolution
1804

Slaves
1719-1812

prisons and houses of correction, including 88 "working girls" who were given the choice of incarceration or a one-way ticket to matrimonial bliss with a Louisiana colonist. In 1720, the regent of France, Philippe, Duc d'Orleans put a stop to the practice of flushing forth the unsavory elements of France into his New World colony. It may be a coincidence, but it is almost impossible to find any modern citizen of New Orleans who claims an ancestor who came to Louisiana prior to 1727.

One of the city's preeminent cultures is Creole, though the term is one of the most confusing ethnic labels in the United States. Two distinct groups claim the label "Creole" for themselves. White Creoles use the word to describe themselves as people of European colonial parentage. They are very proud descendants of old "aristocratic" families who trace their ancestry back to French and Spanish colonists who came to Louisiana. The other group who lays claim to the title are "mulattos," "quadroons," and "octoroons"—light-skinned, part African-American Catholics bearing many of the same French and Spanish surnames as white Creoles, and tracing their lineage back to some of the same ancestors.

Both groups agree that the origin of the word is *criollo,* a Spanish term which had been used in the West Indies to refer to a person of European descent born in New World colonies. The intent of the noun was to differentiate anyone of Old World stock born in the New World from both recent immigrants and Africans. The noted Louisiana historian Charles Gayarré reports that when the first child of French parents was born in Louisiana, Governor Bienville sent a dispatch to the French government to announce the fact. A document of March 4, 1731, proves that the French government paid a bounty to Claude Jousset de la Loire, the infant son of a Canadian trader.

By 1790, the city had a population of 8,000 souls, including "Creoles, free people of color, and slaves." European New Orleanians wanted to distinguish themselves from the Americans after 1803. Similarly, it is thought that French-speaking free people of color adopted the Creole label after the Union army occupation in the 1860s as a means of differentiating themselves from the English-speaking former slaves who were pouring into the occupied city. Interestingly, while slavery existed in New Orleans until the 1860s, most Seventh Ward Creole-of-color families had been free people since the late 1700s.

Both sets of Creoles cling to their history as tenaciously as powdered sugar sticks to beignets. There is an old local riddle, "What do Creoles have in common with the Chinese?" The answer is that both eat a lot of rice and pay homage to their ancestors. Creoles, of either group, take great pride in their European heritage, despite the fact that France never showed much support for its emigrés. Perhaps this had to do with the fact that every time things "hit the wall" in France, many of the old guard packed up their pedigrees and pretensions and high-tailed it to Louisiana. Among white Creoles, the most popular ancestors are the members of the nobility who still had their heads after the French Revolution. From the sound of most local family histories, these nobles were as numerous and as prodigious breeders as the casket girls.

At the dawn of the 19th century, a time of social and political upheaval throughout much of the world, another group of French-speaking refugees arrived

Portrait of Dr. Hardin, a Creole of color in 1895. (Historic New Orleans Collection)

who were to have a major social impact on the city—those fleeing from Toussaint L'Overture's slave revolution against the French settlers in Saint-Domingue (Haiti). Many cane planters packed up their households and fled to Louisiana. One of the new emigrés was John James Audubon, the famous naturalist painter, whose mother—alleged by some to have been a Creole of color—had been killed in the revolution. Another was James Pitot, who from 1804 to 1805 served as the second mayor of the city under American rule. His country home, built circa 1780 and purchased by Pitot in 1810, is now a museum home at 1440 Moss Street on Bayou St. John, where it was moved in the 1960s.

The next group of Frenchmen to leave their imprint on the city were the followers of Napoleon. When Napoleon was exiled to the island of Elba in 1814, many of his dejected soldiers sought passage to the newly American New Orleans. Among these refugees was Napoleon's trusted aide from the Battle of Waterloo, General Charles Lallemand. Evidently many of the soldiers had come to Louisiana to prepare for Napoleon's victorious return. (One legend has it that Jean Lafitte did rescue Napoleon, but that the emperor had a heart attack off the coast of Mexico and was buried in the pirate enclave later called Lafitte, in Louisiana.)

New Orleans waterfront during the antebellum period. (Historic New Orleans Collection)

The gallery of Pitot House, 1440 Moss Street in Bayou St. John. Built circa 1780, the house was purchased in 1810 by James Pitot, the second mayor of the city under American rule.

Another of Napoleon's exiled lieutenants, Pierre Benjamin Buisson, designed the second New Orleans Customhouse and served as the surveyor for the Village of Lafayette, later known as the Garden District. He is given credit for naming Napoleon Avenue and for affixing the names of Napoleon's victories on Milan, Austerlitz, Marengo, and Constantinople streets in the Uptown section, an American part of the city.

By the time Napoleon ended up at St. Helena, Dominique You (also spelled Youx), the brother of pirate Jean Lafitte, had been persuaded to lead an expedition to free the former French emperor and bring him to Louisiana. The Napoleon House, the bar that stands at the corner of Chartres and St. Louis in the French Quarter, was the home of Mayor Nicholas Girod, who offered it as a residence for the great Bonaparte. Napoleon did not live long enough to be rescued, but Napoleon's personal physician, Dr. C. F. Antommarchi, did move from St. Helena into Girod's house and practiced medicine there for the next 13 years. In 1834, Antommarchi gave one of Napoleon's three bronze death masks to the Louisiana State Museum's Cabildo (the other two are in Paris), and it is now in the collection of the Louisiana State Museum. On December 20, 1821, an elaborate Grand Mass honoring Napoleon was celebrated in a black-draped St. Louis Cathedral.

■ CAJUNS

The term "Cajun" is an elision of the term "Acadian," Acadia being the name of the French Canadian colony founded in 1604 by Samuel de Champlain and now called Nova Scotia. Champlain was joined in 1632 by 300 settlers from Poitou who were fleeing religious persecution in France. The Acadians lived in relative isolation for over 100 years until the French and Indian War in 1754, after which the British demanded that these French-speaking people pledge allegiance to England and renounce their Catholic religion. When the Acadians refused, they were rounded up, separated from family and household members, and deported with the few possessions they could carry. Some were sent as indentured servants to the American colonies; others were sent back to France; some were sent to concentration camps in England; and a few managed to hide and remain in Nova Scotia.

The Acadians would have remained a people divided had not the Spanish invited them to relocate to Louisiana. As the Acadians were Catholic and staunch enemies of the British, they were considered ideal Louisiana settlers. By 1763, the first Acadians had begun to burrow deep into the southern Louisiana swamps, adapting quickly to both the open prairies and the bayous—land of alligators, poisonous snakes, and bountiful fresh foods. It was a place of primordial beauty, and the Cajuns dug in like crawfish, spending more time with the Indians than with the uppity Creoles. They learned to build canoe-like cypress *pirogues* that were light enough to skim on dew. Their raised cottages were built along lazy, meandering bayous tangled with palmettos and moss-draped cypress, where "Dutch nightingales" (frogs) croaked an antiphonal opera and moccasins and alligators slithered from one spot of dry land to the other.

Cajuns were isolated from the urban French in New Orleans, and their language

A palmetto house, late 1890s—a typical Cajun trapper's shack. (The Louisiana State Museum)

retained much of the 17th-century France their ancestors had left. Although both speaking versions of French, the Creoles and Cajuns probably have no common ancestry. The immigrants from Wales, Scotland, Germany, and Spain who moved into southwestern Louisiana soon fell into the Cajun ways, gallicizing their surnames and learning to, in the words of the famous Cajun song, *"Laissez le Bon Temps Rouler"* ("Let the Good Times Roll").

The Cajun homeland lies to the southwest of New Orleans, in the area around the city of Lafayette and between Baton Rouge on the east and Lake Charles on the west. Today the descendants of the original Acadians are thought to number close to three-quarters of a million.

CAJUN CULTURE IN NEW ORLEANS

■ **RESTAURANTS**

K-Paul's Louisiana Kitchen. 416 Chartres St.; (504) 524-7394. Paul Prudhomme put Cajun cuisine on the international culinary map. K-Paul's, the mother ship of his empire, has recently been revamped.

■ **BARS AND CLUBS**

Several red-hot Cajun-style bars and dance clubs thrive in the **Warehouse District**, where you can learn to line dance or two-step to the chinka-chinka beat of a live Cajun band. To read about Cajun music, see pp. 209–211.

Michauls. 840 St. Charles Ave.; (504) 522-5517. **Mulate's**. 201 Julia St.; (504) 522-1492. Both clubs are city cousins of popular Cajun clubs in the Lafayette area.

Patout's Cajun Corner. 501 Bourbon St.; (504) 529-4256, has a music line-up that mixes Cajun, zydeco, and local R&B.

■ **FESTIVALS**

Louisiana Swamp Fest. *Late September to early October.* Audubon Zoo and Woldenberg Riverfront Park; (504) 861-2537. Cajun food, music, crafts.

New Orleans Jazz & Heritage Festival. *Late April to early May*. Fairgrounds Racetrack; (504) 522-4786. Cajun music is always a feature of this68 major music event.

Festivals in Lafayette:

A two-hour drive from New Orleans (take I-10 West to the Lafayette exit), Lafayette hosts several Cajun festivals: **Festival International de Louisiane**. *Late April*. **Cajun Heartland State Fair**. *Late May*. Cajundome. **Festivals Acadiens**. *Late September*. Call the Lafayette Visitors Commission at (800) 346-1958.

Blessing of the shrimp fleet. Many Louisiana shrimpers are of Cajun descent. (Michael P. Smith)

■ AMERICAN INDIANS

One of the country's earliest large Native American communities, constructed approximately 2,700 years ago, can be found in the northeastern part of the state near Monroe (a five-hour drive from New Orleans), at Poverty Point. This ancient Native American city is remarkable not only for its size—an estimated 5,000 people lived here—but also for the fact that it was erected between 800 and 600 B.C., at the beginning of the American Neolithic Age. The village at Poverty Point represents the earliest record of the southward movement of Hopewell Civilization.

The ancient community sustained itself in a fixed location, though it remains a mystery how they managed this, since the site predates any evidence of the domestication of animals or the planting of crops. The site is dominated by a mammoth eagle-shaped mound, 600 feet long and 70 feet high, the second tallest Indian mound in North America. Close by is another mound that measures 600 feet by 55 feet. Archaeologists marvel at the fact that the Indians had to dig the earth with sticks and that they transported over a half-million tons of dirt in baskets.

This civilization seems to have been overtaken about 1,000 years ago by a group of Indians who moved north from Mexico, bringing with them agricultural

---

AMERICAN INDIAN CULTURE IN SOUTHERN LOUISIANA

■ FESTIVALS

Louisiana Indian Heritage Association Powwow. *Early May.* Tchefuncte Campground in Folsom, about an hour from New Orleans. (504) 241-5866.

Calumet Powwow. *Mid-May.* Louisiana Nature and Science Center, 11000 Lake Forest Blvd., New Orleans East; (504) 246-9381.

■ MUSEUMS

Bayou LaCombe Rural Museum. St. Mary St., Lacombe; (504) 882-5146. Late 19th- and early 20th-century exploration of local native populations.

Cannes Brûlée Native American Center. 303 Williams Blvd., Rivertown, Kenner; (504) 468-7232. Traditional folklore demonstrations and a re-creation of an outdoor village of the 1750–1820 period.

Chitimacha Tribal Office. Charenton, Bayou Teche in the St. Mary Parish; (318) 923-7215. Displays of distinctive Chitimacha vessels.

techniques and more efficient weaponry. Most of the tribes who lived in permanent fortified villages on navigable waterways around Marksville, Louisiana, wove baskets and made a wide variety of pottery. It is estimated that at that time there were 13,000 Indians in the entire land area that was to become the state of Louisiana.

By the time the French colonists arrived, Indians in southern Louisiana spoke versions of three different languages: Tunican, Caddoan, and Muskhogean. The Acalopisas, the Chitimachas, the Tunicas, and the Bayougoulas taught the earliest colonists the survival and food-gathering skills that saved their lives. But sadly, while the Indians showed them how and where to grow crops and procure meat, fish, skins, and timber, the legacy of the white man was disease, particularly smallpox, which reportedly wiped out entire villages.

Today the 283-acre **Chitimacha Reservation** lies within Jean Lafitte National Park, on Bayou Teche in the St. Mary Parish—less than a two-hour drive from New Orleans. The intricately patterned Chitimacha baskets are included in museum exhibitions around the world and are also on display in the museum adjacent to the tribal office. Due to the shortage of mature five-year-old swamp cane, these baskets now sell for about $20 per square inch and are smaller in scale than the ones of a generation ago. Also there are fewer weavers who have mastered the difficult and time-consuming craft. By the early 1990s, there were only six weavers skilled in making the traditional black, red, and ochre motifs such as the "alligator entrails," "worm tracks," and "blackbird eyes." Many of the elders have predicted that with the arrival of gambling establishments on the Indian reservations, all of the ancient skills will be lost to a younger generation who may prefer to become roulette operators and bingo callers.

■ AFRICANS

On nights when a breeze pushes the pungent smells and the sounds of metal against metal from the holds of football-field-sized ships docked along the wharves, the heart of downtown begins to feel like Pireaus or Istanbul. But then those two port cities don't have the soul of black New Orleans. The evocative rhythm that dominates the sounds of the city and the pace that resonates from its streets puts New Orleans in ethno-cultural harmony with Rio or Dakar. Since the mid-18th century the evolving culture of African Americans has been a driving force of the city.

Dancing the bamboula, as depicted in an old print. (Historic New Orleans Collection)

The first Africans who came to Louisiana were brought in 1719 from the Senegambia region (near Senegal) by French slavers. Recent research shows that between 1719 and 1731 the French Company of the Indies brought in 7,000 slaves. In 1727, the *Code Noir,* a set of regulations for the treatment of slaves, made Louisiana a less oppressive place for blacks to live than in some areas dominated by the British. Though the importation of slaves was outlawed in the United States in 1808, New Orleans was not exempted from this law until 1812. Slavery continued for another sixty-odd years, and local slave auctions were well attended. By 1860, there were some 12 small, year-round slave auction houses, in addition to grander affairs conducted in late winter and early spring—ironically the season of Lent. At these events, New Orleans auctioneers would dress the slaves up in European clothes, hoping to make the Africans look less fearsome. Slave auction sites included the Cabildo, the St. Louis and the St. Charles hotels, and Maspero's Exchange, now a cafe on Chartres Street.

Records show that as early as 1805, the *Place Congo* or Congo Square (now known as Louis Armstrong Park) was a grassy plain on the edge of the swamps at the far side of the French Quarter where *gens de couleur libre* (free blacks) and slaves would congregate. It became a place where African rituals and ceremonies were kept alive and where disparate peoples from a variety of tribal groups found a cultural bond in their improvised music. The immigration of the *gens de couleur libre,* slaves, and former slaves from Haiti in the early 19th century served to infuse other African tribal traditions into those of the Louisiana slaves, many of whom were by then third-generation Louisianians.

An account of 1853 describes the *bamboula,* a dance performed by the blacks: "The head rests on the breast or is thrown back upon the shoulders, the eyes closed, or glaring, while the arms, amid cries, and shouts, and sharp ejaculations, float upon the air, or keep time . . . to music which is seemingly eternal."

Not all of the African Americans living in Louisiana were slaves. There are reports from the 1720s of free blacks, often former slaves who moved to Louisiana from the Caribbean. Between 1763 and 1803, the numbers of free people of color increased from 99 to 1,355, partially due to immigrants from the Indies, and partially due to the number of light-skinned mixed Euro-African citizens. Between 1840 and 1860, the census reported over 7,500 free people of color. By the time of the Civil War, many blacks in Louisiana were 20 generations removed from Africa and 10 from slavery. Additionally many a Frenchman left property to his mixed-race offspring. The initials F.P.C. (Free Person of Color) came to be used after the name of a person of mixed race who might be mistaken for being white and therefore try to assert his civil rights. Oppressive as this was, however, New

Plantation life. (Historic New Orleans Collection)

Orleans afforded free blacks more rights than any other American city north or south, allowing African Americans to own property and to seek justice through the judicial system.

President Abraham Lincoln's Emancipation Proclamation of January 1, 1863, freed slaves in all of the areas of the United States that were in rebellion. By a peculiar stroke of bad luck, slavery was to last in New Orleans longer than in any other part of the United States, as the city was under federal control. Slavery was allowed to continue for almost a year by federal occupation forces. From this period on, one segment of black culture was to be permanently set off from the other by a sociocultural Hadrian's Wall. Uneducated, poor, often darker-skinned, and raised on English-speaking plantations, these recently freed slaves were ostracized by Creoles,

AFRICAN-AMERICAN CULTURE IN NEW ORLEANS

■ FESTIVALS

Black Heritage Festival. *Second weekend in March.* At the Audubon Zoo, 6500 Magazine; (504) 581-4626/(800) 774-7394. Features two days of music, awareness activities, characters from black history, and foods and crafts.

New Orleans Jazz & Heritage Festival. *Last April weekend to first May weekend.* Fairgrounds Racetrack; (504) 522-4786. Spotlights the extraordinary contribution of the black community to New Orleans and to music.

■ MUSEUMS

Amistad Research Center, 6823 St. Charles Ave. (on the Tulane University Campus), (504) 865-5535. The nation's largest black archive and an invaluable research resource. Contains an impressive collection of works by noted African and African-American artists.

■ TOURS

Roots of New Orleans: A Heritage City Tour. 1215 Prytania St., Suite 238; (504) 596-6889/(888) 337-6687. Roots offers a variety of regularly scheduled and custom-designed routs of the city's plethora of fascinating African-American sites. The Sunday morning **Roots n' the Church** combines a gospel mass, brunch, and city tour; **Roots n' the Nite** includes dinner and visits to several jazz and blues clubs; and **Roots of New Orleans City Tour** is an insightful four-hour mini-bus tour.

For further information on African-American culture in New Orleans, contact the **Greater New Orleans Black Tourism Network**, (504) 523-5652/(800) 725-5652.

GROWING UP IN NEW ORLEANS

I'm always wondering if it would have been best in my life if I'd stayed like I was in New Orleans, having a ball. I was very much contented just to be around and play with the old timers. And the money I made—I lived off of it. I wonder if I would have enjoyed that better than all this big mucky-muck traveling all over the world. . . .

But man I sure had a ball there growing up in New Orleans as a kid. We were poor and everything like that, but music was all around you. Music kept you rolling.

When I was about four or five, still wearing dresses, I lived with my mother in Jane's Alley in a place called Brick Row—a lot of cement, rented rooms sort of like a motel. And right in the middle of that on Perdido Street was the Funky Butt Hall— old, beat up, big cracks in the wall. On Saturday nights, Mama couldn't find us 'cause we wanted to hear that music. Before the dance the band would play out front about a half hour. And us little kids would all do little dances. If I ever heard Buddy Bolden play the cornet, I figure that's when.

—Louis Armstrong, "Growing Up in New Orleans," *Life* magazine, 1966

Louis Armstrong sponsored the "Secret 9" baseball team in 1931.
(The Hogan Jazz Archive, Tulane University)

and free people of color and American slaves tended to move into an area known as "back-a-town" (Mahalia Jackson and Louis Armstrong were from this area).

Reconstruction proved to be a time of great discord for the people of the "third race." The *gens de couleur libre,* many of whom had owned slaves themselves, lived in relative seclusion and some prosperity in the Seventh Ward downtown, the site of Bernard de Marigny's estate in the 1800s. (Today, its Corpus Christi Catholic parish is the largest predominantly black Catholic parish in the United States.) Many of the wealthiest among them were French-speaking professionals who educated their children in France. Also among them were master craftsmen and the fathers of jazz. Yet after Reconstruction, they found themselves stripped of all of the freedoms and dignity that they had once enjoyed. Consequently, some migrated to Latin America or Europe; and some moved into uptown neighborhoods, married recent immigrants, and permanently crossed from black to white. In many contemporary Creole-of-color families, some members will have white as the race marked on their birth certificates, while a sibling will be categorized as black, depending on the opinion of the mother's doctor. (In the 1920s Huey Long stated that you could feed all the pure white people in the city with one cup of beans and rice and still have some left over.)

Photographs of former slave children, such as this one of three New Orleanian children, were used by the North during Reconstruction to promote the idea that education should be given to former slaves. (Historic New Orleans Collection)

Ethnic strife is well known in New Orleans. After ugly riots in 1866, the Louisiana Constitution was passed in 1868, insuring rights for blacks that included enfranchisement and the prohibition of segregation in schools and in public spaces. By the end of Reconstruction in 1876, 45 percent of the black population was registered to vote, and by 1897, this figure increased to 95 percent. But the enforcement of Louisiana's infamous grandfather clause and "Jim Crow" laws reduced the percentage to less than 10 percent the following year, and to one percent by 1901.

■ SPANIARDS

The Spaniards were, in a manner of speaking, the state's first white tourists. Hernando de Soto first arrived on the western coast of Florida in 1539, and in the years that followed he explored as far as Arkansas in a fruitless search for silver and gold. While Castilian rule of Louisiana lasted a mere 34 years (1769-1803), the city was nevertheless wedged in between, and profoundly and permanently influenced by, flourishing Spanish settlements in Texas, Florida, and the Caribbean.

Spanish rule was greeted by more than a little "unpleasantness" from French settlers and required military force to quell the unrest. Spanish officials must have

---

SPANISH/LATINO CULTURE IN NEW ORLEANS

■ FESTIVALS

Look in the "Lagniappe" section of the *Times-Picayune* for listings of Latin festivals—always a ball to check out—usually held in the fall and spring. Of special note:

Honduran Independence Day Festival. *Second weekend in September.* French Market.

Minsaje Festival. *April.* In Kenner; (504) 468-7527.

■ MUSEUMS

Islenos Museum. 1357 Bayou Rd., St. Bernard Village; (504) 682-0862. Founded in 1976 by the Spanish Heritage and Cultural Society, the collection affords an intriguing look at photographs and artifacts of a culture that traces its origins to the Canary Islands.

Middle American Research Institute and Museum. Dinwiddie Hall, Tulane University; (504) 865-5110. An exceptional collection of Mexican and Central American archaeological treasures and Guatemalan textiles.

For further information about Latino culture in New Orleans, contact the **Louisiana Hispanic Chamber of Commerce, Inc.**, P.O. Box 5985, Metairie, LA 70009, (504) 885-4262.

seen that their only hope was to marry the problem, and Governor Luis de Unzaga obliged by marrying Mlle. St. Maxent, and a few years later, the third governor, Don Bernardo de Galvez, wed the brilliant Felicie d'Estrehan—a particularly popular first lady of Louisiana.

During his eight-year administration, from 1777 to 1785, Galvez supplied the American frontiersmen with weapons to use against the British, and seized any British ships he could get his hands on. This was of great assistance to the American Revolutionary army. In September of 1779, Galvez captured Baton Rouge and Natchez; in 1780 he took Mobile; and in 1781 he overtook Pensacola. This is why the Daughters of the American Revolution (the D.A.R.) will admit members who trace their ancestry back to those who fought with Galvez.

The fourth governor, Miro, did his marital duty to the locals by taking as his bride the extremely wealthy Celeste Elenore Elizabeth Macarty, daughter of one of the city's premiere Irish Creole families. (The family's original name was Macarthey-Mactaig, an Irish family who had fled Ireland for France to escape the tyranny of the British.) Mlle. Macarty's father and uncle had come to New Orleans in 1731 as part of a French marine detachment. Bienville honored both men by making them *Chevaliers de Saint Louis,* and assisted them in gaining large land grants.

One of the most interesting enclaves of Spaniards is the *Islenos* who came to Louisiana over 215 years ago from the Canary Islands, a Spanish colony off the northwestern coast of Africa. Today close to 500 of the group who live in St. Bernard Parish (one of the four parishes that make up metropolitan New Orleans) still speak their 18th-century Creole Spanish, in an area where 25 percent of the 67,000 residents are of Isleno descent. They live in the communities of Delacroix Island and Reggio and make their living as fishermen and trappers. Since 1976, when the group formed the Spanish Heritage and Cultural Society of St. Bernard, they have actively sought to keep the Spanish heritage of Louisiana alive.

The Latin influence was re-activated in the mid-20th century when political upheaval caused mmigraton from Honduras, Guatemala, Nicaragua, El Salvador, Panama, and Cuba. By 1940, more than 2,000 Latin American-born immigrants were registered in the state. Forty years later the number had risen to more than 100,000 statewide.

■ GERMANS

In the 18th century, it became crucial to the survival of the fledgling colony that John Law's Company of the Indies find enough sturdy immigrant farmers to grow something for French settlers to eat. Toward this end, the company inundated southern Germany and Switzerland with handbills promoting Louisiana as a "paradise." The first large German-speaking Catholic groups arrived in November 1719 on the vessel *Les Deux Freres.* The last great 18th-century German-speaking migration started out two years later with over 1,000 Germans. No sooner had the four ships left the French port than a cholera epidemic broke out.

Once they arrived they were in for more bad news; they soon realized that New Orleans, the "Paris of the New World," was in reality the capital of mildew and malaria, and far from an idyllic place to farm. When John Law's pyramid scheme failed in France, he fled to Italy, leaving the German farmers stranded in the soggy French-speaking Louisiana colony. Law had promised the Germans money and land, but they were still waiting for both when they learned that their new homeland had been given to the Spanish. The Germans pulled out of New Orleans and found dry land to farm 25 miles upriver in an area that became known as the *Côte des Allemands,* or the German coast.

The German farmers did their job well, supplying the city with an abundance of fresh produce. Surnames such as Schexnaider and Hymel (pronounced "Heemel," the Francophone version of Himmel) are still prominent in the suburban

---

GERMAN CULTURE IN NEW ORLEANS

■ BARS AND CLUBS

Fritzel's European Jazz Club. 733 Bourbon St.; (504) 561-0432. German oompah blends with jazz nightly.

■ OKTOBERFEST

Oktoberfest de l'Acadian at **Ormond Plantation.** Destrehan, about 30 minutes from the French Quarter; (504) 764-8544. One of the nicest of these autumn celebrations, celebrated on the third weekend in October.

Deutsches-Haus holds celebrations at 200 S. Galvez St.; (504) 522-3014. Every Saturday in October.

communities of Jefferson Parish. Other Germans intermarried with the French or simply found that it was easier to adapt their names to the language of the region.

Not only were the Germans excellent farmers, but they also soon gained a reputation for being among the finest bakers of French bread and pastries. Even today most of the top local bakeries bear Swiss and German names, and much of the French bread for local poboys comes in paper wrappers printed with

German settlers were brought to Louisiana to grow wheat and became the city's preeminent bakers. (Sharon Dinkins Collection)

the name Leidenheimer. The Germans also built many impressive churches, and introduced commercially brewed beer.

In the middle of the 19th century and at a time when New Orleans still enjoyed a reputation as an Old World European-style city with New World possibilities, political upheaval in Europe brought yet another wave of Germans to Louisiana. Between 1820 and 1850, more than 50,000 Germans passed into the United States from the port of New Orleans. By 1870, an estimated 17,000 people spoke German as their principal language. This wave of immigrants was proud of its Teutonic heritage. Moving into commerce and banking alongside Americans, these newly arrived Germans seemed to have managed to straddle the fence between the old French social strata and newly moneyed Americans. Many of them settled alongside the Creoles in Faubourg Marigny, which would be nicknamed "Little Saxony" by the end of the 19th century.

By the early 20th century, New Orleans' German diaspora was sharing its vibrant musical tradition with other New Orleanians: German oompah bands found appreciative audiences when they played outdoors in the city's parks and plazas. Their use of instruments and upbeat tempos would later influence New Orleans' famous marching bands.

■ IRISH

From its founding, New Orleans proved an attractive destination for enterprising Irish Catholic grandees who loathed the British. Many found their way to New Orleans through military service with the French and Spanish. Once there, they tended to marry into Creole families, and/or adapt their own last names accordingly. The builder of the Gallier House, now a museum house in the French Quarter, was a Mr. Gallagher. Records show that he changed his name before his arrival in the French-speaking colony. The Galliers, the father and the son of Ravensdale, Ireland, are responsible for some of the city's finest architectural treasures, including Gallier Hall, the original city hall, and St. Patrick's Church on Camp Street, as well as many of the city's finest private residences.

The experiences of the old-line, 18th-century Irish Creoles (known as "lace-curtain Irish") upon their arrival in New Orleans, and those of the mid-19th-century potato famine immigrants who followed them were as different as a chestnut horse and a horse chestnut. In the years after the 1845 potato blight, hundreds of thousands of starving Irish poured through the Port of New Orleans, arriving in a city where every section of dry land had already been claimed, where housing was scarce, and where menial labor was usually done by slaves. The new arrivals couldn't afford passage north

Gallier Hall, New Orleans' former city hall.

or west; so they were trapped in a city where they were unneeded.

In 1860, New Orleans had about 175,000 inhabitants, with approximately one quarter of all white New Orleanians being native-born Irish. Potato famine-era Irish could be hired for next to nothing and were often assigned to tasks considered too dangerous for a valuable slave or servant. One of these tasks was to dig the city's canals. Fortunately, the Irish being a hearty lot, many of them managed to survive not only a brutal work load and yellow fever, but also the injustices dished out by both Creoles and Americans. The first statue ever erected in honor of a woman in the United States was dedicated to an illiterate Irish peasant, Margaret Haughery, credited with caring for hundreds of Irish children orphaned after one of the yellow fever epidemics. Her statue stands in a small park at Camp and Prytania with an inscription that simply reads "Margaret."

IRISH CULTURE IN NEW ORLEANS

■ **PUBS**

O'Flaherty's Irish Pub. 514 Toulouse St. (at Decatur); (504) 529-1317. O'Flaherty's often hosts live concerts by musicians who favor the ceili, fiddle, and whistle over the electric guitar and the saxophone. Not to be missed is a local Celtic music group, **The Poor Clares.**

Parasol's Bar. 2533 Constance St. (at Third St., in the Irish Channel); (504) 899-2054. This small neighborhood bar is known year-round as the home of the best roast beef and gravy po-boys in town.

■ **ST. PATRICK'S DAY PARADES**

French Quarter parade. Starts in the 1100 block of Decatur, the Friday before March 17. Call **Molly's at the Market**, 1107 Decatur, (504) 525-5169.

Irish Channel parade. On the Saturday before St. Pat's, the Irish Channel St. Patrick's Day Marching Club begins its celebration by attending the 1:00 P.M. mass at St. Alphonsus or St. Mary's Assumption, then begins its parade at the corner of Felicity and Magazine streets. On St. Patrick's Day Parasol's Bar (see above) opens at 7 A.M. More than 7,000 revelers join the Irish marching clubs to form spontaneous parades and drink such holiday-specific libations as green beer and "Liquid Leprechauns" (don't ask!), dance to live music, and participate in the many live radio broadcasts. The party usually shuts down by dawn the next day.

Another lasting memorial to Irish women and men are the festivities of March 17. Some suspect that there may be a papal dispensation allowing Catholics to break their Lenten abstinence to celebrate St. Patty's Day with gusto And yes, there are many parades. All hardship is forgotten when St. Patrick's Day rolls around, though the festivities often start the Friday before in the 1100 block of Decatur Street in the French Quarter. Here the Decatur Street Marching Club leads a parade that includes other festive groups, such as Joe's Jungle Marching Club, the Kazoozie Floozies, and the Pipes and Drums of New Orleans. Just about everybody in town dons green and takes to the streets to enjoy the party. At noon on St. Patrick's Day, businessmen in pinstripe suits and emerald green derbies can be seen jaunting down Camp Street for mass at St. Patrick's.

The weekend following St. Pat's, there's even an Irish-Italian parade in the suburbs that features Pete Fountain's Half-Fast Walking Club. At these parades float-riders throw cabbages and potatoes, as well as doubloons and plastic necklaces (usually recycled Mardi Gras jewels), to the crowds; and green and white paper carnations are traded for a kiss.

■ ITALIANS

Throughout the 18th century Italians were attracted to New Orleans's Latin/Catholic culture and mild climate. As with the Irish, many aristocratic Italians made their way to Louisiana in the service of the French and Spanish governments. Enrico Tonti was part of the La Salle expedition that discovered the mouth of the Mississippi in 1682. Famed Confederate General Pierre Gustave Toutant Beauregard was the son of Helene Judith de Reggio, of the family of the Duke of Reggio, part of the House of Este. (Another Reggio descendent is married to Senator Edward Kennedy.)

Many other Italians came later, part of the last large wave of immigrants to come to New Orleans in the 19th century, most of them arriving from Sicily. By 1890, there were 15,000 Italians living in the city. Many moved into the crumbling French Quarter, which had fallen out of favor with Creole families. After New York, New Orleans was the largest port of Italian embarkation in North America. Ninety percent of Italian Americans in New Orleans trace their ancestry to Sicily.

One powerful group among these immigrants came from the village of Contessa Entellina in Sicily. On September 8, 1886, these Sicilians founded the Contessa Entellina Society, one of the oldest Italian-American organizations still in existence. Each fall their descendants hold a Mass of Thanksgiving at St. Louis Cathedral to commemorate their coming to America.

The late-coming Italians were treated just a shade worse than the Irish and a tiny bit better than blacks. But like the Irish and blacks, they too survived. One notable Italian was Joseph Vaccaro, who rose from being a door-to-door fruit peddler to founding the company that would later become Standard Fruit and Steamship Company. A second notable immigrant was Mother Frances Xavier Cabrini, the first American citizen to be canonized by the Catholic Church. Mother Cabrini came to New Orleans in 1892 as a missionary to the French Quarter, which was by then 90 percent Italian. Within her lifetime she established 67 different institutions to aid recent immigrants to the city, including orphanages, hospitals, and day-care centers, as well as St. Mary's Italian Church, which served as the focal point in the lives of French Quarter residents.

During the 1970s, four of New Orleans's seven city councilmen, as well as the mayor and the chief of police, were of Italian heritage. Today a visit to the vegetable stalls in the French Market, to the Italian grocery stores near Jackson Square on Decatur Street or to one of the many Italian ice cream shops will confirm that Italian culture continues to thrive in New Orleans.

The American-Italian Renaissance Foundation Museum, at 537 South Peters in the Warehouse District, is a treasury of artifacts and historical documents reflecting the struggles and resourcefulness of Italian immigrants. Call (504) 891-1904 for information.

The Italian community still pays homage to St. Joseph—the patron saint honored as the protector of the family—for delivering the Sicilians from famine in the early 1800s. On St. Joseph's Day, March 19—the day the Creoles called "La Mi-Carême," the middle of Lent—the Italian community gives the city yet another reason to celebrate. On this day, many Italian-American New Orleanians bake and bag several thousand cookies to give away; others cook up gallons of fava beans, the food that saved their 19th-century ancestors from starvation in Sicily. These dishes and dozens of other meatless Sicilian delicacies are prepared, including stuffed artichokes and mirlitons, pasta Milanese, *baccala* (codfish), *sfingi* (an

A St. Joseph's Day altar, an Italian tradition. (Michael P. Smith)

eggplant and olive oil dish), a magnificent array of decorative breads, and pastries and cakes such as *dolci* and *cuccidati*. Once prepared, the food is set on special St. Joseph altars around the city. After each altar has been blessed by a priest, it is opened to the public for viewing and sampling. Afterwards, the foods that have been displayed are served to the poor.

Ads in the *Times-Picayune* classified section invite the public to partake at St. Joseph altars in homes, churches, and businesses. The St. Joseph's Church at 1802 Tulane Avenue presents one of the largest outdoor altars in the world.

St. Joseph's Day also brings yet another parade to the streets of New Orleans. On the Saturday nearest to March 19, the French Quarter fills with 1,500 tuxedo-clad members of the Italian-American St. Joseph Parade Marching Club. Horse-drawn buggies and marching bands accompany floats, each of which depicts a different Italian province. Those in the parade trade red, white, and green carnations for kisses and throw fava beans and doubloons.

ITALIAN CULTURE IN NEW ORLEANS

■ **FESTIVALS**
St. Joseph's Day. *March 19.* (See pp. 82–84 for more information.)

■ **MUSEUMS**
The American-Italian Renaissance Foundation Museum and Research Library.
537 S. Peters St., Warehouse District; (504) 522-7294. A must for Italian-Americans doing family research or for those interested in historical documents and artifacts reflecting the struggles and resourcefulness of Italian immigrants to Louisiana.

■ **SPECIALTY FOODS**
Angelo Brocato's. 527 St. Ann St.; (504) 535 9676
214 N. Carrollton Ave.; (504) 486-1465. For the flavors of Italy New Orleans style, don't miss having Brocato's Italian ice and cookies, a muffuletta sandwich, and a "wop salad" (yes, that's what it's called on local Italian menus).

For a subscription to the Italian-American voice of the Southeast: *Italian American Digest,* P.O. Box 2392, New Orleans, LA 70176; 504-522-7294. Locally, copies of the four seasonal issues can be picked up in most Italian restaurants and bakeries in the city.

FRENCH QUARTER
VIEUX CARRÉ

SPRAWLING, SULTRY, SEDUCTIVE, AND AGELESS, the original neighborhood that was New Orleans still exists as the French Quarter just where Sieur de Bienville, its French founder, left it when his 30 convicted salt smugglers first hacked down razor-sharp palmetto thickets to clear a spot for a few ramshackle houses. An area about three-quarters of a mile long and a quarter-mile wide, the Quarter remains both the heartland of old New Orleans and its most progressive neighborhood. As the decades pass, **Jackson Square**—the old town square that faces the river—continues to be vitally alive with new generations of neighborhood children playing ball, lovers having a lunch-time smooch over a muffuletta, pigeons looking for handouts, and itinerant artists sketching the passersby. The neighborhood remains part residential and part commercial. **Bourbon Street clubs** still serve as a finishing school for local musicians, and both strip joints and gay dance clubs co-exist with T-shirt shops on carefully maintained pedestrian walkways. Not far from all this ebullience and sleaze, expensive antiques are sold from posh shops. Also within the borders of the old city are a thriving public elementary school, an A&P (small by American standards), numerous bakeries, and praline and perfume shops. Above all this exuberance, contradiction, and energy looms the new city of New Orleans—20 or so office and hotel towers that poke up in the uneven pattern of a child's toothy smile. On one side are the twin bridges that span the Mississippi River. The other side of the skyline is dominated by a gigantic aluminum soufflé, the 128,000-cubic-yard **Louisiana Superdome**.

The first step to establishing a relationship with old New Orleans is to stay in one of the small hotels or guest houses operated in one of the older neighborhoods—places such as the Soniat House, the Lafitte Guest House, and the Maison de Ville in the French Quarter; the Columns or the Josephine in the area near St. Charles; or the Parkview near Audubon Park (see pp. 264–272). The second step involves food and drink—meals at Antoine's, the oldest restaurant in America; sandwiches at Uglesich, one of the oldest neighborhood po-boy places; and drinks at the Napoleon House and Lafitte's Blacksmith Shop.

Next to taking a professionally guided tour, a fine way to get the feel of the architecture of the French Quarter is to take a carriage ride—that is if you can stand being seen in a carriage displaying advertisements for the Wax Museum and pulled

French Quarter Walking Tour

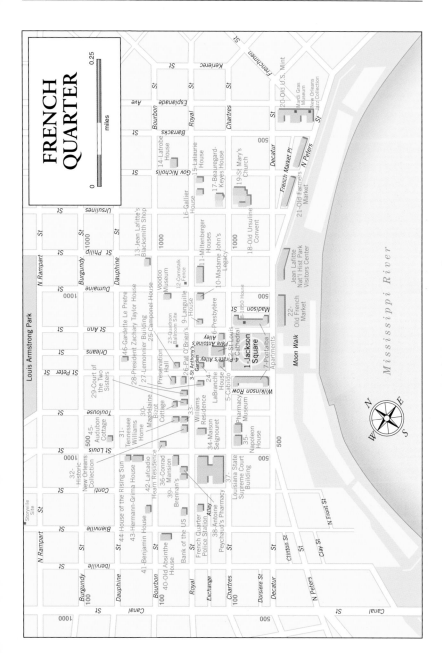

FRENCH QUARTER

0   0.25
miles

French Quarter Walking Tour

Louis Armstrong Park

Storyville Site

Mississippi River

1-Jackson Square
2-St. Louis Cathedral
3-St. Anthony's Garden
4-Pirate's Alley
5-Cabildo
6-Presbytère
7-Pontalba Apartments
8-1850 House
9-Languille House
10-Madame John's Legacy
11-Miltenberger Houses
12-Cornstalk Fence
13-Jean Lafitte's Blacksmith Shop
14-Latrobe House
15-Lalaurie House
16-Gallier House
17-Beauregard-Keyes House
18-Old Ursuline Convent
19-St. Mary's Church
20-Old U.S. Mint
21-Old Farmers Market
22-Old French Market
23-Quadroon Ballroom Site
24-LaBranche Buildings
25-Camponel House
26-Pat O'Brien's
27-Lemonnier Building
28-President Zachary Taylor House
29-Court of the Two Sisters
30-Magdalaine Bizot Cottage
31-Tennessee Williams Home
32-Historic New Orleans Collection
33-Williams Residence
34-Maison Seignouret
35-Napoleon House
36-Conrad Mansion
37-Louisiana State Supreme Court Building
38-Antoine Peychaud's Pharmacy
39-Brennan's
40-Old Absinthe House
41-Benjamin House
42-Lafcadio Hearn Residence
43-Hermann-Grima House
44-House of the Rising Sun
45-Audubon Cottage
46-Gardette Le Pretre

Preservation Hall
Voodoo Museum
Pharmacy Museum
French Quarter Police Station
Bank of the US
Peychaud's Pharmacy
Jean Lafitte Nat'l Hist Park Visitors Center
Moon Walk
Mardi Gras Museum
New Orleans Jazz Collection
Wilkinson Row

Mississippi River

by a mule sporting diapers and a straw hat festooned with plastic flowers. (If this sounds like too much, you might consider wearing a mask. Passersby will not give you a second glance, because in the Quarter there are always a few hard-core partyers who celebrate Mardi Gras year round.) It is preferable to make this half-hour excursion at dusk, when the streets are less crowded and a dreamy lassitude settles over the old city. A few of the drivers who give tours will even point out the balcony in the 1000 block of Royal from which "The King" sang in *King Creole*. But listener beware: these drivers are not licensed guides, and their monologues tend to be more folksy than accurate. One group of local preservationists was horrified to overhear a carriage driver referring to Spanish moss as "Mardi grasses." The point is to sit back and enjoy studying the buildings of the French Quarter from the second floor on up.

■ EARLY HISTORY

In 1721, the governor of New Orleans sent for a French engineer named Adrien de Pauger to create a grid of European-style streets and a grand public square on the ramshackle outpost. Of course, this entailed convincing the crusty settlers that their new city would be more aesthetically pleasing if they knocked their homes down and reconstructed them in an orderly fashion. A document dated September 5, 1722, describes how Pauger and a man named Traverse got into a violent fistfight over the engineer's scheme. Nevertheless, Pauger's 66-square-block network of streets was soon established.

But the French sense of civilized orderliness and the well-considered architecture of the buildings that soon graced New Orleans eventually proved no match for the natural disasters that continually plagued the city. On March 21, 1788, a fire began at the Spanish paymaster's house on Chartres and Toulouse Streets that destroyed all but a tiny portion of the fledgling colonial city. When the city was rebuilt, the (by-now) Spanish governor, Baron Francisco Luis Hector de Carondelet, initiated many improvements, adding the first streetlights—80 oil lamps suspended from poles on street corners—and a drainage canal along Carondelet Street; editing the city's first newspaper; and encouraging the establishment of a theater. Then in 1793 and 1794, the newly improved city was struck by three hurricanes; and in 1794 another terrible fire raged through the city, destroying almost 200 French-built buildings, most of them private homes, in less than three hours. Yet once again the Vieux Carré was rebuilt, and if its well planned streets were sometimes filled with rotting sewage, slops, and garbage, the graciously appointed interiors of many of its homes belied this reality. Some of these, such as the Hermann-Grima Historic House, the Gallier House, and the Beauregard Keyes House and Garden, are still standing and are described later in this chapter.

Note: The French Quarter museum houses keep short hours and are often open only for regularly scheduled tours. Call ahead or check the Friday *Lagniappe* Entertainment Guide in the *Times Picayune* under the "Historic Homes" listing. Also, ★ indicates the sight is important and/or especially interesting.

■ JACKSON SQUARE AREA

★ Jackson Square **1**

The heart of the French Quarter remains its central plaza, Jackson Square, originally constructed in 1721 as a drill field and called the **Place d'Armes.** Bounded by Decatur, St. Peter, Chartres, and St. Ann Streets, the square was renamed in 1848 to honor Andrew Jackson, the hero of the 1815 Battle of New Orleans. In 1851, the Baroness Pontalba installed the fences and gardens landscaped in the sun

The early Place D'Armes, the center of the Vieux Carré, which later became Jackson Square. This drawing is of the second of three cathedrals on this site. (Historic New Orleans Collection)

French Quarter Walking Tour

pattern made popular in France during the reign of Louis XIV, the Sun King.

The pigeon-covered statue of Jackson ("Old Hickory") atop a rearing steed was fashioned by sculptor Clark Mills. It was the world's first equestrian statue in which the horse has more than one foot off the base. The statue now bears the inscription, "The Union must and shall be preserved," which was added in the 1860s by the occupying Union army during the War Between the States.

★ **St. Louis Cathedral** **2**

Jackson Square is dominated on Chartres Street by St. Louis Cathedral, the oldest continually active cathedral in the United States, and the third church to be built on this site. (The first, constructed in 1722, was lost to fire, as was the second.) The present cathedral dates in part from 1794, but was largely remodeled in 1845-1851 by J. N. B. de Pouilly. Its interior contains magnificent stained glass, murals, frescoes, and the graves of many early New Orleans dignitaries. The cathedral's rectory serves as the repository for church registers that date back to 1731. Nearby Père Antoine's Alley is named for the late-18th-century priest; lying behind the cathedral, **St. Anthony's Garden** **3** is named for the padre's patron saint. A monument in St. Anthony's Garden is dedicated to those caregivers who were stricken in the epidemic, which killed over 11,000 people.

Pirate's Alley **4**

Père Antoine's Alley runs from Chartres to Royal along the northeastern side of the cathedral and garden; bounding the opposite side of these sites, Pirate's Alley sounds like its evil twin. In 1925, William Faulkner lived in a humble garret at 624 Pirate's Alley while writing his first novel, *Soldier's Pay.* Today **Faulkner House Books** occupies this space, allowing you to pick up a copy of *As I Lay Dying* and commune with the writer's ghost.

★ **Cabildo** **5** **and Presbytère** **6**

St. Louis Cathedral is flanked by original late 18th-century Spanish Colonial government buildings, the Cabildo (to the left of the cathedral) and the Presbytère. The Presbytère stands at 713 Chartres Street on the site of an early French monastery. A wealthy Spaniard, Don Almonester, financed this new building as a home for the priests of the Cathedral. While the building was

St. Louis Cathedral in Jackson Square was built between 1849 and 1852. See page 89 for a drawing of the cathedral which preceded St. Louis Cathedral.

French Quarter Walking Tour

under construction, in 1794 a fire destroyed much of it. The Presbytere sat abandoned until 1813, when the Americans rebuilt it for use as a courthouse.

The Cabildo was once a Spanish government building, the *Casa Capitular* where the "Very Illustrious Cabildo," or city council, met. Destroyed in the 1788 fire, it was rebuilt with an ornate wrought-iron balcony rail attributed to Marcelino Hernandez. The Louisiana Purchase was turned over to the United States in the left-side room on the second floor of the Cabildo on December 20, 1803. From its chambers French, Spanish, Confederates, and Americans have ruled the city. In 1847, mansard roofs were added to both these Colonial-style buildings in an effort to modernize them. In 1988, yet another fire greatly damaged the upper floors. Today both buildings are part of the Louisiana State Museum system.

Pontalba Apartments 7

Flanking Jackson Square on either side of the park are the Pontalba Apartments, which some call the first urban renewal project in the New World, and begun in 1849 by the Baroness Micaela Pontalba, the daughter of Don Almonester y Rojas. The infamous Baroness married her French cousin, the Baron Celestin de Pontalba; had a near fatal altercation with her father-in-law; and fled to Louisiana cloaked in scandal. The Pontalba buildings originally included commercial space on the ground floor, and palatial living quarters and slave quarters above. The first stage of the development includes the 16 elegant row houses along St. Peter Street. The complementary row, facing St. Ann Street, on the opposite side of the square, was completed in 1852. The rows of ground-floor offices and shops with residences above were conceived as a means of attracting up-and-coming Creoles to reinforce the commercial and social life of the Vieux Carré at the time that Americans were establishing their own commercial district across Canal Street.

Note the elaborate ironwork in the balconies and galleries, characteristic of many Vieux Carré buildings. Introduced by the Spanish governors between 1762 and 1800, the French Quarter's first lacy iron balconies and grilles were hand-wrought by artisans whose work was a translation of North African metal-working traditions that date back over 2,000 years. Such work may have been beautiful, but it was also expensive and impractical. It was the baroness who introduced the use of cast rather than hand-wrought iron for her balconies and galleries. Their elaborate design intertwines the initials "A" and "P," her maiden and married initials.

Today the St. Peter Street Pontalba building is maintained by the city, while the one on St. Ann Street is owned by the state. The apartments are quite sought after, and one must be well connected to secure a lease. At Christmas when there is candlelight caroling in the square, local people consider themselves to be fortunate if they are invited to one of the parties hosted by Pontalba inhabitants. At 523 St. Ann Street, in the middle of the state's building, is the **1850 House** **8**, a three-story period restoration; call ahead for times, (504) 524-9118 or (504) 568-6968. The square itself remains an active plaza. The Old World–style cathedral, the Pontalba buildings, the Presbytère, and the Cabildo serve as a backdrop for street musicians, tarot card readers, Lucky Dog and ice cream vendors, mimes, and artists—slightly more upbeat replacements for the public executions that once took place there.

■ LOWER FRENCH QUARTER

The Quarter is conventionally divided into sections, with Jackson Square marking the midpoint between the Lower Quarter (the northeastern half) and the Upper (the southwestern). The following tour of the Lower Quarter begins at the northern corner of Jackson Square, loops through the northeastern half of the Quarter, takes a quick detour along the Mississippi, then returns to Jackson Square along the river. From the square, head northwest on St. Ann Street to Royal and turn right.

Languille House **9**

The Languille House at 800 Royal Street was the tallest building in the city for many years after its completion in 1801. It soon earned the reputation as the hangout for French Royalists, many of whom met at the Cafe des Exiles on the building's ground floor.

Madame John's Legacy **10**

Turn right onto Dumaine Street to visit Madame John's Legacy at 632 Dumaine, a rare remnant of the West Indian/Colonial-style architecture of the early French Quarter. Built in 1726, the house was partially destroyed by the Good Friday fire of 1788, rebuilt a few years later, and survived the fire of 1794. Some argue that it is one of the oldest buildings in the Mississippi Valley, predating the Ursuline

French Quarter Walking Tour

Convent. The name "Madame John" comes from the short story written by George Washington Cable about fictional owner Captain Jean Pascal, who was killed by the Natchez Indians, and the free woman of color who was his mistress and the inheritor of his home.

Return to Royal and turn right to see some fine examples of cast ironwork. Some of the nicest examples of cast ironwork can be seen in the 900 block of Royal Street in the three attached brick houses, the **Miltenberger Houses** **11**, which date from 1838. It was here that Alice Heine, the first American princess of Monaco, was born in 1910. Miss Heine married the Duc de Richelieu, and later married Prince Louis of Monaco.

Don't miss the **Cornstalk Fence** **12** across the street at 915 Royal, with its 1850s cast-iron motif of ears of corn and morning glories. The story goes that a doctor commissioned the fence from Philadelphia as a present for his wife, who missed the cornfields of her native Midwest.

★ Lafitte's Blacksmith Shop **13**

Another structure evocative of the Colonial Period is Lafitte's Blacksmith Shop at 941 Bourbon Street. The building dates back to circa 1780 and was built with the timber and soft-brick construction used by the first colonists. Jean Lafitte and his fellow pirates are said to have sold their booty out of the back door of a blacksmith shop at this address, and it was here that illegally imported slaves were traded after the importation of slaves was outlawed in 1807. Some claim that the name comes from legend rather than fact, and that no one really knows where Lafitte's shop was located. No matter, the building now houses one of the city's most colorful bars.

Latrobe House **14**

In 1814, the then 19-year-old master local architect, Henry Latrobe, built the house at 721 Governor Nicholls Street—probably the first example of Greek Revival architecture in the city. Latrobe is credited with inspiring New Orleans's love for the architectural style.

Lalaurie House **15**

Also known as the **Haunted House,** the Lalaurie House at 1140 Royal Street (at the corner of Governor Nicholls, formerly Hospital, Street) was sacked by an angry mob in 1834. Louis McCarty built the house and presented it to his

(opposite) Jean Lafitte's Blacksmith Shop is one of the oldest extant buildings in New Orleans, having been constructed in 1780. His fellow pirates reputedly sold their booty out of the shop's back door.

daughter, Marie Delphine McCarty Lalaurie, in 1831. Unfortunately, Madame Lalaurie found pleasure in torturing her slaves and enough of them "committed suicide" that the neighbors started to talk. When her neighbor called the volunteer fire brigade to her house to put out a fire on April 10, 1834, they discovered seven shackled, starving slaves. The lady of the house fled before the mob, determined to kill her, got there. Shrieks of the slaves are still said to fill the night air in that block of the Quarter. Mrs. Lalaurie later died in Europe, and her body was brought home to New Orleans to be buried in secrecy in St. Louis No. 2.

★ Gallier House 16

In 1857, 30-year-old Anglo-Irish Protestant architect James Gallier, Jr. began work on an elegant townhouse for himself, his Creole wife Aglae Villavaso, and their four young daughters. Today the Gallier House at 1118-1132 Royal Street, located three blocks from the Mississippi River in what was formerly the orchard of the Ursuline Convent, is a National Historic Landmark. James Gallier, Jr. (son of the architect, James Gallier, Sr.) was the noted architect of the famed French Opera House that stood on the corner of Bourbon and Toulouse Streets from 1858 until it was destroyed by fire in 1919. Gallier's Bank of America Building (1866), designed in the Northern Italian Renaissance style, can still be seen at 111 Exchange Place. It is thought to be the first building in New Orleans to have a structural cast-iron front.

Gallier House reflected the latest architectural innovations of its time, including an operable etched-glass skylight above the upstairs landing, ventilators in the master bedroom, and a flush toilet. Departing from custom, Gallier attached the kitchen directly to the house. An English cast-iron, coal-burning range minimized the cooking odors and fire hazards that had for so long made detached kitchens a necessity. Two 3,500-gallon cisterns provided water directly into the indoor faucets. Hot water circulated from a copper boiler through the range and then upstairs to the copper bathtub.

The home remained in the hands of the Gallier's three unclaimed treasures, his spinster daughters, until 1917, when they sold the house and moved Uptown. One of these daughters, Clemence, worked at the New Orleans Public Library from 1898 until her death in 1941. The Gallier House Museum was opened to the public in 1971 and painstakingly restored along the lines of the 1868 inventory of Gallier's estate. Of special interest are the portions of the house that are couched in "summer dress," the stylistic tricks employed to combat the brutal heat and humidity of Louisiana summers. Straw matting replaces the wool carpets. Mirrors, chandeliers, and all gilded objects are covered with netting to protect them from the permanent black-spotting damage of "flyspecks." Throughout the house in summer, upholstered furniture is covered in white cotton slipcovers that are cooler to the skin than velvet or brocade. Call (504) 525-5661 for hours.

Return to Ursulines and turn left to continue your tour of the Lower Quarter.

★ Beauregard-Keyes House and Garden **17**

Located at 1113 Chartres Street—at the corner of Ursulines Street, across from the convent—this house possesses one of the most captivating gardens and courtyards in the French Quarter. Built in the Greek Revival style (see chapter "ARCHITECTURE," pp. 116–117), it dates from 1826. The original home was owned by the grandfather of chess champion Paul Morphy, who spent a portion of his early years here. Confederate General P. G. T. Beauregard rented a room here from 1866 to 1867. Later, the prolific writer Frances Parkinson Keyes (rhymes with "eyes") took up residence here, and moved her doll collection into the house. Ms. Keyes also took inspiration for her work from the prior inhabitants of her home, writing books about both a chess player and the general.

Ms. Keyes' doll collection and huge Victorian dollhouse remain special treats for guests. Each Christmas the museum house hosts the Doll's Tea Party on the second Saturday of December. Children of all ages are invited to bring their dolls along to have tea with the dolls in the collection. The children themselves enjoy Christmas caroling and cups of punch from the silver punch bowl.

While the house is decorated in a style appropriate to the turn of the century, its beautiful garden is authentic to 1830s New Orleans. The interior courtyard is dominated by a magnificent live oak tree which serves as a gigantic umbrella, keeping the garden 10 degrees cooler than the rest of the French Quarter. About the tree bloom pink ruffle azaleas, a profusion of ferns, Purple Dawn, and Louisiana Peppermint camellias. Like the garden in Jackson Square, the side garden is a "parterre" (a garden with ornamented plots separated by paths) which is laid out in a sunburst pattern. The Garden Study of New Orleans (Garden Clubs of America) maintains a formal, white, **French garden** that blooms year-round with white magnolia, petunias, azaleas, the parterre, and an herb garden. If a tour of the house isn't possible, peek through the gate at the garden. Call (504) 523-7257 for hours.

French Quarter Walking Tour

French Quarter Walking Tour

★ **Old Ursuline Convent** 18

The earliest Ursuline Convent and the country's first Charity Hospital were located at 301 Chartres Street, in a townhouse leased to the Sisters of St. Ursula from 1727 until 1734. Here they founded the first convent and the first girls school—the Ursuline Academy—in the United States. The sisters then moved to the Old Ursuline Convent at 1114 Chartres Street when it was completed around 1752. Having survived the fire of 1788, it has stood longer than any brick-and-post building of the French Colonial style in the Mississippi Valley. The Sisters continued to serve the community in their second location, later starting the first black and Native American school in the United States. Adjacent to the old convent is the Chapel of the Archbishops erected in 1845. Today it is called **St. Mary's Church** 19, and it serves as the St. Lazarus National Shrine.

Old U.S. Mint 20

One of the oldest mints still standing, is at the back of the Quarter at 1300 Decatur Street at Esplanade Avenue near the French Market. On the site of one of

(above) The Ursuline Convent, founded by nuns from France, housed the first girls' school in the nation. (opposite) Ironwork such as that at the Soniat House (down the street from the Ursuline Convent) distinguishes New Orleans architecture in the popular imagination.

the city's original five forts, Fort San Carlos, it was designed by William Strickland and begun in 1837. While in service it minted almost $300 million in United States coins. The State of Louisiana took possession of the mint when the Civil War broke out in 1861, and it became the mint for the Confederacy. When the city fell to Union hands, it became a prison for captured Confederate soldiers. After the war, it functioned as a federal mint again until 1909. Today, the building is part of the Louisiana State Museum system and houses the extensive **New Orleans Jazz Collection** and **Mardi Gras Museum**.

★ Old Farmers Market 21 and Old French Market 22

Make your way back to Jackson Square along North Peters, and pass by (or visit) the Old Farmers Market between Governor Nicholls and Ursulines. In this WPA building, local chefs professional and amateur peruse the garlic-draped stalls for vegetables, fruit, seafood, and spices, all for sale 24 hours a day. At the corner of Decatur and Dumaine stands the Old French Market, originally an Indian trading post where Creoles bought spices and other goods such as sassafras leaves (from which filé powder is made) from the Choctaws. Later, French and Spanish made this the site of their open-air market: Creoles have been shopping at this location since the early 1700s. The current building went up in 1813, and was renovated in the 1930s and again in the '70s.

To continue touring the Quarter, return to Jackson Square, and make your way to the site of the Quadroon Ballroom.

■ UPPER FRENCH QUARTER

Quadroon Ballroom 23

The Quadroon Ballroom and the Negro Sisters of the Holy Family's orphanage chapel were both once located at 717 Orleans Street. Originally built on this site were the Orleans Theatre and the Orleans Ballroom, which were destroyed by fire in 1816. The following year John Davis rebuilt the Orleans Ballroom at this address. (Davis also brought the French Opera to America, but his empire of theaters and dining rooms was lost in the aftermath of the defeat of the Confederacy, which he backed.) It was here that the famous quadroon balls were held, and here that mulatto daughters were presented by their mothers as potential mistresses to masked white Creole men. Wealthy Creole men sometimes supported quadroon mistresses and families in addition to their own "legitimate" white families. These balls lasted from 1838 until the early 1860s. In 1874, a free man of color, Thomy Lafon, bought the ballroom for an order of black nuns, the Negro Sisters of the Holy Family, founded in New Orleans in 1842 by the daughter of a quadroon mistress. The Quadroon Ballroom is now a restored meeting room within the **Bourbon Orleans Hotel.**

La Branche House 24
Return to Royal Street and turn right to see a fine example of ironwork: the oak boughs-and-acorns motif of the La Branche House, 700 Royal Street at St. Peter. The house was completed in 1840, and the ironwork was added in the 1850s.

Camponel House 25
One of the loveliest homes of the early free people of color is at 717 St. Peter Street. This New Orleans home of the wealthy Parisian Bartholome Camponel was built in 1811.

Pat O'Brien's 26
Just across the street at 718 St. Peter, the Tabary Theatre, the first Spanish theater in the United States, was built in 1791 by a Spanish military officer; it now stands as the bar Pat O'Brien's. Today, the bar sells more mixed drinks than any other establishment in the world. Built in 1791, the house found new life in 1933 as the home of the notorious pink drink—the "Hurricane."

Lemonnier Building 27
Return again to Royal to see this four-story building at 640 Royal Street. Locals were truly horrified in 1821 when this honest-to-God skyscraper was built two blocks from the Languille House, until then the tallest house in the Quarter. For several generations neighbors predicted that the Lemonnier would collapse and kill pedestrians. (It is also known as the setting of the story by George Washington Cable, "'Sieur George.")

President Zachary Taylor House 28
Cross the street to see 621 Royal Street. "Old Rough and Ready," the Mexican War hero, often stayed with his daughter and her husband in the 1840s at this

address. In 1847 the city gave him a monumental celebration and in 1848 he was elected President of the United States, later dying mysteriously while in office.

Court of Two Sisters Restaurant 29

Spanish settlers favored private, shaded interior courtyards and patios. One courtyard that is particularly lovely can be found at 615 Royal; it's named refers to the two sisters who ran a dry goods store here from 1886 to 1906. Originally the site was occupied by the house inhabited by two Spanish governors, but that building was destroyed in the 1788 fire. Later, the president of the Banque d'Orleans built his house here with one of the largest slave quarters in the city, as he is said to have had over 35 household servants.

Magdelaine Bizot Cottage 30

Turn right onto Toulouse to see 719 Toulouse Street, given to a free woman of color by Joseph Bizot, who had it built in 1799. In the 1930s and '40s it was the home of writer Roark Bradford, and it was here that Bradford and his wife entertained William Faulkner and Ernest Hemingway. Another writer—Tennessee Williams—once rented rooms across the street at 720 Toulouse Street 31. where he wrote and set his play *Vieux Carré*.

★ Historic New Orleans Collection 32

Return to Royal Street to visit the Historic New Orleans Collection. The main entrance is at 533 Royal, though the collection is housed in seven historic French Quarter buildings. The earliest was built in 1792 by a merchant and is one of the few existing buildings spared by the fire of 1794. The privately endowed research facility mounts exceptional exhibitions related to the history of New Orleans; their wonderful gift shop specializes in fine historical reproductions. Also in the complex, the **Williams Residence** 33 is an elegant 19th-century townhouse restored in the 20th century by its then new occupants, General and Mrs. L. Kemper Williams. The house itself stands at 718 Toulouse, across from the Magdelaine Bizot Cottage, but entrance is at 533 Royal; call (504) 523-4662 for days and hours.

★ Antique Shops on Royal and Chartres

Both Royal and Chartres Streets are lined with a plethora of antique shops specializing in fine French and English antiques. Both areas also have many shops offering

AUDUBON

*J*ohn James Audubon, ornithologist, naturalist, and artist, was born in Haiti in 1785, the natural son of a French slave trader and a Creole woman. After Audubon's mother was killed in a slave insurrection in Haiti, John James was raised in France by his father's wife. As a young man of 18, Audubon fled from conscription into Napolean armies, smuggled himself out of France, and came to the United States.

He tried and failed at a series of money-making schemes before he turned to painting. Once he did, his dogged pursuit of feathered subjects led him on hunting parties with the Osage Indians, whose language he spoke, and even into the company of Daniel Boone.

Audubon's spare and stylized paintings—accomplished by first killing and stuffing the birds he so admired—served as a foil to his chaotic life. The subjects' highly mannered poses bespeak the painter's romantic sensibility, and his pictures tell almost human stories of flirtation, pride, and anger.

"Wanderlegs" is how Audubon described the affliction that kept him adrift in the forests and swamps of nineteenth-century America. He once wrote to his anxious wife, in a letter written in New Orleans and dated May 3, 1821: "Thou art not, it seems, as daring as I am about leaving one place to go to another, without the means . . . without one cent." Audubon did hold for a time in 1821 at a cottage at 505 Dauphine in the French Quarter, working on his *Birds of America* series in his studio at 706 Barracks Street. Audubon never lost his French accent, and even permitted rumors to spread that he was the lost Dauphin of France. But when he returned to France on a few occasions to visit, Audubon posed as the wild outdoorsman of the frontier—a noble French savage in buckskin and leggings.

New Orleans has since honored the painter in its naming of Audubon Park and Audubon Zoo.

—Dan Duane

John J. Audubon. (Historic New Orleans Collection)

The French Quarter is well known for fine antique stores such as Lucullus on Chartres Street.

antique jewelry and porcelains. Two of the most famous 19th-century furniture makers created their masterpieces in the Quarter. One is the Frenchman Prudent Mallard, who came to the city in the 1830s and opened his shop in the French Quarter. Mallard's Magasin was located at 301 Royal Street. The other is another Frenchman, Francois Seignouret, who fought at the Battle of New Orleans and was a wine merchant as well as a furniture maker. In 1816, he built a house and wine-importing business at 520 Royal Street, **Maison Seignouret** 34. His furniture (which is represented at the White House in Washington) always bears the initial "S" somewhere in the design.

If you'd like to visit another wonderful antique store, stop by Lucullus at 610 Chartres. It specializes in culinary antiques, from fine china to kitchen chairs.

★ The Napoleon House 35

By now you may be ready for a break. Make a detour and turn left at St. Louis to visit The Napoleon House at 500 Chartres. Built in 1814, it's a quiet place to stop in for a Pimm's Cup and a game of chess while enjoying the Mediterranean feel of crumbling plaster and the smell of antiquity. The French Colonial building is topped by the original tile roof and an octagonal cupola. The original owner, Mayor Girod, was said to have offered his home as a residence for Napoleon should he be able to escape.

Conrad Mansion 36

To continue seeing this Quarter, return to Royal via St. Louis. Just past Royal at 722 St. Louis stands the Conrad Mansion, built by physician Joseph Conrad circa 1808 and later sold and turned into a pension. While the French Opera House thrived at 541 Bourbon Street from 1859 until 1919 (when it burned), many chorus members stayed here. The more famous performers stayed at the Rouzan Mansion, 522 Bourbon Street, which became the French Opera Hotel in 1884.

Louisiana State Supreme Court Building 37

Covering the entire 400 block of Royal Street, this grand Victorian structure was built 1908–09. After decades of neglect, the building was renovated and the Louisiana State Supreme Court moved in. Oliver Stone fans may recognize it from the film *JFK,* part of which was shot here.

French Quarter Walking Tour

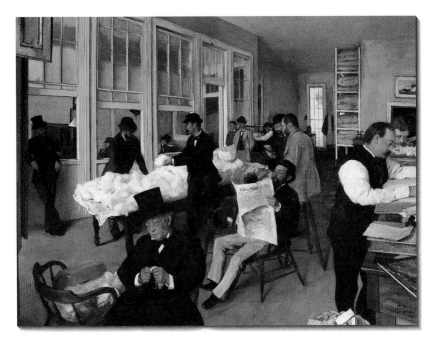

Edgar Degas's painting of his uncle's New Orleans cotton office in 1873, now hanging at the Musée des Beaux Arts, Pau, France. (photo by Erich Lassing, Art Resource/NY)

Peychaud's Pharmacy 38

The cocktail is thought to have been invented at 437 Royal in the late 1800s, when Antoine Peychaud concocted the first bitters and stirred them into his brandy—along with a little absinthe. The word "cocktail" itself derives from the egg cups, or *coquetiers*, in which Peychaud originally served his mixture—a drink known as a Sazerac. Today's Sazerac is a bit different: bourbon replaces the brandy, and absinthe flavoring stands in for the outlawed extract.

Brennan's Restaurant 39

Circa 1796, prominent merchant Vincent Rillieux, Edgar Degas's great-grandfather, built the home at 417 Royal Street. Later it became the Banque of Louisiane, hence the "BL" in the balcony rail. The Gordon family purchased it shortly thereafter, hosting Andrew Jackson in 1828. In subsequent decades, chess champion Paul Morphy was raised here. The building now houses the popular Brennan's.

★ Bourbon Street

Bourbon Street may not seem to be the Vieux Carré's most picturesque byway —it's the only street in the Quarter with neon—but a wander amidst the rowdy crowds and a drink at a noisy club are a part of the New Orleans experience, an should be done, if only once. For more on Bourbon Street clubs, see pp. 214–215.

★ Old Absinthe House 40

Although most people do not visit Bourbon Street to savor the architecture, there are several structures that are worth strolling by. At the corner is the Old Absinthe House, thought to be the oldest bar still in operation in the state; note the Creole-style building that houses it. A block away, at 327 Bourbon Street, is **The Benjamin House 41**, the 1835 townhouse that was the home of Confederate Secretary of State Judah P. Benjamin.

The nearly destitute writer Lafcadio Hearn rented a room at 516 Bourbon Street **42** during his stay in the city from 1877 to 1887.

The free spirit and good times of Bourbon Street are enhanced by the performances of famous exotic dancers such as Chris Owen, shown above. (Syndey Byrd)

French Quarter Walking Tour

✴ Hermann-Grima Historic House 43

Located at 818-820 St. Louis, this was one of the earliest Georgian-style residences in the French Quarter. With the only functioning 1830s kitchen in the city, the house is the scene of fascinating open-hearth cooking demonstrations each Thursday from May until October. Throughout the year many homemade delights are available in the gift shop, including potpourris, pralines, and unusual jellies and vinegars.

Roughly from mid-October until All Saints Day, the museum house is transformed into a scene of "Sacred to the Memory," depicting the Creole funerary and burial customs of the 1830s. Black drapes cover the pictures, and a casket occupies the parlor. In addition to its other charms, the house is said to be haunted by a friendly spirit who smells of lavender and lights the fireplaces on chilly mornings.

Between the first of December and New Year's, the house is decorated Creole-style for the Christmas holidays. Decorations and furnishings are authentic down to the mop bucket filled with water that stands beside the candle-lit Christmas tree, just in case it should catch fire. An added enticement are the cooking demonstrations. Call (504) 525-5661 for days and hours.

The House of the Rising Sun 44

If the French Quarter claims charming family homes, it has also played host to more than a few houses of ill repute. The house at 826 St. Louis Street, is politely known as "The Dancing Master's House" by those who claim this has always been the home of only the most prominent citizens. Its more common name is of uncertain derivation. The home was sold by the city's most famous dancing master in 1847 to widow Elizabeth Levant; *levant* in French means "rising," which may explain the other name. (Buggy drivers also like to pass along the rumor that Hotel Villa Convento at 616 Ursuline Street may have been that famous bordello.)

Audubon Cottage 45

The cottage at 505 Dauphine Street, is where the artist John James Audubon lived from 1821 to 1822 while at work on his *Birds Of America* series. (Also see p. 103.)

Gardette-Le Pretre House 46

The house at the corner of Orleans and Dauphine (716 Dauphine), dates from 1836. In June 1861, victorious Confederate General Beauregard sent part of the captured flagstaff from Fort Sumter to this house, where it was given to the Orleans Guards. Formerly occupying this site was the home of Cousrouf, brother to Sultan Selim III of Turkey, where both he and his five child-wives were murdered in 1792. In her 1922 account of the story, Helen Pitkin Schertz warned, "Highstrung, imaginative folk cannot abide in such ghostly quarters. . . . Holy water has proved ineffective in laying the little veiled figures which evanesce through corridors and up stairways, moaning in flight."

ST. ROCH'S CHAPEL

North of the French Quarter, on St. Roch near North Roman, St. Roch's Chapel was dedicated on August 16, 1876, in thanksgiving to St. Roch for sparing the congregation of the Holy Trinity Catholic Church from the yellow fever epidemic in 1868. The church looks as though it were a scale model of a Gothic cathedral or, as some locals have described it, a Victorian parlor clock. The belief is that for every miracle St. Roch grants, he takes something away: the offerings shown in the photo are meant to appease the saint.

The tiny shrine only has a few pews and an altar with a statue of St. Roch and his faithful dog. It is not unusual to see Catholic school girls in their white blouses and pleated skirts coming from school to one of the city's shrines, praying to St. Ann to take away a broken heart or deliver the perfect boyfriend. "St. Ann, St. Ann," they sing, "send me a man."

Inside St. Roch's Chapel

(following pages) Crowds gather in Jackson Square for a Fourth of July music festival. (Syndey Byrd)

ARCHITECTURE

IN MUCH OF AMERICA THE PURPOSE OF ARCHITECTURE is to create isolated monuments. In New Orleans, to be considered successful, a structure must live in harmony with those buildings which have come before. The New Orleans style of architecture is a tantalizing repertoire of motifs and periods whose style is caught between romanticism and the first rumblings of functionalism.

In its early days, the city gave rise to a variety of styles from brick-and-post cottages to West Indian planters' houses; from columned antebellum mansions to Italianate townhouses; from Spanish-inspired stucco shops with living quarters above and hidden courtyards below to working-class shotgun houses with decorative scroll work. Many houses can boast of having been made of the barge boards from the keelboats that the hillbilly "Kaintock" traders broke up and sold to the Louisiana colonists in the early nineteenth century. Following is a brief description of classic New Orleans architectural styles.

■ CREOLE COTTAGE

The first French settlers framed their houses with cross-braced cypress and heart pine beams, then bound them together with mud, Spanish moss, and animal hair. These early one-room cottages were topped with palmetto-leaf roofs, which seemed to resist the swarms of termites, the torrents of rain, and the rot so common in a damp climate. Sometimes local bricks were used as infill, with clay or mud holding the structure together. This style can be seen at **Lafitte's Blacksmith Shop,** 941 Bourbon Street, which was constructed in 1780. Bricks were often covered in plaster, sometimes scored to resemble stone, as water tended to seep through those bricks left uncovered. Buildings were built on brick piers to avoid floodwaters, a construction which also increased ventilation. The Creole cottage soon adapted to a more urban context, often being built two-stories high and containing four rooms and no interior hallways. The Creole cottage was most often built flush to the sidewalk, with whatever small patch of garden space located in the rear. The exterior was finished in either woodlap siding or stuccoed brick and frequently painted in light-reflecting colors. The most common style of roof is side-gabled with chimneys breaking through the roof pitch at the centerline of the house, which is sometimes flanked by arched dormer windows.

The front porch of the Laura plantation house. (Syndey Byrd)

Audubon's former residence is a good example of a Creole cottage.

Many homes of the urban Creole cottage style can be seen in the **Faubourg Marigny Historic District** (bounded by Esplanade Avenue, St. Claude Avenue, Press Street, and the Mississippi River). The area was the first "suburb" of the original city and the original plan dates from 1806. One of the finest examples of the Creole cottage can be seen at 1809 Dauphine, which dates from the 1830s.

Another area with some fine examples of this architecture is the city's largest local historic district, encompassing some 250 city blocks, the **Esplanade Ridge Historic District** (roughly the area from Bayou St. John to North Rampart and Philip Street and down Orleans Avenue to North Villere Street). Its earliest section, Faubourg Treme, contains several lovely Creole cottages dating from the 1830s. These include the residences at 1020-1022 Treme and 1308 St. Claude.

■ SPANISH COLONIAL

The great fires of the late 18th century destroyed most of New Orleans's earliest buildings. To limit the disastrous spread of such fires in the future, Governor

Carondelet instituted building codes requiring tile roofs and adobe or brick walls for all structures two stories or taller. The grandest and most baroque of these post-fire, Mediterranean-style buildings was the Renaissance-inspired Cabildo, the seat of the Spanish government. The present building was built in 1795 and was followed by its sister, the Presbytère, on the other side of the cathedral.

■ CREOLE TOWNHOUSE

The general plan of these houses consisted of a ground floor including the service rooms, which opened into a courtyard. Stairs were mounted outside the galleries in the courtyard. At the back was a two-story *garçonniere* (also known as a "carriage house") for older sons, male relatives, and guests; the kitchen was on the ground floor. The entertaining area was located in the main house on the second floor above the stench, noise, and mud of the street. The family bedrooms were on the third floor and the servants were quartered in the oppressively hot attics. **The Pharmacy Museum**, built in 1837 at 514 Chartres, is an excellent example of this architecture.

Pitot House, with its open first floor, is representative of raised plantation architecture.

■ RAISED PLANTATION STYLE

As the city filled in its late colonial years, houses reminiscent of West Indian plantation houses were constructed on the outskirts of the town. The main living floor was built over a brick above-ground "basement," which served as protection from floods. West Indies-style double-pitched roofs extending over the galleries (galleries are balconies supported by columns or colonettes instead of brackets) created shady areas and allowed windows to be left open when it rained. As in the Creole cottage, there were no hallways; rooms were built parallel to each other, each opening onto the gallery through French doors.

The **Mayor Pitot House** at 1440 Moss in Bayou St. John, the oldest of the city's museum houses, is a fine example of the colonial Louisiana plantation style. It is constructed with stucco-over-brick and wide, airy galleries. The house, built about 1780 by the Ducayet family, was bought in 1810 by James Pitot, the city's mayor from 1804 to 1805, as the country home for his family. The house sits atop the 1708 site of the first French settlement in the New Orleans area. The Pitot House is open several days a week for tours; call (504) 482-0312.

■ AMERICAN STYLES

A few districts in New Orleans, developed after the city became American in 1803, recall (heaven forbid) the Yankee architecture of Boston or Philadelphia. In them one finds asymmetrical three-story brick townhouses organized around a side hall which served as the main entrance. Creoles scoffed that these American houses were "lopsided." A few American-style townhouses began to appear in the French Quarter prior to the 1820s, but the largest blocks of them were constructed between 1830 and the War Between the States. The finest concentration of these buildings can be seen in the **Lafayette Square Historic District** (bounded by Baronne, Magazine, Lafayette, and St. Joseph streets); the oldest homes still standing were built in 1832 at 535-545 and 602-646 (called Julia Row) on Julia Street.

■ GREEK REVIVAL

It was the Americans who were to add the classical stamp of the new republic to the city. Local architects such as James Gallier, Sr. (the St. Charles Hotel, the Boston Club), James Gallier, Jr. (the French Opera House), and Henry Howard were but a few who were able to influence the style of the burgeoning metropolis in the first half of the nineteenth century. The style's trademarks include galleries

Author Anne Rice's Garden District home with its distinctive Greek key motif around the door.

supported by columns, window architraves, and fanlight transoms.

The publication of Stuart and Rivett's *Antiquities of Athens* gave every architect and draftsman free access to a wide assortment of motifs for moldings and door frames which could be easily copied in wood. In addition, prefabricated cast-iron detailing also became available in 1855, replacing the more expensive wrought-iron versions. These innovations allowed other decorative styles to flourish as well, particularly the Italianate, Gothic, and Romanesque.

■ AMERICAN MANSIONS

Some of New Orleans's newly rich Anglo-Americans built free-standing villas with columns and wide porches, creating a style that took advantage of the rectangular lots and allowed for fresh air and landscaping. The houses were set back from the street, and often faced onto side gardens. They were embellished liberally with Greek Revival motifs, and later with Romanesque, Italianate, and other styles.

The nicest examples of this grander style are located in the Lower Garden District. The house at 1531 Camp is thought to have been built in the 1850s.

Bracketed shotgun houses.

Other examples include 2000, 2018, 2026, and 2113-15 Prytania.

New Orleanians also built free-standing, sprawling homes which utilized larger lots and landscaping, recalling the houses some Americans were then building outside the city. The style refered to as "center hall villa" is characterized by a floor plan consisting of a center hall stretching from the front of the house all the way to the back, with rooms on either side. First appearing in the city in the 1840s, most of the homes were wood-framed, with wide, columned verandas. The proportions of the homes were lavish: 12- to 16-foot ceilings were designed to trap hot air in the warm months; wide galleries allowed interior furniture to be used outside in the hot evenings. Louvered shutters controlled the blistering rays of the sun and let in filtered breezes. The **Lower Garden District Historic District** (roughly from Prytania to Chippewa and Erato to Jackson) contains many examples of this style of house which date from the period 1850 to 1880. The home at 1226 Camp is thought to date from the 1870s. On Jackson Avenue there is a center hall villa at 1007 and another at 1435; other fine examples stand at 1431 Josephine, 1805 Coliseum Street, and 2127 Prytania.

■ SHOTGUN HOUSES

Between 1840 and 1910, thousands of these railroad-car-shaped wooden houses covered in wood siding were built in each of the up-and-coming suburbs of the day, because they were an economical and cooler way to utilize narrow lots. The shotgun usually has no hallway and has from three to six rooms going straight back, with room opening into room. The American shotgun has a side corridor, allowing more privacy. And occasionally, a smaller wing has been added to one side, creating an L-shaped shotgun. Some shotguns have two stories, but more common is a second story only in the back, referred to as a "camelback" shotgun.

Shotgun houses were decorated elaborately and eclectically with details borrowed from Baroque, Greek Revival, Italianate, and even Moorish and Oriental styles. Galleries, overhangs, railings, columns, and bays were common design elements added to the basic shoebox homes. Prefabricated cast-iron decorations could be ordered from catalogs or purchased in New Orleans shops.

The shotgun, the side hall, and the camelback can be seen in abundance in Faubourg Marigny, Esplanade Ridge, Mid-City, Algiers Point, and the Irish Channel. In March the **Preservation Resource Center** hosts several special Shotgun House Tours and Seminars. Call (504) 581-7032 for more information.

GARDEN DISTRICT
ST. CHARLES AVENUE STREETCAR

JUST A 10-MINUTE DRIVE away from the French Quarter is the Garden District, a residential area whose architecture bespeaks the exuberance of the Southern Belle Epoque of the early 19th century. After the Louisiana Purchase in 1803, New Orleans officially became an American city, a thriving port just a stone's throw from the rural sensibilities of the rest of the South. By 1810, it had 17,000 residents, making it the fourth largest city in its new country. Within 10 years, the population had more than doubled to 41,000, which caused something of a problem as the French Quarter was already jammed with Creole citizens, and the surrounding dry land was controlled by powerful Creole planters.

If the Creoles were the old-line aristocrats of New Orleans, the Americans were growing very rich indeed on cotton, sugar, and lumber. Just the same, the Creoles excluded them from their neighborhoods, and the Americans found themselves

Dating back to 1835, the St. Charles Avenue streetcar line is the oldest operating street railway system in the country. (Syndey Byrd)

Spring meet at the Metairie Jockey Club. (Historic New Orleans Collection)

corralled in a wedge of land between Canal Street, the end of the French Quarter, and Jackson Avenue, bordering the vast plantation of the powerful Jacques Francois Esnould Dugue de Livaudais. Livaudais, noted for building the first racetrack in New Orleans, had land holdings extending along the river to the beginning of what is now the Uptown area.

Livaudais greatly expanded his holdings when he married Celeste de Marigny, daughter of Philippe de Marigny de Mandeville, who owned a large plantation called "Fontainbleu" on the banks of Lake Pontchartrain. Mandeville's city residence was thought to have been in the Elysian Fields/Esplanade area, and an avenue of trees connected his white-pillared mansion to the banks of the Mississippi. The historian Grace King reports that in 1798 he entertained the Duc d'Orleans (who was later to become the king of France) and his two brothers the Duc de Montpensier and the Comte de Beaujolais. The area of the city where they lived is still known as the Faubourg Marigny.

After marrying Celeste, Monsieur Livaudais, possibly seeking to outshine his father-in-law, began construction on what many at the time considered to be the most palatial plantation house in all of Louisiana. Before the fabulous house could be finished, his land was visited by one of the worst spring floods of the decade.

His sugar crop was destroyed and his new house severely damaged. In 1825, Celeste up and left her husband and moved to Paris. After her divorce, she ended up with the plantation, which, as a result of the flood, had been left with rich alluvial sediment that made it the most fertile soil around. In 1832, she sold the Livaudais land for half a million dollars to a group of real estate developers who carved it up to make a new neighborhood for the emerging American gentry and nouveau riche. The area was to become a 14-block square bounded by St. Charles Avenue and Magazine Street, and by Jackson and Louisiana avenues.

One of the first things that the developers did was to hire a good engineer. Due to turmoil in France, one was available: Benjamin Buisson, fresh from his service to Napoleon. He divided the plantation into the pattern of streets that exists today. The oldest home in the area is thought to be **Toby's Corner,** built in 1838 (2340 Prytania Street) in the Greek Revival raised cottage style. The owner, a Philadelphia native, helped to finance his friend Sam Houston's revolt in Texas. The house was eventually sold in a sheriff's sale for $5,000 after the Union occupation.

The French and Spanish continued to exclude the Americans from their own neighborhoods and society. Nineteenth-century Creole writer Kate Chopin in her story "A Matter of Prejudice" describes the cold shoulder that a Creole mother gives her son when he marries an American girl from the Garden District. Creole society remained rooted in urbanity, exclusiveness, and the Latin traditions of Catholicism, while the leaders of the Americans personified the nineteenth-century ideals of exuberant decorative arts and straight-laced Protestant Victorian manners. Since the Creoles had a stranglehold on the politics of the area, they withheld city services from the ostentatious American sector of the city, and the American millionaires had to step from their palatial homes into the muddy streets. In an effort to control their own property, the Americans incorporated the section of the Garden District into the city of Lafayette. It remained as a separate city until 1852, when the Americans felt that they had attained enough clout in New Orleans to rejoin the city.

The grand era of Garden District development lasted only a few decades, but it was one of unbridled architectural innovation. The Greek Revival style was incorporated with great enthusiasm, with houses painted in Mediterranean colors complemented by wrought iron, louvered shutters, white columns, and elaborate gardens. By the 1830s, builders borrowed eclectically from Italianate, Moorish, Asian, and other design elements to suit the client's fancy.

■ GARDEN DISTRICT TODAY

In historic times Canal Street was the dividing line between the Creoles and the Americans; today it marks the division between the Central Business District and the French Quarter. At 171 feet wide, Canal Street is one of the widest main thoroughfares in the United States. Both its name and width come from the fact that it was intended to be a canal. Though it didn't actually become a street until 1806 during Claiborne's governorship, all the addresses on the streets that cross Canal Street begin at 100 there, and move out to the north and south. All the streets to the north of Canal Street are prefixed "North," e.g. North Broad Street, and those to the South are prefixed with "South."

WHAT'S IN A NAME?

*M*errill Shackleford happened to be a poor man, but he knew New Orleans society. Actually, he *was* New Orleans society, a certain segment of it. Merrill's segment lived uptown in the hundred-year-old houses that were in states of legendary disrepair, where faulty wiring caused the crystal chandeliers to dim whenever the wind blew; where the parlor windows were hung with hemmed white bed sheets; where worn-out colored mothers worked for sixty cents an hour, serving Vienna sausages on heirloom silver trays to the ladies of the house.

ᔆ ᔆ ᔆ

Because he knew the caprices of his native city's ruling class, Merrill did not make the mistake of instantly assuming that a New Orleans girl named Aimée Desirée was a whore, working Esplanade Avenue to the river. Hadn't he danced at the Comus ball with a frozen-lipped debutante called Lola, a name for a hot-blooded barmaid? Didn't he share a box each season at the symphony with a pedigreed divorcée christened Royal like a jockey out at the Fairgrounds? Once he'd gone to a funeral luncheon with a highborn, gilded widow called Evangeline, as if she were a Cajun housemaid.

In New Orleans, the chances were excellent that an "Aimée Desirée" was the darling of some madcap French aristocrat's frail heart and his robust last will and testament.

"What's her last name?" said Merrill.

. . . "That's Dreuil Vairin's only child," he said, rising. "She's richer than God. . . ."

—Sheila Bosworth, *Slow Poison,* 1992

The other navigational points of the American city are the river and the lake. Locals will say that their house is on the lake side or the river side of St. Charles Avenue, the uptown or the downtown corner. Up at the end of St. Charles Avenue is the University Section, where the St. Charles Avenue streetcar veers off to the right and rambles onto the neutral ground of Carrollton Avenue. The streetcar stops at Claiborne Avenue, but Carrollton Avenue continues under the expressway right through Mid-City, and Mid-City butts up on City Park. Past that the lake-front neighborhoods come into view.

Architectural styles were freely borrowed and added to (see essay on architecture). Many Italian "villas" were garnished with wrought iron and Greek Revival features. The Italianate and Greek Revival **Colonel Short's Villa** at 1448 Fourth Street was built in 1859, and stands behind an elaborate wrought-iron fence of intertwined cornstalks and morning glories. (The fence is remarkably similar to one in the French Quarter.) The **Musson House** at 1331 Third Street also exhibits magnificent lacy iron work. It was built in 1850 by Michael Musson, the president of the cotton exchange and the uncle of Edgar Degas. **The Bervard House**, 1239

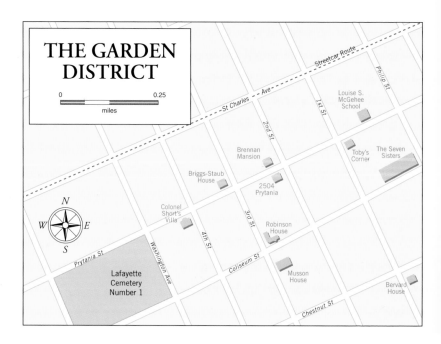

Belle Epoque interior of a Garden District mansion.

First Street, is embellished with lovely cast-iron grilles festooned in a rose motif. The home thought to have had the first indoor plumbing in the state is the **Robinson House** at 1415 Third Street. Built in 1865 with Italianate and Greek Revival features, this mansion is one of the largest private residences still in use in the city.

One of the loveliest streets to use as a starting point for explorations is Prytania Street. The street's name goes back to Bartheleme La Fon's original plan for part of the subdivision owned by Pierre Robin Delonge. La Fon had left a large plot of land for a school, and the owner offered the land to anyone who wanted to construct the "Prytaneum." One lavish architectural treasure is the **Louise S. McGehee School** for girls which stands at 2343 Prytania Street. It was constructed during the carpet-bagger era in 1872 by Bradish Johnson for $100,000 and transformed into a girls' school in 1929. Several other homes of special note include **2504 Prytania Street** built in 1859 in a marriage of Italianate and Greek Revival styles and capped with an octagonal turret. It now serves as the headquarters of the **Women's Opera Guild** and is open for group tours. Across the street is the **Brennan Mansion,** at 2507 Prytania Street, once the palatial home of some of the members of the Brennan restaurant dynasty (owners of Commander's Palace, Brennan's). Built in 1852, the Greek Revival home contains Ionic- and Corinthian-columned galleries and a magnificent gold ballroom. One of the few surviving Gothic Revival-style homes is at 2605 Prytania Street, the **Briggs-Staub House,** built in 1849.

Coliseum Street was named after a large public facility that never materialized. Other homes of interests include the row of cottages in the 2300 block of Coliseum Street, known as the **Seven Sisters.** The **Payne Home** at 1134 First Street, built in 1849–50, is not only a mansion of magnificent proportions, but was also the residence where the former U.S. Senator and the only president of the Confederacy, Jefferson Davis, died on December 6, 1889, while a guest of Judge Jacob U. Payne.

The area abounds with gorgeous foliage. Many of the live oaks belong to the **Live Oak Society** (membership dues are 45 acorns a year). During most of the year, the fragrance of sweet olive, jasmine, and gardenia mask the odors of the city. They were first planted in the 19th century to shield the inhabitants from the stench of the neighboring slaughterhouse. In the late summer many of the streets are lined with white, lavender, and pink crape myrtles, magenta bougainvillea, and white or purplish oleander. The winter brings camellias, and in the spring most of the gardens are bathed in the stunning colors of azaleas.

■ St. Charles Avenue Streetcar

To get a true feel for the city, it's worth your while to take a streetcar ride from Canal Street uptown along the oak-lined St. Charles Avenue—which runs along the edge of the Garden District. (Another famous New Orleans streetcar once ran along Desire Street, and inspired the title of Tennessee Williams's *A Streetcar Named Desire*.)

The St. Charles Avenue Historic District runs along the streetcar tracks from Jackson Avenue to Jena Street. The 13-mile route (which goes outside the historic district) takes about an hour and a half, round trip. As it is the city's only commuter train and each of the cars can only accommodate 52 people, it is best to avoid rush hours and the end of the school day, about 3 P.M. The streetcar runs continuously 24 hours a day, roughly every quarter of an hour between 7 A.M. and 8 P.M. After 8 P.M. it runs every half hour until midnight, then every hour until 7 A.M. (It is never a mistake to know where a nearby bus line is or to have cab fare ready, as there is occasionally trouble on the line.) After 9 P.M. opt for the cab, as it is unsafe to wait on streetcorners at night, even on St. Charles. Along the route, the car will stop about every two blocks if passengers want to enter or exit.

The St. Charles Avenue streetcar line is the oldest operating street railway system in the country, dating back to 1835 when the New Orleans and Carrollton railroad connected the city of Carrollton to New Orleans. The 35 olive green cars in use today are Perley Thomas Arch Roof 900 Series cars built in High Point, North Carolina in the 1920s.

The good news is that as we roll into the millennium the street car has proven its environmental worth. One of the city's old lines has recently been resurrected along the waterfront. Called "The Ladies in Red," these six vintage red and gold cars travel Canal Street to the French Market. Plans are afoot to expand the service to better serve tourists and locals alike.

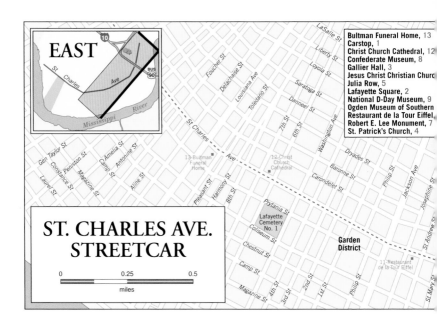

EAST

ST. CHARLES AVE.
STREETCAR

0   0.25   0.5

miles

Bultman Funeral Home, 13
Carstop, 1
Christ Church Cathedral, 12
Confederate Museum, 8
Gallier Hall, 3
Jesus Christ Christian Churc
Julia Row, 5
Lafayette Square, 2
National D-Day Museum, 9
Ogden Museum of Southern
Restaurant de la Tour Eiffel,
Robert E. Lee Monument, 7
St. Patrick's Church, 4

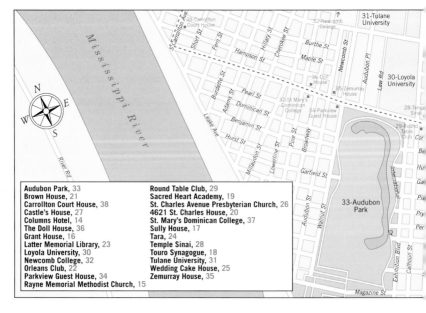

Audubon Park, 33
Brown House, 21
Carrollton Court House, 38
Castle's House, 27
Columns Hotel, 14
The Doll House, 36
Grant House, 16
Latter Memorial Library, 23
Loyola University, 30
Newcomb College, 32
Orleans Club, 22
Parkview Guest House, 34
Rayne Memorial Methodist Church, 15

Round Table Club, 29
Sacred Heart Academy, 19
St. Charles Avenue Presbyterian Church, 26
4621 St. Charles House, 20
St. Mary's Dominican College, 37
Sully House, 17
Tara, 24
Temple Sinai, 28
Touro Synagogue, 18
Tulane University, 31
Wedding Cake House, 25
Zemurray House, 35

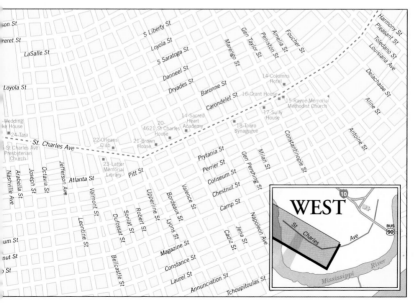

■ St. Charles Avenue Streetcar Tour

The following tour begins at the **1** **St. Charles Avenue/Common Street carstop** off Canal Street. (In the French Quarter, Royal Street becomes St. Charles Avenue when it crosses Canal Street.)

2 **Lafayette Square,** 500 block of St. Charles Avenue. This was the central park of the early American sector. The statue on the white pedestal is of John McDonough, benefactor of many of the public schools in New Orleans.

3 **Gallier Hall,** 545 St. Charles Avenue. Designed by James Gallier, Sr., this magnificent Greek Revival structure was the city hall from 1852 to 1957, also serving as the seat of the Reconstruction government. It's now used to hold receptions.

4 **St. Patrick's Church,** 724 Camp Street. Patterned after Yorkminster Cathedral in England, it was opened in 1838 for an English-speaking congregation.

5 **Julia Row,** between Camp Street and St. Charles Avenue. To the left are 13 American-style townhouses in which prominent Americans lived during the 1840s.

6 **Ogden Museum of Southern Art,** 615 Howard Street. Local collector Roger Ogden's 1,000-piece collection (valued at over $13 million) will serve as the core of this museum, dedicated to the evolution of the visual arts in the South. Opening in 1999.

7 **Robert E. Lee Monument,** Lee Circle at the intersection of St. Charles Avenue and Howard Street. Since 1884, a 7,000-pound bronze statue of General Robert E. Lee by sculptor Alexander Doyle has stood atop a 60-foot (18-m) white marble column. Facing north, it is said, he will never be surprised.

8 **Confederate Museum,** 929 Camp Street. Built in 1891, it's the oldest museum in Louisiana, housing local Civil War artifacts.

9 **National D-Day Museum,** Howard and Magazine streets. More than 25,000 square feet of D-Day memorabilia transported from a French miltary-history museum. Opening in 1999.

10 **Jesus Christ Christian Church,** 1137 St. Charles Avenue. The 1916 building (formerly the Jerusalem Temple) features a beautiful tile mosaic.

11 **Restaurant de la Tour Eiffel,** 2040 St. Charles Avenue. This structure houses the painstakingly shipped and re-assembled interior of a restaurant that once operated in the Eiffel Tower. It found new life for a brief time in 1986 as a trendy bistro, and was later acquired by the Pontchartrain Hotel (across the street) as a banquet facility.

12 **Christ Church Cathedral,** 2919 St. Charles Avenue. Completed in 1887 at the height of the Victorian Era, the cathedral is the diocesan headquarters of the Episcopal Church.

13 **Bultman Funeral Home**, 3338 St. Charles Avenue at Louisiana Avenue. This amalgam of three wood-framed houses dating from 1852 was cut and pasted together in the 1930s to create the city's most opulent funeral home. The business was sold by the Bultman family in 1991.

14 **Columns Hotel**, 3811 St. Charles Avenue. This columned private home was built in 1884 and later turned into a hotel. Louis Malle used the interior in his film *Pretty Baby.*

15 **Rayne Memorial Methodist Church**, 3900 St. Charles Avenue. This Gothic style church was completed in 1875.

16 **Grant House**, 3932 St. Charles Avenue. Architect Thomas Sully built this home in 1887 in the Queen Anne Style.

17 **Sully House**, 4010 St. Charles Avenue. Architect Sully's private gingerbread palace.

18 **Touro Synagogue**, 4238 St. Charles Avenue. Named for the philanthropist Judah Touro when it was built in 1908, its new wing contains a rose window by sculptress Ida Kohlmayer.

19 **Sacred Heart Academy**, 4521 St. Charles Avenue. An elite Catholic girls' school opened by the Sisters of the Sacred Heart in 1899.

20 **4621 St. Charles House.** Once a country house, 4621 dates from the 1850s and is probably the oldest house on the avenue.

21 **Brown House**, 4717 St. Charles Avenue. No, it wasn't named for its color, and yes, this really is a single-family dwelling. Even back in 1902, this Romanesque Revival landmark cost $250,000.

22 **Orleans Club**, 5005 St. Charles Avenue. The Orleans (pronounced "Or-lee-*yawn*") was built as a private home in 1868, but was transformed into an exclusive ladies' club in 1925.

23 **Latter Memorial Library**, 5120 St. Charles Avenue. This Beaux Arts style mansion was built in 1907. In the 1920s, screen star Marguerite Clark lived here, and in 1947 the owners donated it to the city; it is now an elegant library.

24 **Tara**, 5705 St. Charles Avenue. A replica of the plantation in the film classic *Gone With the Wind.*

25 **Wedding Cake House**, 5809 St. Charles Avenue. A late 19th century mansion in the Georgian Revival style.

26 **St. Charles Avenue Presbyterian Church**, St. Charles Avenue at State Street. Built in 1930, the Gothic structure hosts a group descended from the second Protestant congregation established in New Orleans.

27 **Castle's House**, 6000 St. Charles Avenue. The interior of this Georgian Revival House, completed in 1896, is often featured in design magazines. Architect Thomas Sully took his inspiration from Longfellow House, built in 1759 in Cambridge, Massachusetts.

28 **Temple Sinai**, 6227 St. Charles Avenue. Built in 1928, the temple hosted the first Reformed congregation in the city.

29 **Round Table Club,** 6330 St. Charles Avenue (near Audubon Park). A men's club that uses a King Arthur's court theme for its annual Carnival ball.

30 **Loyola University,** 6363 St. Charles Avenue. The Jesuit order established the college of the Immaculate Conception downtown in 1840. The college merged with Loyola College, which existed on the present site, in 1904. The Tudor- and Gothic-style university complex houses the largest Catholic university in the South.

31 **Tulane University,** 6400 St. Charles Avenue. Founded in 1834 as a medical college, Tulane was moved to its present Romanesque buildings in 1884. Its school of business is the oldest college of commerce in the United States.

32 **Newcomb College,** 1229 Broadway Street. At the back of the Tulane campus, and not seen from the streetcar, is the female wing of the university, Sophie Newcomb College.

33 **Audubon Park,** across from the two universities. This 400-acre park was named for naturalist John James Audubon, and was designed by noted landscape architect Frederick Law Olmsted. It contains lagoons, a golf course, picnic areas, and the zoo. It was developed after the close of the 1884 World's Industrial and Cotton Centennial Exposition which had occupied the site.

34 **Parkview Guest House,** 7004 St. Charles Avenue. This hotel was opened in 1884 to accommodate the visitors to the Cotton Centennial.

35 **Zemurray House,** 2 Audubon Place. This white-columned mansion was built in 1907 as the home of Sam Zemurray, president of United Fruit Company. The house now serves as the official residence of the President of Tulane University.

36 **The Doll House,** 7209 St. Charles Avenue. The small Tudor dollhouse in front of the home it duplicates actually has its own postal address.

37 **St. Mary's Dominican College,** 7214 St. Charles Avenue. The Dominican Sisters started a school for girls here at the end of the Civil War; later it became a college for women. The Sisters sold much of the campus to Loyola University in 1985, though their residence is still maintained on the site.

38 **Carrollton Court House,** 719 South Carrollton Avenue. Built in 1855, this columned structure once served as the townhall for the city of Carrollton, which became part of New Orleans in 1874. It is now the Lusher Extension, the junior high school portion of a public magnet school.

The American-style townhouses of Julia Row near the route of the St. Charles Avenue streetcar.

CITIES OF THE DEAD

The term "Cities of the Dead" came from both St. Louis No. 1 and No. 2 cemeteries, as their oven-like tombs, called *"fours"* by the Creoles, give the cemeteries the appearance of rows upon rows of windowless brick-and-stone dollhouses. Spaces in these cemeteries were completely sold out by 1820, though the original families may still reuse their family tombs, and do. Many of the more elaborate tombs were designed by J. N. B. de Pouilly, who designed St. Louis Cathedral and the St. Louis Exchange Hotel.

Thanks to the efforts of a local non-profit organization called "Save Our Cemeteries," many of the fine old tombs that were no longer being cared for have been restored and preserved. Until recently, unkempt tombs would bear notices such as, "Important: Anyone interested in the remains of persons interred in this vault, call the cemetery office." There are still many that have their slabs broken and ferns growing from empty crumbling tombs. Many are embellished with magnificent wrought-iron fences, balconies, crosses, and other objects.

St. Louis No. 1, the famous cemetery filmed in *Easy Rider,* stands just outside of the French Quarter, near the Iberville housing project (that stands atop most of what used to be Storyville). It is a maze of randomly spaced tombs, jammed into each other in no particular order.

Here Étienne de Boré, the man noted for perfecting the sugar-refining process, spends eternity in the company of Paul Morphy, the famous chess champion; Homer Plessy of the 1892 Supreme Court case Plessy vs. Ferguson, which allowed Jim Crow laws in the South; Bernard de Marigny; and voodoo queen Marie Laveau I.

St. Louis No. 2 Cemetery was opened in 1822, four blocks away on Claiborne Avenue between Canal and St. Louis. It is here that Marie Laveau II, the daughter of the original voodoo queen, is supposedly buried, as are 19th-century mayors Pitot and Girod, and pirate captain Dominique You.

St. Louis No. 3 Cemetery, known as the Bayou cemetery, was founded in 1833 on the site of the city's early leper colony. It is at the end of Esplanade Avenue near Bayou St. John. Here James Gallier, Jr. designed his family cenotaph.

By the 19th century, due to the influx of large immigrant populations and the severity of the yellow fever epidemics, it became necessary for professional, ethnic, religious, trade, and social groups to band together to create benevolent societies for the purpose of providing medical assistance, burial services, and whenever possible actual tombs. The first black "perseverance, benevolent, and mutual aid society" was formed in 1783; about 200 more would soon be formed.

By the mid-nineteenth century New Orleans had become an amalgam of ethnic neighborhoods, each with its own cemetery. Along Washington Avenue, in the American sector, were **Lafayette Cemetery No. 1,** opened in the Garden District in 1833 as a final resting place for yellow fever victims; **St. Joseph's** opened in the 1850s, and **Lafayette No. 2** in 1853.

St. Roch came into existence in 1868 to serve the new wave of French Quarter Italian immigrant residents. Down at the far end of Canal Street near Metairie, land was plentiful and cheap, and it was accessible by the transit system. Thus, a whole other group of "specialty" burial grounds grew up. The most interesting of these is the Egyptian-style Cypress Grove. Cypress Grove and Greenwood Cemeteries were started by the Fireman's Charitable and Benevolent Association in the 1840s for the volunteer firemen and their families.

Another oft-repeated local legend is about how **Metairie Cemetery,** the 155-acre former grand racecourse, got its start. Charles T. Howard, who created the state's first lottery in the 1870s, was also responsible for this cemetery. The story goes that Howard was blackballed from joining the Metairie Jockey Club in 1871. Instead of fighting a duel over it, he got even. In 1872, he bought the racecourse and turned it into an elegant cemetery where all of society would have to "die for admittance." Now Mr. Howard lies permanently where the track used to be. His neighbors once included Josie Arlington, the Storyville madam. However, Ms. Arlington's niece recently sold the tomb to the Morales family, had the famed madam's name chiseled off the face, and had the remains reburied in a humble, unmarked grave. But local legend has it that the $17,000 tomb still glows red on certain nights.

There's the miniature version of the Temple of Nike on the Acropolis where William Hellis lies encased in a ton of imported Greek soil. The largest tomb is that of the Moriarty family, part of the group of Irish immigrants shunned by "polite" society. When Mary Moriarty died, her husband, a bar owner and grocer, vowed to give her the grandest monument in the city. The massive granite monument is flanked by four female figures: Faith, Hope, Charity, and Mary Moriarty.

The favorite landmark of many a child is the tomb decorated with a dog that has a marble tear falling from his eye. It lies at the head of the tomb of Francis Masich.

Evidently when his master died, the dog followed the funeral and remained at the cemetery to mourn. It isn't unusual to find notes, flowers, or bows left for the

continues

"Good Doggy."

Another tomb noted for its architecture is that of David C. Hennessy, the slain Irish police chief. This 26-foot memorial erection is worth the trip to the cemetery. The broken shaft is covered by a pall, over which is draped a police belt and nightstick. Its designer won a contest and received $3,300 for the finished masterpiece.

Self-guided walking tours can be obtained free of charge, seven days a week from the offices of the adjacent Lake Lawn Metairie Funeral Home Office. The information was gathered by Henri Gandolfo, who worked for the company for 72 years, and compiled a history entitled *Metairie Cemetery: Tales of Statesmen, Soldiers, and Great Families.*

† **Lakelawn Metairie Cemetery Tours.** 5100 Pontchartrain Blvd.; (504) 486-6331. Free cassettes and maps for driving tours of this expansive, park-like cemetery are available at the funeral home within the compound, seven days a week, 8:30 A.M. to 4:00 P.M.

† **Save Our Cemeteries Tours.** P.O. Box 58105, 70158; (504) 525-3377 or (888) 721-7493. Mondays, Wednesdays, and Fridays, beginning around 10:00 A.M.

- **St. Louis No. 1 Tour** (French Quarter). Given each Sunday morning at 10 A.M. by dedicated volunteer guides. The price of the hour-and-a-half walking tour includes the protection of a New Orleans police officer. Tours assemble in the French Quarter. Reservations required. $12.00.

- **Lafayette Cemetery No. 1 Tour** (Garden District, across from Commander's Palace Restaurant). Three tours a week at 10:30 A.M., Mondays, Wednesdays, and Fridays. Reservations not required. $6.00.

† **Hidden Treasures Cemetery Tour.** 1915 Chestnut; (504) 529-4507. Charlene Sinclair provides the first daily tour of St. Louis No. 1 beginning at 9:00 A.M. Complimentary coffee is included in this highly informative hour-and-a-half walking tour. Seven days a week, except holidays. (Police escort only on Sundays.) Reservations accepted. $15.00.

Several of the city tours also stop at the cemeteries. See pp. 285–289 in "PRACTICAL INFORMATION" for details.

Note: All the historic walled cemeteries are extremely dangerous and should not be visited without an organized group.

The tomb of voodoo queen Marie Laveau I in St. Louis Cemetery No. 1.

CULTURE BEHIND THE SCENES

NEW ORLEANS HAS LONG SERVED as a breeding ground for a rich assortment of pleasures and vices. It is a city whose culture percolates from the ground up; where passions, intrigue, and funk intermingle on street corners to create cultural traditions that move up the socio-cultural scale, rather than down it.

■ CREOLE WOMEN

As early as 1743, when the Marquis de Vaudreuil-Cavagnial, known as the "Grand Marquis," arrived as governor, New Orleans was taking a stab at having its own aristocracy. By all accounts the governor and his entourage of gold-braid-adorned officials led a life, amid the stench and cockroaches, as close to that of the Court of Versailles as they could muster. If the marquis' drop-dead elegance and stubborn courtliness provided inspiration to those who struggled daily against mud and fever, he was not similarly inspired by the colony, describing it as besotted with rum and "a chaos of iniquity and discord."

Nevertheless, the few "proper" families in town tried to avoid sinking into this chaos by maintaining strict control over their daughters. The Creole maiden was forbidden not only to wear velvet, but also to glance into the eyes of a young man, at least when her mother was watching. No young man was allowed to call on her at home after her first viewing; contact had to be made by relatives or friends and first approved by the girl's father or male head of the household. During the period between the Louisiana Purchase and the War Between the States, proper families showed off their daughters to society but once: at the opera, where accompanied by her parents and grandmothers she would sit in the family box and receive callers. Parents had from their daughter's sixteenth birthday until her twenty-fourth to find an appropriate mate for her. Spinsterhood was a fate worse than death in a society that viewed marriage or the convent as the only two worthy vocations for women.

Once the proper husband or wife was found, the two families negotiated over the prospective bride's pedigree in order to determine dowry. A bonafide aristocrat—even a somewhat impoverished one—was worth more in the family tree than was a newly rich, salt-smuggling grandaddy.

Needless to say, the bride and groom were never allowed to be alone before their wedding. If they met at all, it was on a few carefully staged occasions and in the company of their families. Monday and Tuesday evenings were the proper days for Creole weddings. A detail of Swiss guards added pomp to weddings performed at St. Louis Cathedral (a practice that ended after 1803). Other than that, the Creole wedding was simple. After the service the bride's bouquet was sent to the convent where she had been educated.

On her wedding night, the young bride was dressed in a hand-embroidered peignoir and boudoir cap and left to lie in her own bed to await her first private moment with her new husband. The couple's "getting-to-know-you" phase lasted from three to seven days during which they were not even allowed to leave their room; all meals were brought to them. A newly married girl didn't show her face in public for several months after the marriage, and certainly never when she was with child.

Once married, Creole women had things a bit easier. For many, beauty and fine clothes were a passion. In letters written to her home in France, a young 18th-century Ursuline nun, Sister St. Stanislaus, observed, "Not withstanding the expense, the women (married) are dressed in velvets and damasks covered in ribbons, materials which regularly sold in the country for three times that in France."

"The Creole of New Orleans."
(Historic New Orleans Collection)

ELEGANT CREOLE LADIES

I cannot help to refute with great indignations, as a woman and as a French woman, the lines of Madame de G.: "The Creoles of the plantations talk mostly the Creole French . . . and their neglect in their clothes and their lack of education is such that it completely hides their pretty faces. Everything in them appears to be ugly and stupid."

I think that I can say with great certainty that Madame de G. during her very short visit in Louisiana has never been invited on a plantation. This is the reason she shows such bitterness against the Creoles living on plantations. But the ladies on the plantations have a right to be prudent and wanting to know to whom they give hospitality. They are so hospitable and so gracious to their guests, but they are very reticent in inviting strangers to participate in the life and customs of plantation life. Madame de G. mentions also that these Creole ladies in the plantations are a sort of savages who hide from strangers or laugh at them not knowing how to address them.

These ladies do not live isolated and alone as they would live in a desert. . . . These ladies have their city home. They usually spend the winter in New Orleans, they go to receptions, balls, theaters, operas. They have gone to hear the conference of Mrs. G. Finally they are part of society and form the very best society of Louisiana. Their mothers, sisters, friends are ladies living in this city. Their daughters are sent to the best boarding schools of the city and in the convents of the Ursulines, either one, for there is one on the levee outside the city limits and the other one on Rampart and St. Claude. The Ursulines have the reputation of giving a complete course of instruction giving excellent music lessons.

To give an idea of the hospitality of the Creoles I will relate a day spent on a plantation at the beautiful home of Mrs. X. . . . Received with the greatest of cordiality, I was given the best room in the house. It opened its wide windows in all directions and faced the wide river that rolled along the contours of cyprieres, the fir tree and the immense fields of sugar canes.

With the perfect service from the well trained servants, the exquisite politeness of the young master of the house, the simple manners of the young girls and the amiability of the ladies of the house, one could easily imagine oneself to live in one of the most elegant and refined French castles. But . . . there was a difference. A big fan was suspended above the dining room table sending us its refreshing breezes, near the dining room could be seen the orange trees covered with fruits, the young Negro butler and his assistants proved to us that we were not in France but in America. The breeze from the river brought to us the exquisite and elusive fragrance of jasmine.

. . . In the afternoon, we met in the big parlors to talk, embroider or sew, and read in instructive [literature] in a loud voice, some one taking the book, reading

The Musson sisters, relatives of Degas, quintessential Creole ladies. (Historic New Orleans Collection)

while the rest occupied themselves with their needle. We did not read novels or newspaper clippings, but we read works of well known writers. For instance: *Tableaux de l'Eloquence chretienne au IV siecle* par M. Veillemain. La Bruyere, Pascal, beautiful plays from Racine. The young girls would then learn those verses by memory and recite them to friends and visitors. The touching story of *"La Servante"* of Lamartine, the charming *Novelles Genevoises* by Topffer, and many other renowned authors.

After dinner we took a walk on the river bank, sometimes we went in the carriage to visit other plantations, but we preferred to walk near the river admiring the splendid effects of the sunset reflecting itself in the great water of the Mississippi River, beautiful crimson and blue clouds losing [themselves] into an immense horizon bordered by the dark cypress forests, extending in the distance. This majestic effect of nature that I have seen only in America spoke to our heart in such a tender manner that it lifted our souls beyond this world, in the regions of the infinite.

—Helen d'Aquin Allain,
letter written in 1850s in Paris describing life in Louisiana

During this period, colonial families moving up the social ladder usually tried to send to France for a private chef. An invaluable status symbol, a chef also served as the facilitator for admittance into the whirl of the provincial "court." Nothing was more important than hosting a banquet in order to dazzle a newly arrived French aristocrat.

For over 175 years, proper Creole entertaining revolved around an event called the "soirée." In their purest form, these were supper dances for close family friends. They took place in the double parlor of a home, where a small band provided music for dancing and the dining table was laden with delicacies.

Creole society could be a joyous place for men, who were wont to ride about town, gamble, duel, and carouse with mistresses, but for unmarried upper-class women, the rules were as rigid as a whalebone corset.

■ DUELING

The Spanish both embraced and added to the culture of Louisiana when they arrived on the scene unexpectedly after a treaty between France and Spain. After they established themselves, the masculine tradition of brawling gave way to an entirely new, and more "orderly," means of settling disputes. The *duello* became the forum through which men of honor soothed their wounded pride, often killing one another in the process. The European-inspired etiquette governing these altercations was remarkably strict and demanded great proficiency with the rapier.

While both illegal and condemned by the church, duelling thrived in the Creole community until well into the nineteenth century. Aristocrat Bernard de Marigny is still remembered with admiration for the vast number of successful duels he fought.

Things didn't change much when the U.S. government took over the city: one of the combatants in the first duel fought in New Orleans under American rule (in 1803) was supposedly none other than the governor of the Louisiana territory, William Claiborne. The *Daily Picayune* of July 29, 1837 reported that "duels are as common these days as watermelons." *The Code of Honor* was published in 1866 by an expert duelist who settled in New Orleans from Cuba, and became a favorite text for those to whom loss of face was a fate worse than loss of life.

St. Vincent de Paul Cemetery located on Louisa Street was one of the business ventures of New Orleans' most famous duelist and proprietor of a *salle d'armes,* Señor Jose "Pepe" Llula. He operated the cemetery from 1857 until 1888 (when he died of old age) and was buried alongside some of his victims. The cemetery is now owned by Stewart Enterprises, the same corporation that owns Metairie Cemetery.

As Americans became gentrified they increased the use of their weapon of choice: the pistol. The "Dueling Oaks" off Bayou St. John, now in City Park, was an ideal spot to settle scores, for it allowed the duelists to stand exactly the right distance apart and yet stay out of earshot of the worried ladies in the Vieux Carré (French Quarter). (The site has also served as a location for pivotal scenes in literature, including Tennessee Williams's *Suddenly Last Summer.*) One of the last times a duel was mentioned in the press occurred in 1889, when the police arrested two duelists who had raised a ruckus after managing to miss each other with three rounds.

■ DEATH

European colonists brought with them their Old World funeral and mourning traditions. As in Catholic European countries, New Orleans Creole society required months of mourning following a relative's death. During the Victorian era, mourning periods became more codified and rigid: wives mourned husbands in carefully prescribed fashion for over a year. Even slaves were required to mourn the people who had enslaved them.

Traditional and often elaborate funerary rituals were also carefully observed. At the hour of a loved one's death, the lady of the house was responsible for stopping all clocks. Black crêpe was hung on the front door, and mirrors were draped in black; the wake and the funeral service were conducted at home, and funeral directors sometimes loaned fine furnishings to the home of the deceased so that the bereaved might make a better impression. Cabinetmakers built the caskets, and livery business owners arranged the transportation for funerals. Funeral coach drivers dressed in black top hats and tails. Their horses wore black plumes on their heads and were specially trained to march in funeral high step. The burial wagon would be followed by a procession of black coaches filled with black-clad mourners.

On one Sunday in 1849, ten duels were fought in the city. (Historic New Orleans Collection)

BITTER SORROWS

*W*e must also say that the Americains, who are, for the most part, all protestants, follow with great zeal the rites and practices of their cult. How could it be otherwise in a city where death is constantly reaping its prey? Here in this city at each stop, one meets with a funeral. Why? Because we have not only the yellow fever epidemics but also cholera, pernicious fever, scarlatina with such violence that at times they exist and bring havoc together. We do not only have one disease . . . but several at the same time. These funerals that are seen at every corner, do they not talk of the short span of existence? of the rapid passing of time? and of the useless necessity of making plans for this world, terrestrial hopes should be abandoned. Each year every family counts several members who are victims to these epidemics. These bitter sorrows are so hard to bear. These sudden catastrophes are much more frequent here than anywhere else, and bring to the hardest sinner thoughts of a better world, religious and deep thoughts.

—Helen d'Aquin Allain,
memoir describing New Orleans c. 1830s.

Frank Dorsey's funeral march on its way to the cemetery in 1973. (Michael P. Smith)

Despite their fancy dress, not all funeral coach drivers were entirely respectable. *Gumbo Ya-Ya: Folk Tales of Louisiana* includes the following story from the *New Orleans Bulletin,* of May 29, 1875: "Buried alive. Sickening tale of our hospital dead: A man in the charity wagon revives. He attempts to get out of his coffin. The driver smothers him." The story goes on to detail eyewitness accounts of how the driver, Jim Connors, struck the still-living man, a 19-year-old black smallpox victim named George Banks, with a brick. "You—," Connors shouted, "I have a doctor's certificate that you are dead, and I'm going to bury you." Witnesses reported that the driver took off the coach seat and smothered the man with it.

Graves that might receive the dearly departed represented a distinct problem for New Orleanians. Because much of the city is below sea level, coffins buried in the ground during the first days of the colony had the horrible habit of washing into the streets whenever floods hit. By the late 18th century, wealthy colonists solved the problem by laying the dead to rest in above-ground vaults. Of course, throughout the city's history, the poor had to be buried in the cheapest way possible, which meant planting the corpses in holes in the ground and hoping that they stayed put. Early accounts describe caskets being stomped into pools of viscous mire. During the yellow-fever epidemics, cast-iron coffins with glass faceplates, thought to protect the mourners from disease, became popular with those who could afford them. Then, as now, all New Orleanians showed respect for both their loved ones and their tropical climate by promptly entombing the dead.

Today Louisianians faithfully preserve the time-honored tradition of visiting family graves on **All Saint's Day**. In the rural areas of Cajun country, a nocturnal mass is performed in the graveyards on Halloween night. Families light candles and spend the night praying over their departed love ones. Burial sites all over New Orleans are whisk-broomed; tombs are scrubbed with brushes and often white-washed. Ladders are used to place chrysanthemums on top of the vaults. While these cemeteries may be visited, they are also dangerous—not because of the ghosts, but because of thieves who lurk around the tombs. It's best to visit by taking a tour: see esay "Cities of the Dead," pp. 134–137, for cemetery tours.

Although the use of funeral parlors did not become popular until this century, New Orleans today has many opulent funeral homes, some hosting more than funerals. The **Bultman Funeral Home**, at 3338 St. Charles Avenue, holds free public classical music concerts several Sunday afternoons a year, Call (504) 895-7766.

Former tomb of Josie Arlington in Metairie Cemetery. This cemetery was once the Metairie Jockey Club racetrack.

■ VOODOO

Voodoo, the ever-evolving practice akin to black magic and spirit worship, originated from the syncretic melding of the ancient practices of Africa's Fon (or Dahomey), Yoruba, and Kongo tribes. The practice of voodoo probably originated in Santo Domingo (modern-day Haiti) where slaves devoted rituals to the power of nature and the spirits of the dead. The term "voodoo" that the slaves adopted to describe their rituals probably derives from the name of the African Fon spirit, "vodu."

For many enslaved Africans such spiritual traditions and practices provided a vital means of mental and emotional resistance to bitter hardship. Indeed, although their beliefs and rituals may not have freed them, Africans do seem to have successfully frightened their captors: slavers so feared the powerful spirits of their human cargoes that by the mid-eighteenth century, they made certain to mix their load of Africans, breaking up tribes in order to prevent captives from banding together and taking over the ship.

Slaves who'd worked for a time in the Caribbean brought to New Orleans some of the rituals which were being practiced in Haiti. Once they got to New Orleans, slaves originally from different tribes were drawn together by what they did have in common—miserable living conditions, music, and spiritual practices. By 1782, the governor of Louisiana sought to outlaw the practice of voodoo out of the fear that its evil forces would serve as a rallying point for a slave uprising, especially as white colonists were greatly outnumbered by those they held in bondage.

Such fears came true in Haiti, where slaves ultimately used these African-born rituals to fuel their own rebellion. Between 1791 and 1804, a series of slave revolts inspired by spirit worship finally culminated in the expulsion of the French from the island. Many of the French who were able to escape fled to Louisiana, some accompanied by their French-speaking, occult-practicing slaves.

When these Haitian slaves arrived in New Orleans, voodoo began to emerge as a specific religious system that incorporated elements of the Catholic church's icons and rituals. At its core was the act of sacrifice as a means of establishing a direct link with the sacred. Forging that link were voodoo practitioners who through intuition, devotion, and practice, offered solace to their followers. Voodoo practices themselves evolved through each priest's or priestess's successful methods. If one priest or priestess succeeded in soliciting the aid of the spirit world—and thereby cured a straying lover, prevented illness, or harmed an enemy—then his or her practices would be emulated.

A doctrine for the practice of voodoo was first formulated by the witch queen of New Orleans, Marie Laveau, or "Madame L," an early nineteenth-century folk heroine whose reputation has been kept alive in songs, movies, and novels. Born in New Orleans, sometime during the 1820s she became the wife of a cabinet-maker named Glapion, whose descendants are now involved in the funeral business and local politics. Marie worked as a hairdresser in many prominent Creole homes, but on the side, this practicing Catholic was also a voodoo spiritual advisor to slaves and masters alike. She presided at the voodoo rites of St. John's Eve (June 23) and at many of the rites in Congo Square, and she was tireless in her efforts to care for the victims of the various fever epidemics. To this day, true believers in her power mark her tomb, located just a few steps from the Basin Street entrance of St. Louis No. 1, with red X's. The tomb of the "Widow of Paris," as she is called, is a white-washed, three-tiered structure bearing the inscription "Marie Philomen Glapion dece'de'e le 11 Juin 1897."

A drawing of a voodoo dance as it appeared in an issue of Harper's Weekly *in the 1880s.* (*Historic New Orleans Collection*)

QUEEN OF THE VAUDOUX

Now one word about the Vaudoux. In the center of a great plain, that is no doubt covered with houses today, there was formerly a wooden house, painted in grey and isolated completely from other houses. It was surrounded by a high grey wooden fence. I remember even today the feeling of terror when my young friends and myself would pass close to . . . that mysterious place. We would never walk close to these sad and lonely high fences. No trees, no flowers, no galleries, no traces of any one living there. . . . One day by the greatest of chance, I happened to meet face to face with the queen of the Vaudoux. . . .

We had hired to work in our garden of Bayou Street a small negro boy, intelligent but a liar and a hypocrite. When he had spent all his wages in playing scraps, or "caniques" (marbles) he would spend his nights away from home. He greatly feared that Vaudou Queen who happened to be his grandmother. One day, wanting to inquire about her grandson, she came to our home and I found myself face to face with this Vaudou Queen. I was not thirteen anymore and instead of being paralyzed with fear, as I would have been if it had happened in my childhood, I was calm and composed and rather took pleasure in finding myself in the presence of this beautiful woman. She was tall and elegant, well proportioned, slim waist line, and dressed with a good deal of taste. Her features were regular, piercing eyes, and intelligent expression, and a queenly bearing. Her walk was really imposing. She expressed herself not only in very correct grammar, but she had a melodious voice and a great deal of elegance in her speech. She talked of the many important people she had met, and if my memory is clear, she mentioned a trip to France. She did not seem to be bad, and had nothing to frighten any one. She was a queen without a throne and had all the imposing manners of a queen. However Baptiste did not seem to share my admiration for his grandmother. He entered in the room with his head low, trying to duck the blows that his grandmother was inflicting on his ears and his head.

Marie Laveau I and II appear in this print looking as witchy as possible. In fact, both were said to be quite beautiful. (Historic New Orleans Collection)

—Helen d'Aquin Allain, memoir describing New Orleans c. 1830s

It was Marie I's daughter, Marie II (born in 1827), who set 19th-century society afire with her elaborate rites. Legend has it that her advice was sought by politicians, well-born matrons, and even conventional religious leaders. Marie II may have been buried at the back of St. Louis No. 2 (in a tomb that can be distinguished by all of the tiny X's on the wall made with a scrap of soft brick), but almost every Catholic and Protestant cemetery in town claims Marie II's remains. Both Laveau women were protéges of the mid-19th-century voodoo priest, Dr. John Creaux, a flamboyant slave-owning free person of color, who was purported to be descended from Senegalese royalty. (Dr. John the singer adopted his name.)

Voodoo continues to evolve today, and its ferocious appetite for new ideas and practices has kept it alive and vital. Like its symbolic snake, voodoo swallows and is nourished by other cultural practices, religions, and philosophies. New Orleans still has Spiritual churches, some of whose practices bear a resemblance to the original voodoo rituals. These small, tightly-knit Christian congregations are characterized by ritualistic dancing and exotic altars. (See essay, "Spiritual Churches," pages 218-219.)

Voodoo traditions also live on in other forms. Many folklorists claim that the reason why the Mardi Gras Indians parade on March 19, St. Joseph's Day, is that it is actually the date of *Legba,* the voodoo feast of spirit communication.

A visit to **F&F Botanica** at 801 North Broad; (504) 482-9142, or any of the other neighborhood groceries that sell "potents" (voodoo charms) will attest to the fact that voodoo in various manifestations is still alive and well. The shop sells candles to ward off evil spirits, incense to promote potency, medicinal herbs to enhance longevity, and powders to sap the strength of an enemy. It is a commonly held belief that once a woman adds her menstrual blood to a man's food he will never be able to stray, and if she can possess some of his hair or fingernails she can make an effigy doll of him and control his every move from afar. Some men are so tormented by the potential threat of a voodoo-practicing damsel that they refuse to eat any food she may prepare and guard every strand of their own hair with their lives.

■ PROSTITUTION

The city's earliest female settlers were the first to establish the world's oldest profession on the North American continent. In 1744, a French officer commented that there were not 10 women of blameless character in the entire city. Whether this is a criticism or a compliment is unclear, but perhaps he appeared to be such a rake that no man wanted to take him home to meet his sister. But what kind of a port city would New Orleans have been if it didn't offer a bit of companionship to sailors after months at sea, or to those frontiersmen who had braved the voyage down the Mississippi River on flatboats?

After the more puritanical Americans took control in 1803, they attempted to clean up the rampant bawdy atmosphere of certain quarters of the city. As the practice of prostitution was prohibited on the ground floor of any building, the street level of such establishments became reserved for gambling and the serving of alcohol. By 1857, madams and their "girls" were required to obtain licenses, and their taxation was personally administered by the mayor.

If the solution did not mollify upstanding Protestant Americans, the soldiers of the occupying Union army seemed to be less scrupulous about their virtue. A clump of bordellos along the old basin canal became popular with the lonely Yankees, and in the early 1870s Josie Arlington, New Orleans's most famous madam, formally opened her "sporting house" in the neighborhood.

Forty years after licenses were first issued, Alderman Sidney Story proposed an ordinance to rid the better residential neighborhoods of the repugnant activity. Sporting houses were restricted to a single area on the far side of the French Quarter from "the north side of the Customhouse (Iberville) from Lower Basin Street to South Robertson streets, to the south side of St. Louis from South Robertson to Basin." Ironically, the area came to be called "Storyville" after the fastidious alderman. It was during this time that the photographer E. J. Bellocq (the subject of the Louis Malle film *Pretty Baby*) made his famous photographic portraits of prostitutes. (See essay and photo, pp. 154–155.)

In Storyville, women such as the "Countess" Willie Piazza and Josie Arlington ran posh and decorous houses with "real" oil paintings and potted palms. Many of the houses were staffed by the madams' stunning quadroon and octoroon "nieces," usually girls whose families had fallen on hard times. The popularity of female Creoles of color among the patrons of bawdy houses caused many old-line Creoles of color to cloister their strictly raised daughters. Even today many Creoles of color will not let their daughters date until they make their debuts in the senior year of all-girl Catholic school.

For those who sought the services of the district's prostitutes, the *Blue Book* could be had for a mere 25 cents. Subtitled *Tenderloin 400,* this combination guidebook and *Who's Who* advertised the attributes of each establishment and listed over 700 ladies of trade in alphabetical order. Those who misplaced their copy of the *Blue Book* might consult a local newspaper called *The Mascot.* The paper ran a column called "On the Turf" that detailed the newsy goings-on from Storyville.

For many years, the central authority in the area was Tom Anderson, a member of the state legislature who owned three salons in the district. The official sanction Anderson represented, however, was soon a thing of the past. When World War I began, Josephus "Tea Totalling" Daniels, Secretary of the Navy, threatened to close down the New Orleans naval base if Storyville was not shut down. Thus, the district was officially closed by ordinance in 1917, and prostitution once more became a clandestine activity. Ladies of the evening relocated to the French Quarter, Julia Street, Tulane Avenue, and North Rampart Street. Most of the area of Storyville itself was demolished in the 1930s to make way for the Iberville Housing Project.

THIS place is one of the few gorgeously furnished places in the Storyville District, located so that the most particular person in the world can reach it without being seen by anyone.

This mansion is under the sole direction of Frances Morris, who is one of the handsomest landladies in the District and is a princess. Her ladies are of like type.

The success and reputation enjoyed by this establishment in the past is more than surpassed under the able management of Miss Morris, who has not overlooked anything that goes to make a place famous and select.

You make no mistake in visiting 1320. Everybody must be of some importance, otherwise he cannot gain admittance.

PHONE MAIN 2318

Advertisement for a house of ill repute in the "Blue Book." (Historic New Orleans Collection)

(following pages) This Enrique Alferez sculpture in City Park appears to symbolize the "good life" of New Orleans.

E. J. BELLOCQ

Early this century, New Orleans photographer Ernest James Bellocq took a series of portraits of Storyville prostitutes, and today those candid images still resonate with vitality. While earning his living as a commercial photographer, Bellocq spent much of his leisure time capturing the city and its residents with his Kodak Bantam Special. Sadly, most of that work—including images he took in New Orleans' Chinatown homes and opium dens—cannot be found. His Storyville series would be lost as well, had the plates not been discovered in his desk after his death. The collection fell into the hands of New Orleans art gallery owner Larry Borenstein, from whom photographer Lee Friedlander bought the plates in 1966. Friedlander produced prints from these plates for a 1970 show at New York's Museum of Modern Art. (Aside from Friedlander's collection, a few other Bellocq plates are known to exist; some reside in the New Orleans Museum of Art.)

Little is known about the life of this very private man. A monograph published for the MOMA exhibition includes excerpts from conversations with Bellocq's acquaintances, among them Johnny Wiggs, the cornetist; Adele, one of Bellocq's Storyville subjects; and a few New Orleans photographers. They describe him as somewhat malformed—no taller than five feet, with a hydrocephalic head—and often brusque, suspicious of others. Adele, however, notes that she and the other prostitutes he photographed found Bellocq polite and kind.

The portraits themselves suggest that these women did trust Bellocq. The subjects seem relaxed, allowing their individual personalities to emerge. John Szarkowski, who curated the show at MOMA in New York, summarized this ability in his preface to *E.J. Bellocq: Storyville Portraits,* published by the Museum of Modern Art.

*I*n his own way, in these pictures, Bellocq consummates many love affairs. Johnny Wiggs understood this when he saw, to his amazement, that Bellocq's prostitutes are beautiful ... Beautiful innocently or tenderly or wickedly or joyfully or obscenely, but all beautiful, in the sense that they are present, unique, irreplaceable, believable, receptive. Each of these pictures is the product of a successful alliance.

A skillful photographer can photograph anything well. To do better than that he must photograph what he loves. Some love geometry; some love sunlight on mountains; some love the streets of their city. Bellocq apparently loved women, with the undiscriminating constancy of a genius.

Women playing cards in Storyville, circa 1911–13, from a gelatin silver print by E.J. Bellocq. (New Orleans Museum of Art, museum purchase)

One Storyville operation that did escape notice until the 1950s was run out of the building at 1205 North Rampart, now occupied by the New Orleans Jazz & Heritage Foundation. When the Jazz Festival's music production staff began renovation of the building in the 1980s, the first thing they had to do was remove the wash basins from all of the rooms.

■ GAMBLING

New Orleans, the unofficial American capital of stylish indulgence, not only boasted the first grand casino in the United States, opened in 1827, but is also credited as the American birthplace of the game of craps. It was the popular European game of hazard, imported through the port of New Orleans, which became the inspiration for craps. The name "hazard" comes from the Arabic word *az-zahr,* or dice. The game came to Louisiana with both the French and the Spanish in the 18th century. Bernard de Marigny, nicknamed "Johnny Craps," is given the credit for introducing the game to Creole society when he returned from being educated in Paris; "craps" probably derives from *crapaud,* or frog, for the frog-eating reputation of the French held by some American New Orleanians. From New Orleans the game was spread up and down the river by the hill-dwelling Kaintocks.

French soldiers who had fought under Napoleon in the Middle East are given credit for bringing a card game called *as nas* to Louisiana, incorporating elements of the game into a more interesting version of the French game of *poque.* Again the Kaintocks gave it a name that was easier on the American tongue: poker.

Blackjack, or twenty-one, is another of the gambling games that was born of the cultural assimilation of various nationalities in New Orleans. In the 1700s, faro, a guessing game played with cards (similar to blackjack) had taken the royal courts of Europe by storm. At the same time the French aristocracy were enjoying other card games called *vingt-et-un* and *chemin de fer* (or shimmy), while the Spanish had an Arabic-conceived game called one-and-thirty. By the time that New Orleans had her own grand casino, twenty-one was on the menu.

Legal gambling fell out of favor after the Civil War, but in 1868, during Reconstruction, the legislature chartered a state lottery to a group who agreed to pay $40,000 toward the operation of the Charity Hospital. (Lotteries were relatively common fund-raisers for schools and hospitals in 19th-century Louisiana.) The lottery operators advertised a $600,000 prize, kept the proceeds minus the hospital donation, and maintained a slush fund of $15,000 to pay off state legislators. When the scam was in danger of failing in 1877, Confederate generals Jubal Early and P. G. T. Beauregard were hired to appear decked out in full dress uniform to conduct the weekly drawings. The federal government finally shut the lottery down in 1895, prosecuting all state officials implicated.

Up until 1887, gaming establishments were operating in the French Quarter, but pressure from American government officials led police to begin closing them down. Nevertheless, New Orleans's attraction to such decadence never waned, and in the 1930s populist demagogue Senator Huey Long is thought to have given the nod to mobster Frank Costello, allowing him to install slot machines in the city in return for a contribution to local widows and orphans. Whether or not the widows and orphans benefited is unclear at best, but there are still a few old-fashioned one-arm bandits dotted around town that have escaped detection.

In the 1950s, Mickey McDougall, the self-styled "greatest gambling detective in the world," stated to the local paper, "As Mayor Morrison so often points out, there is no wide-open gambling in New Orleans proper. But in Jefferson Parish the temples of luck seem to outnumber temples of God; in St. Bernard more paved roads apparently lead to gambling houses than to schools." Meanwhile, the Southport Club, an illegal gaming casino, advertised that it was just 10 minutes from downtown New Orleans. The Southport Club was owned by the local organized-crime kingpin, Carlos Marcello. (See "The Mob," p. 159.)

The Beverly Country Club, a gilt-and-marble miniature Monte Carlo-style gambling villa, was the brainchild of Meyer Lansky, Frank Costello, and Carlos Marcello, who had a 12.5 percent stake in the operation. The club opened in 1945, a year before Bugsy Siegal opened the Flamingo in Las Vegas. This strictly illegal gambling palace had its own version of the Rockettes—the Beverlettes, who backed up headliners such as Danny Thomas and Rudy Vallee. Celebrities (among them, Rita Hayworth) were photographed against the dining room's tufted silk wall-covering. World War II American military officers lived it up at the lavish Beverly on summer nights, cooled by its 120-ton air conditioner. In the early 1950s, a Senate investigative committee led by Senator Estes Kefauver came to New Orleans to look into the Beverly's entertainments. The sheriff of Jefferson Parish swore that he'd see to it that the federal law against gambling would be upheld, and the Beverly was closed. (The Beverly reopened in 1972 as a dinner theater, but closed in 1983 when the building burned.)

After World War II a reform movement in Louisiana sought to wipe away the taint of gambling, and over 20 gambling operations were closed in Jefferson Parish, 12 in New Orleans, and an equal number in St. Bernard.

It wasn't until 1991 that legal gambling came back to the city with the passage of state legislation authorizing a lottery, riverboat gambling, and a single land-based casino. The move was prompted by the state's dire financial straits.

But flagrant gambling, and not unobtrusive, behind-the-scenes gaming, seems to bother the local community. A 1977 University of New Orleans study revealed that an estimated $144 million was spent on illegal gambling in the area, and no one said much about it. By 1987, local law enforcement officials argued that the figure was well over a quarter of a million a year. On weekends bookies are a common sight in many neighborhood bars or at streetcorner pay phones where they balance their bulging notebooks with fistfuls of quarters. Legal charity-based bingo games in the area bring in close to $30 million annually as well.

Harrah's land-based casino squats at the end of Canal Street near the river. It has

Lucky Dog stand on Bourbon Street.

Paddle-boat river casinos have fallen on hard times recently. (Syndey Byrd)

been riddled with controversy and bankruptcy since 1994. As the State Legislature and the Governor wrangle with Harrah's investors over taxes, size, etc., the pentecostal-church style architectural monolith remains incomplete. Several suburban gambling boats remain operational, as do the mega-gambling enclaves along the Mississippi Gulf Coast and those low-roller boats in Natchez and Vicksburg.

■ THE MOB

One of the most notorious crimes of 19th-century New Orleans involved the assassination in 1890 of David C. M. Hennessy, the first superintendant of the New Orleans Police Department. Nineteen members of a Sicilian gang were accused of the crime. When they were acquitted of the crime in 1891, an angry mob broke into Parish Prison and lynched 11 of the Italians. For years afterwards, the slur "Who killed the Chief?" could lead to a renewed outbreak of violence against Italians. (Today Hennessy's tomb remains a popular attraction in Metairie Cemetery.)

The upstanding Italian community has been dogged by the unsavory reputation of a handful of their kinsmen, in part because New Orleans, port of entry for most Sicilians into the United States, served as the cradle of America's first Mafia families. Most moved on to Chicago and New York.

The most notorious Mafia boss to stay in New Orleans was Carlos "Little Man" Marcello. Born Calogero Minacori in Tunisia in 1910, Marcello came to Louisiana as a baby. His family settled in Algiers, the community across the river from New Orleans, and as a young man Marcello launched his career by stealing autos, selling marijuana, and operating a bar in Gretna on Teche Street. He moved into the big time in the 1940s, when he went to work for New York mobster Frank Costello in the slot-machine business. In May of 1947, Carlos Marcello was made the head of the local Louisiana-based crime family at a ceremony held at the Black Diamond, a club that stood at the corner of Galvez and Conti.

At his federal bribery trial 34 years later, Marcello swore that he was nothing more than a humble tomato salesman employed by the Pelican Tomato Company. But he never denied owning a little bit of property, estimated to be worth $30–40 million. His eventual conviction kept him in prison for six years. In 1989 he returned to his suburban brick home in Jefferson Parish, where he resumed his life as a doting husband, father, and grandpop of 11.

When Carlos Marcello died in his sleep at the age of 83 in March of 1993, many touted the event as the end of the godfather era. To some he remains a folk hero, a modern-day Jean Lafitte. To others—if books such as *Contract on America* and *The Mafia Kingfish* are to be believed—the five-foot-three don was the power behind the Kennedy assassination.

CULTURAL TIMELINE

1764 Sieur Braud sets up the first printing press.

1792 Tabary Theater opens featuring raucous French political satire. Ultimately closed-down by a shocked Spanish government.

1794 Publication of first newspaper, *Le Moniteur de la Louisiana.*

1796 Staging of first opera in North America, André Grétry's *Sylvain.*

1803 The University of New Orleans is chartered.

1817 Betting on fights between bulls and dogs a popular pastime.

1821 Naturalist painter John James Audubon rents studio in the French Quarter.

1829 Composer Louis Moreau Gottschalk born in New Orleans.

1837 First issue of the *Picayune* is published. Chess player Paul Morphy is born.

1838 First Mardi Gras parade takes to the streets of New Orleans.

1847 New Orleans becomes leading horse racing center in the United States.

1857 Mystick Krewe of Comus presents its first Carnival procession.

1870 Writer Kate O'Flaherty Chopin comes to New Orleans.

1872 Rex presents its first parade—in honor of the visit of His Imperial Highness Alexis Romanoff, Grand Duke of Russia.

1885 Ferdinand "Jelly Roll" Morton born in New Orleans.

1890 Andy Bowen and Jack Burke fight the longest boxing match in history, lasting 100 rounds and ending in a draw.

1894 The Original Illinois Club, reputably the oldest black carnival and debutante presentation organization in the world, is founded.

1917 "Tarzan of the Apes" filmed amongst moss-draped oaks, pecan trees, and palmettos. Members of the New Orleans Athletic Club play apes.

1920s William Faulkner lives at 624 Pirate's Alley; Sherwood Anderson in the Pontalba Apartments.

1925 The *Louisiana Weekly,* a black newspaper, begins publication.

1935 Tulane defeats Temple, 20 to 14 in the first Sugar Bowl.

1941 Tennessee Williams makes his first extended visit to New Orleans, staying for three months at 1525 Louisiana Avenue.

1953 Duel is fought with automobiles at Tulane and South Broad.

1985 The New Orleans Saints are sold for approximately $71 million to Ted Benson.

1991 Oliver Stone's *JFK* is filmed in Louisiana.

C A R N I V A L
M A R D I   G R A S

IN CHRISTIAN COMMUNITIES around the world, the 40 days preceding Easter comprise Lent, a period of fasting and penitence. It begins with Ash Wednesday, the day many Catholics (and some Protestants) go to church to receive the sign of the cross marked in ash on their foreheads—its purpose being to remind them of their own mortality. For much of the country, the Tuesday before Lent is just that, a Tuesday, but in New Orleans this Tuesday is "Mardi Gras" (literally, "Fat Tuesday") and represents the last gasp of frivolity before a period of austerity. The date on which Mardi Gras Day falls is determined by the church calendar—always 41 days before Easter, and as early as February 3 or as late as March 9.

In New Orleans, the term "Carnival" refers to the season of balls and parades that begins on Twelfth Night, or January 6, and continues until Mardi Gras. On January 6, Christmas decorations come down, Carnival colors go up, and the six-to-eight-week season begins. Also on that day, one krewe (club)—the Twelfth Night Revelers—hosts the first ball of the season. (A "krewe" is a club that mounts a ball, a parade, or both.) The high point of Carnival is the parade-filled, four-day weekend that begins on the Saturday before Ash Wednesday and culminates in an all-out bash on Mardi Gras Day with the daytime parade of Rex, King of Carnival—the main event of Carnival.

MARDI GRAS DATES (TUESDAYS)

1998	February 24
1999	February 16
2000	March 7
2001	February 27
2002	February 12

BASIC WEEKEND SCHEDULE

Saturday	Iris and Endymion parades
Sunday	Bacchus parade
Monday	Lundi Gras, Spanish Plaza
Tuesday	Rex, the main-event parade

Be sure to check the *Times-Picayune* for routes, times, and parade participants.

(opposite) The Rex float is adorned to look like a Thai royal barge during the main-event parade of Mardi Gras Day. (Syndey Byrd)

■ HISTORY

Mardi Gras was celebrated in the Christian countries of Europe long before the founding of the Crescent City. The day French-Canadian explorer Sieur d'Iberville and his men camped 60 miles south of New Orleans in 1699 happened to be Mardi Gras, March 3, so he named the place Pointe du Mardi Gras. It didn't take long for the French to start celebrating this holiday in the New World. Historians say that Mardi Gras was observed by masked balls and bawdy street processions in New Orleans as early as the 1700s. A report issued in 1791 to the Louisiana colonial government warned that Mardi Gras provided dangerous opportunities: "People of color, both free and slaves, are taking advantage of carnival, going about disguised, mingling with the Carnival throngs in the streets, seeking entrance to the masquerade balls, and threatening public peace." By 1806, the festivities had gotten so rowdy that Mardi Gras celebrations were forbidden, but by all accounts, this law was summarily ignored. In 1817, masks were declared illegal. But by 1823, the celebration that had been going on all along became legal again, and by 1826 even masking was legalized. "Bals masque" (masked balls), also known as "tableau balls," were so fashionable in the 19th century that by law the season was limited to January 1 through Mardi Gras Day in order to keep the population from celebrating all year long. In 1827, it was reported that John Davis's *Theatre d'Orleans* was such a glorious event that it continued straight from Mardi Gras until St. Joseph's Day (on March 19). By 1837, the "season" was lengthened to last from November 1 to June 1. There is much debate as to whether the first formal parade was held in 1835 or 1838, but no matter, the parades that traversed the muddy streets are said to have been wicked and satirical. The first krewe to parade was the Mystick Krewe of Comus (see "Krewes," p. 166).

Much of the pomp employed by the old krewes comes from the entertainments planned in 1872 when the Russian Grand Duke Alexis Romanoff came to New Orleans at Carnival time in hot pursuit of actress Lydia Thompson. Forty businessmen got together and founded the Krewe of Rex, mounting a daytime parade in the archduke's honor. Every Rex from 1888 to 1997 has belonged to the exclusively white and male Boston Club. The city's upper-crust folks, always socially ambitious, decided to adopt the Romanoff household colors—purple (signifying justice), green (faith), and gold (power)—as the official Carnival colors. The local gentry also learned that the Grand Duke Alexis's favorite song was a regrettable ditty called "If Ever I Cease To Love" from the New York musical *Bluebeard* that starred Ms. Thompson. All these years later, it remains the official song of Carnival. (The song is indeed so forgettable that many a jazz band gives up on the melody and plays a tune akin to "Little Brown Jug.")

■ PARADES

There is no question that Mardi Gras is about parades. About 60 Carnival parades fill the schedule between January 6 and Ash Wednesday, particularly during the two and a half weeks before Mardi Gras. But the four-day Carnival weekend is when parading reaches its crescendo. The *Times-Picayune* should be able to supply you with the parade routes and the list of who parades on each. Among those held during the four-day weekend are two super-parades. The first is the **Endymion parade** on Saturday, which bills itself as the largest non-military parade in the world. Endymion first paraded in 1967 and continues to make good its motto, "Throw 'til it hurts!" The second is the **Bacchus parade** on Sunday.

In 1993, musician Harry Connick, Jr. and friends established the Orpheus parade, named for the musician whose music moved everthing it touched. One thousand riders throw special Greek medallion beads and glitter theme cups, a first for the city. Each year a local legendary musician is honored and numerous celebrity musicians serve as riders/performers at the Orpheuscapade Ball. It is held the Monday before Fat Tuesday.

The crowds who attend these celebrity-studded parades tend to be denser, louder, and more aggressive than at other parades. Because these events fall on the weekend, people drive in from a 300-mile radius just for a chance to see the likes of Henry Winkler or John Goodman dressed up in crown and blond wig, and to have their tax attorney or former professor throw them handfuls of 12-inch pearl strands.

Carnival Day (Tuesday) is more for families. Eager parade-goers wake up before dawn and stake out a spot along a parade route. By 7:00 A.M., St. Charles Avenue is blanketed with parade-watching equipment and essentials: special ladders, folding deck chairs, ice chests, generators; crockpots filled with red beans, barbecue pits, and buckets of Popeye's fried chicken; and video cameras and hand-held TVs.

KREWES

Krewes are the masking and parading clubs for which New Orleans is both famous and infamous. Several of these are described below.

Babylon. Started by a New Orleans dentist, Frank Oser, in 1939, it remains one of the 10 oldest parading krewes in the city. Its membership of 200 is made up largely of physicians. The **flambeaux** are Babylon custom. These burning "torches"—really tubes filled with chemicals that produce a brilliant, sometimes colored, light—are traditionally carried by African Americans who march alongside the floats. The image of the torch was inspired by the slave ritual of Bois Caiman, performed on August 14, 1791, at the beginning of the Haitian War of Independence. After a fiery parade the slaves swore allegiance to their priest leaders. (When the war ended in 1804, Haiti emerged as the second nation in the Western Hemisphere to gain its independence, and the first free black nation.) Although some parade-goers find it demeaning to black men that they carry these torches, as blacks are rarely, if ever, allowed in this conservative krewe, flambeaux (the term applies to the torch carriers as well as the torches) still accompany the Knights of Babylon.

A loyal member of the krewe of Barkus. (Syndey Byrd)

Bacchus. A large krewe started in the 1970s and known for its innovative floats, Bacchus leads a huge parade the Sunday before Mardi Gras.

Barkus. In 1993, a new krewe was founded with membership limited to dogs and head-

A Bacchus krewe parade float. (Syndey Byrd)

quartered in the vicinity of the "Flea Market." Krewe of Barkus rules include this warning, "Cats, while welcome, will not be provided with security;" as well as, "No dogs may be 'in season' and owners are responsible for their own dog's scoop." This annual French Quarter event is open to the public and is a benefit for local animal shelters and national humane societies.

Comus. From the Greek *komos,* meaning revelers. They are the oldest parading krewe, having originally been called "The Mystick Krewe of Comus." In 1856 six men (all Protestant, white Americans) who had moved to New Orleans from Mobile, Alabama, met at Dr. Pope's drugstore to discuss introducing their brand of Carnival to the city (parades had begun in Mobile a few years earlier). They formed a secret society along with 13 New Orleanians and mounted a tableau ball for 3,000 at the Gaiety Theatre. Their first parade included two floats lighted by flambeaux. Their motto is "Sic volo, sic iubeo" ("As I wish, thus I command").

In keeping with the early Masonic traditions of secrecy, the members of Comus never reveal the name of their king. Comus members are the most discriminatory of the old-liners. In protest to the city council's 1991 anti-discrimination ordinance, some former members of Comus have joined all-white parading krewes across Lake Pontchartrain.

Endymion. Like Bacchus, this large krewe was started in the 1970s. Its Saturday parade is the largest parade of Carnival.

Iris. A ladies-only krewe formed in 1917, this group held its first parade in 1959, and today has over 500 members. They parade during the day on the Saturday before Mardi Gras.

Krewe du Vieux. Inside jokes and a no-holds-barred sensibility characterize the only parade allowed in the Quarter. This is probably the only krewe to capture the old spirit of Carnival, before high society and commercialization put the clamps on naughty expression and behavior.

Momus. Chartered soon after Rex in 1872, the group was named after the god of mockery. Their motto is "Dum vivimus, vivamus" ("While we live, let us live"). Members come from the ranks of the all-white Louisiana Club.

Okeanos. A krewe founded in 1949 by a group of Ninth Ward businessmen who wanted to bring Carnival to St. Claude Avenue, Carnival's original parade route.

Original Illinois Club. One of three old-line black krewes that presents debutantes, the Original Illinois Club was formed by several Creole-of-color community leaders in 1894. The "Chicago Glide" is the dance unique to this club. Though the club has less than 50 members, they mount an elaborate ball for over 700 guests.

Phunny Phorty Phellows. This group of costumed men and women celebrates the official opening of Carnival season by riding a decorated streetcar along St. Charles Avenue. The group eats king cake as they toss throws to the spectators and serenade them with a jazz band. The name comes from a nineteenth-century krewe.

Proteus. Taking its name from the ocean shepherd of Poseidon's seals, Proteus presented its first procession in 1882. One of the more stingy krewes in their parading days, they have now halted parading altogether due to MCS 14984, the ordinance that denies parade permits to discriminatory groups.

Rex. The main-event parade of Mardi Gras Day. The King of Rex is the King of Carnival. He is always a civic and business leader, and, every year since 1888, a member of the old-line Boston Club (an old, conservative, Christian club). The krewe itself has the most liberal admittance policy of all of the old-line groups, as they are a shade more interested in professional stature than in pedigree.

When Frank Howard became Rex's King of Carnival in 1895, he ended up married to his queen, Lydia Fairchild, and it got tongues to wagging. Nowadays kings are old enough to be the grandfathers of queens. A feature of Rex parades is the *boeuf gras,* the fatted beef, bull, or ox that symbolizes the last meat eaten before the beginning of Lent. Rex calls the Queen of the Carnival and the Maids of the Rex Court the "Carnival Court." No other organization is entitled to use this designation.

The charter name for the 600-member Rex organization is "The School of Design," the same group that presented the first daytime parade in the city in 1872. All Rex objects bear the motto, "Pro Bono Publico" ("For the Good of the Public").

Thoth. (Say "Toe-th"). This parading krewe was formed in 1947 to bring Mardi Gras to institutions for children and adults with disabilities.

Tucks. In 1969, two Loyola University students created a rag-tag parading krewe and named it for their favorite local hang-out, Friar Tuck's. Today the krewe maintains its *Animal House* reputation.

Zeus. The krewe that began the Metairie parade tradition in 1956.

Zulu. The Zulu Aid and Pleasure Club was founded in 1909, held its first parade in 1914, was incorporated in 1916, hosted its first celebrity monarch when Louis Armstrong became their king in 1949, and remains the most permeable of the old krewes. It has just under 400 members and several dozen are white. Zulu is the only krewe in which the king gets to choose his own queen. During parade time, any friend of a member can pay a fee and ride in the parade.

Out in Metairie, across the river, and in St. Bernard Parish, the scene is repeated for the suburban parades. By nine o'clock the streets are filled with paraders, dressed in costume and strutting their stuff. The parades begin snaking through the streets in earnest by 11:00 A.M. A lot of the local high school bands also march in parades. The good ones will march in many parades, and the money they earn goes a long way to support their schools.

Anything goes on Mardi Gras Day. *Everyone* dons flamboyant costumes or bizarre make-up. Locals and out-of-towners stroll the streets dressed as packs of Energizer Rabbits, condoms, tap-dancing bottles of Chanel, Nubian royalty, Oscar Wilde, the Romantic Poets, French Revolutionaries leading Marie Antoinette to the guillotine, and troupes of topless clowns. Some people dress as nuns; some nuns dress as bag ladies. Transvestitism reaches the pinnacle of the art form, as the French Quarter hosts one of the most elaborate gay beauty-and-costume contests in the world. Usually, the costumes worn in the Quarter are a great deal more lascivious than those worn by the families in Metairie and along St.

Charles Avenue.

Each year New Orleans festers with rumors concerning the goings-on at Carnival season. As the old-line krewes pride themselves on secrecy, getting the scoop on who is doing what becomes part of the fun. Good sources for the skinny on what's happenin' are limousine drivers who have been booked to tote the royalty around; the lunch crowd at Galatoire's on Friday; the noon streetcorner crowd around Common and Carondelet; alteration staff at Town & Country on St. Charles Avenue; awning installers; and the maids who work on Palmer Avenue and shop at Langenstein's on Arabella Street. Perennial rumors include: one (or all) of the krewes are bankrupt; Schwegmann's Giant Supermarket has sold out of ice picks; a rider in Iris threw her three-carat diamond to the crowd by mistake; or the real queen of Comus got pregnant and the new one is a last-minute replacement.

The biggest gossip in recent times has occurred in connection with the new nondiscrimination rules implemented by the city and aimed at the krewes. It started in December of 1991, when then councilwoman Dorothy Mae Taylor co-authored an ordinance, MCS 14984, prohibiting race and sex discrimination by krewes. Those groups who had exclusive admissions policies were denied access to city services

A Carnival participant in all his glory (above).
Carnival revelers crowd balconies in the French Quarters (right). (both photos, Syndey Byrd)

and parade permits. Of the 60 or so parading krewes, only three old-line krewes whose traditions stem from 19th-century elitist sensibilities viewed this as "cultural terrorism" and refused to comply: they were the Mystick Krewe of Comus, the Knights of Momus, and the Krewe of Proteus. Also as a result of the ordinance, other krewes are changing their routes and schedules. It's best to consult the *Times-Picayune* for the most up-to-date parade information.

Krewe members aren't the only participants in the parades; marching or walking clubs feature prominently as well. The Jefferson City Buzzards is considered the oldest of marching clubs, as it was begun in 1890. They get going about 6:45 A.M. on Mardi Gras morning in the vicinity of Audubon Park and leisurely stroll toward the downtown madness. The Corner Club begins its day before 7:30 A.M. at the corner of Second and Annunciation streets. Pete Fountain's Half Fast Walking Club kicks off from Washington and Prytania streets about the same time.

Truck parades also feature prominently on Mardi Gras Day, when five of them follow the parade of Rex downtown (they follow Argus in another neighborhood). These are comprised of over 350 decorated flatbeds with nearly 15,000 costumed maskers. The trucks are decorated by families and friends who meet on the weekends and do all the decorating and costume-making themselves. In preparation for the parades the riders must get up before dawn, drive to the starting point of the parade, and wait for up to four hours to roll.

To get some meatier info, try visiting the Mardi Gras Museum, the Louisiana State Museum, or the Germaine Wells Mardi Gras Museum on the second floor of Arnaud's Restaurant. For information, see "Gardens, Museums, and Zoos," pp. 275–277, in "PRACTICAL INFORMATION."

■ THROWS

Throughout the parade, masked riders stand atop two- and three-tiered papier-mache, tractor-towed constructions from which they throw plastic cups, panties, and beads, as well as metal doubloons inscribed with the logo of the krewe, to the eager crowd. The riders often spend over $1,000 on their individual stock of "throws" to give out during the parade.

In the early days of the festivities, merry-makers used to carry bags of flour that they would throw at each other. When a mischievous few mixed pepper with their flour, the practice had to be discontinued and safer things thrown. These days, the typical throws are beads, "doubloons" (fake coins), and, in recent years, Zapp potato chips, which come packaged in Carnival colors. Probably the most valued throws are the hand-painted coconuts tossed by the krewe of Zulu. Onlookers vie energetically—sometimes boldly—to catch the most "stuff." In recent years, it's become more commonplace for women to expose their breasts than to shout the conventional phrase, "Throw me sumtin' Mista!" in return for a long strand of faux pearls. *Be warned*—many an ordinarily gentle, little old sterling-headed grand-mother will stomp your knuckles bloody for that aluminum doubloon, and that adorable tyke has no qualms about jerking your knees out from under you for a bamboo-and-rubber spear. Most importantly, never ever put your hand on the ground to pick up anything! If you want those beads or that doubloon, put your foot on it and don't lift your toe until you have it firmly in your hands.

Other tips for catching favors include taking a nun in habit with you, and standing under a street lamp: she'll be a favorite target for the good Catholics on the floats. Or make a posterboard sign that says "John" and hold it up at each float, figuring that there must be at least one guy named John on every float. Or cut a large bleach bottle in half and attach the spout to a broom handle so that you have a handy tool to hold up to the riders. Another version of this is to turn an umbrella inside out and hold it up to the floats. Some parade-goers with kids use a special 8- to 10-foot ladder fixed with a bench at the top for the little ones, while parents stand below balancing them. These pre-made parade ladders can be bought at many local hardware stores and cost about $60. Ladders should not be hooked together, placed at intersections or against barricades, or left unattend-ed—or the police will confiscate them.

Those who live within walking distance from the parade routes sometimes joke that "Mardi Gras" must be an old Creole expression meaning, "May I use your bathroom?" Nowadays the city puts out a lot of Port-O-Lets, and restaurants and bars will let their patrons avail themselves of the facilities. Those groups who have large packs of newly toilet-trained kids or big drinkers in their party might con-sider renting a hotel room on the route.

The estimated size of the Mardi Gras crowd is based on the amount of trash generated. A good crowd is one that has produced 2,000 or more tons of refuse. Each parade is followed by the Sanitation Department with its street sweepers, water-and-brush trucks, and blowers. Watching them is almost as much fun as watching the parade.

■ MARDI GRAS BALLS

Nowadays, there are over 130 krewes who center their year's activities around the Carnival season. Of these, close to 60 mount an annual parade. But all of them host at least one affair: a ball, which is the popular term for a bal masque, masquerade, or tableau representation. The money to mount the tableaux and balls comes from the dues paid by krewe members. These can be as low as $100 or as high as several thousand dollars; the additional initiation fee for new members can be as much as $1,000. The older krewes take their balls very seriously, so these tend to be long on pomp and short on life. At the other end of the spectrum are the gay balls—a combination of Las Vegas and the Lido with just a dash of camp thrown in. They're presided over by a grand female-impersonating queen in a multi-thousand-dollar gown. All of the other krewes' balls fall somewhere in the middle. There are krewes for youngsters, oldsters, neighborhoods, the visually impaired, Italians, artists —you name it and there's probably a krewe and ball for it. Some balls are for members of the krewe only, some are for "PLU" (People Like Us), while other krewes are thrilled to have any visitors enjoy their spectacle. Endymion holds its ball/rock concert in the Superdome, and many revelers eagerly buy tickets to attend.

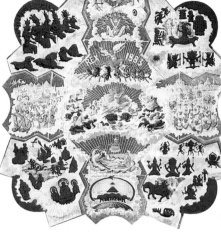

An invitation to a Mardi Gras ball from the nineteenth century.

(Historic New Orleans Collection)

One tradition that krewes (and other partiers) continue is the "king cake" served at Mardi Gras parties. The authentic Carnival version of this confection is a brioche decorated with purple, green, and gold sugar and containing a tiny gold bean. Today the gold bean has been replaced by a plastic baby, a loose reference to the baby Jesus. The person who finds the token in their piece is responsible for hosting the next king cake party.

Elaborate costumes and ritual are the hallmarks of the Meeting of Courts of Comus and Rex. (Syndey Byrd)

■ S O C I E T Y   B A L L S

Among the many balls that krewes give during the Carnival season between January 6 and Ash Wednesday, only a few attract the city's society debutantes to their "courts." The stakes of Carnival are the highest for socially ambitious New Orleanians—a father belonging to one of the "right" krewes will begin a campaign at his daughter's birth to ensure that she will become queen of the ball when the time comes. Little girls who attend private girls' schools such as Sacred Heart and McGehee's learn early that an indiscretion at a childhood birthday party might permanently relegate them to a slot in the court of the queen, while others are tapped to become krewe royalty. Having a mother who was a queen certainly helps a girl's chances. Failing to achieve the status of queen can, within certain circles, lower a family's social status in a way that not even a good marriage can remedy.

Belonging to one of these "old-line" krewes today entails making social standing a priority. A family will make financial sacrifices so Dad can be in the right club, and Sis can make an impressive debut. For those not yet belonging to the right krewe, the willingness to make such sacrifices is not enough to guarantee membership. Regardless of an applicant's credentials, he may still be "blackballed," or rejected, by just one or two members; guests may also be blackballed from some invitation lists.

Few are invited to these "exclusive" balls, and as most krewes do not include an address on their invitation, it is difficult for those who are invited to reply; however, guests may return their admit cards to signify that he or she will not be in attendance. Those who do get invited are expected to wear *costume de rigueur*, or "full dress," consisting of white tie and tails for men, and a floor-length dress for women. Or the ball may be a bal masque, or masked ball, in which an elaborate costume is *de rigueur*. Once you get there, be sure not to take one of the "reserved seats," since space reserved on the floor and balcony is for specific, special guests.

When you get there, you'll notice the members of the court, including the king, queen, dukes, and maids. The king occupies the throne at the ball along with the queen. Attending him is a page, a little boy in costume. The queen is the lucky debutante (probably the daughter of a krewe member) sitting next to the king and wearing a grand, expensive ball gown. Though he may not appear with the other court members, the most powerful member of the krewe is the captain. This elected officer is placed in full charge of the pageantry, including any street parade or tableau ball. Kings may come and go, but it is the captain who decides the krewe's

A debutante is introduced at the Comus ball. (Syndey Byrd)

theme and court. When parading, the captain generally rides a horse, and his identity—particularly in the exclusive krewes —is rarely made public.

Before or after being presented, these royal folk may all be found in the "Captain's Room," or the "King's Room." This dressing room is reserved for the members of the court, the captain, and the aides. Here, champagne and other drinks are usually served by the king. Certain kings provide large quantities of wine and liquors as well as light refreshments. Admittance is restricted to members of the cast of the tableaux and committeemen.

After the king, queen, dukes, and maids are assembled on the throne, the king and queen perform the "Grand March" around the floor followed by their retinue, in the style of Old World royalty. Most European tradition dictates that ladies walk to the left of their escorts because knights of old used their right arms for weapons. But the custom of New Orleans Carnival is that the ladies should always be next to the audience so that they may appear to greater advantage: At most balls the king and queen turn to the right upon beginning the Grand March, and the queen is on the king's right; maids are likewise to the right of the dukes.

Depending on the type of ball, another significant event may be the "tableau," an enactment of the ball's "theme." Following this are the "call-outs," the first three or more dances allocated to members of the cast of the tableau. The term "call-out" may also refer to an invitation to participate in the maskers' dances, or to a person occupying a seat in the call-out section. When a masker calls out a partner, the partner is presented with a "favor," or souvenir. Some favors are obtained by the krewe for their members, while others are purchased by their wives. A few maskers bestow handsome gifts upon favorites: the cost of favors varies from a few cents to thousands of dollars. At the end of the ball, the court and their select guests will attend the Queen's Supper, a late-night party honoring the queen.

■ OTHER CELEBRATIONS

While the obvious focus of Mardi Gras for most is the many parades, New Orleanians and their visitors celebrate the holiday in other ways as well. One big celebration takes place in **Spanish Plaza on Lundi Gras,** the Monday before Mardi Gras. Free and open to the public, the event features the arrivals of the Kings of Zulu and Rex, as well as a free concert and fireworks. For folks with kids, there's also the Mardi Gras Mask-a-Thon, a family-oriented costume contest held on Mardi Gras afternoon in the 600 block of Canal Street.

For those who haven't brought kids along, there's an option that may cure you forever of any desire to party. The **six-block-long party** along Bourbon Street over Mardi Gras weekend somehow manages to be a combination of VE and VJ Day, New Year's Eve on Times Square, *Animal House,* the California Gold Rush, Spring Break in Daytona, and a Fellini movie. When the parades are over, many fun-seekers of the beer-gut and college set line the historic, lacy wrought-iron balconies to shimmy at passersby in return for beads. The aroma of beer, Hurricanes, and bodily fluids can be enjoyed as far away as Garden District. But at midnight on Mardi Gras the street is closed, and police with bullhorns announce, "Mardi Gras is officially over!" This kind of partying is enough to make anyone stumble to a pharmacy the next day for a bottle of XS, the locally produced hangover reliever.

One interesting incarnation of the holiday festivities is the **Courrir de Mardi Gras.** Taking place on the Cajun prairie northwest of Lafayette, this celebration of Carnival strikes a different note. Literally translated, this "Mardi Gras Run" resembles a celebration brought to Louisiana by the early Acadians. The Courrir is a rowdy, exuberant procession of locals going from farm to farm, collecting the ingredients for a pot of gumbo symbolically meant to feed the entire community.

Amid all the revelry, local Catholics do not forget their own heritage—or at least, don't neglect the devotion necessary to compensate for their wild behavior. Many devout Catholic families demand that their children go to confession on Mardi Gras morning *before* the parades to atone for sins, just in case they should over-party and meet their Maker before attending mass on Ash Wednesday. Once that first day of Lent does roll around, hard Mardi Gras partying can cause even pagans to embrace this day of atonement.

■ MARDI GRAS INDIANS

One of the most magnificent spectacles and most elite of all Mardi Gras celebrations is the elaborate tradition of the black neighborhood "tribes" who dress up to honor the Native Americans who first befriended them. Born of a completely original aesthetic tradition, the Mardi Gras Indians have contributed a costuming and parading style that has become integral to Carnival. The inspiration for the

Indians was an event in the 1790s, when several dozen slaves escaped and were hidden by the Chickasaws, who also tried to assist in a slave rebellion. Black oral history kept the contributions of the Louisiana natives alive, and by the time of Reconstruction a few groups from the secret black pleasure clubs (many of whose roots went back to Congo Square) formed their own Carnival clubs. They took to the streets during Carnival dressed in turkey feathers, fish-scale ornaments, and ceremonial regalia to honor the Louisiana Indians.

Tribes soon developed rivalries, and Mardi Gras (referred to as "That Day" in the Indian songs) also provided the perfect opportunity to settle grudges. Dressed as Indian warriors, rival "gangs" could fight outside the law's reach on a day when the rest of the city was celebrating in the streets. Indians then fought ritualistic duels set to music (see "MUSIC," pp. 199–202). Challenges are still made these days, but on strictly aesthetic grounds.

The first official tribe was begun in the 1880s at 1313 St. Anthony Street by Becate Battiste. Hailing from the Seventh Ward, born of both African and American Indian stock, he named his gang the "Creole Wild West Tribe." Today the descendants of the tribe are the **Yellow Pocahontas,** previously led by Battiste's nephew,

A Creole Wild West Mardi Gras Indian member in uniform (above). Mardi Gras Indian tribes are noted for their elaborate plumage (right) (both photos, Syndey Byrd).

Alfred Montana, Sr., and now by his son Allison "Tuddy" Montana. The original Yellow Pocahontas tribe was formed across town in the uptown Garden District in 1896 by a man who was part Louisiana native and part African American, and who married a pure-blooded Choctaw. It is thought that these tribes were in part inspired by the World Centennial Cotton Exposition of 1884, when New Orleans played host to Buffalo Bill's Wild West Show for four months. As part of the show, resplendent (authentic) Indians whooped and hollered, strutting their stuff to New Orleans' people of color. During the Mardi Gras celebration of 1885, American Indians who had performed in the show evidently took to the streets in celebration.

After World War II another wave of tribes was formed, including the Wild Magnolias and the Black Eagles. Tribes are founded by a chief, the man in the neighborhood able to gather the largest personal retinue. Today there are over 20 Indian tribes—among them the Wild Apaches, White Eagles, Wild Tchoupitoulas, and Golden Star Hunters—with between 10 and 40 members each. Most members come from inner-city, working-class black neighborhoods. (One tribe is integrated, however: a Finnish fellow who makes his own costumes has been the Second Chief of the Black Eagles for the past 20 years.) Fifteen of the 17 tribes have decided to "bury the hatchet" and joined together in 1987. The proceeds from their first official poster in 1993 went to benefit the preservation of their Indian culture.

When the tribes march on parade, those watching will see the First Spy Boy, then the First Flag Boy, and several series of Spies and Flags, the number depending on the size of the tribe. Near the end of the procession is the man who carries the Gang Flag, followed by the Wildman or Medicine Man, with the Second Chief and the Big Chief bringing up the rear. The Big Chief is followed by his second-line, his civilian bodyguards, who often carry weapons. Their trademark plumage, which can weigh up to 50 pounds, is designed and crafted by the wearer, an effort that takes months and costs thousands of dollars. Nowadays, the ferocious tribal rivalry focuses on the costumes: the Big Chiefs all seek to be deemed the "prettiest" by other gang members and neighborhood followers. The Uptown tribes —among them Golden Star, Creole Wild West, Black Eagles, Golden Eagles, Wild Magnolia, Carrollton Hunters—are considered to be the fanciest dressers. The Downtown tribe noted for its plumage is the Monogram Hunters. Musician Charles Neville remembers that his mother used to mask as an Indian on Mardi

Gras Day with his uncle, Chief Jolly. She'd carry scissors to keep people around Jolly from stealing his feathers. You can also see the Mardi Gras Indians march a few weeks after Mardi Gras—on St. Joseph's Day, the holiday tradition begun by New Orleans' Italian Americans in the 19th century.

Mardi Gras Indian with a live bird in his feathery hat. (Michael P. Smith)

M U S I C

AMERICA'S ONLY INDIGENOUS ART FORM, jazz is a musical *etouffeé*. It emerged from a base combination of syncopation from Africa and the Caribbean mixed with the melodic structures of Spain and France; was seasoned with Deep South humidity and oppression; and finally was slathered with the rhythmic and harmonic contributions of individual musicians to achieve a unique and delectable stew. Once its early structures were formed, jazz grew up on the collectively improvised back-of-town ragtime and an unbeatable *joie de vivre,* bite, and swagger.

If there is one place in the United States that can be credited with being the spiritual birthplace of jazz, it must be the *Place des Negres,* or Old Congo Square, in what is now Louis Armstrong Park. Here, enslaved Africans were allowed to meet and dance, speaking in their native African tongues and playing their traditional instruments. The square bustled with these activities from 1817 until 1857.

Following the Civil War, bands such as Kelly's Silver Cornet Band performed concerts there. These were times of transition when the melodies of the black minstrel shows, syncopated music, slave work chants, and the blues were mingling everywhere that people gathered. The style of music practiced in the early years of the twentieth century in New Orleans was a buoyant, simple music in 2/4 or 4/4 rhythm. This style of jazz is now often referred to as "traditional" (or "trad," the British term), and in New Orleans there are a good number of 80- and 90-year-old founding fathers still doing nightly gigs.

During these early years, white musicians began to hang out in the streets and clubs of the African-American community, trying to learn their style. Many black musicians were also listening to recordings of white musicians such as Larry Shields of the Original Dixieland Jazz Band. Shields was influential in creating the "trick bag" of jazz riffs common to all New Orleans jazz. The term "Dixieland" was used to connote the syncopated music played by white bands, a distinction made by 1930s jazz critics. The jazz music played by the Creoles of color and the blacks was more improvisational than Dixieland and was rooted in African and West Indian traditions. Added to the mix were Irish, Jewish (cornetist Johnny Wiggs, grandson of the Chief Justice of the Louisiana Supreme Court), and Italian musicians who moved into the same urban neighborhoods and took to the American music form as quickly as the Acadians had taken to the swamps. Some of the early bands often improvised on handmade instruments such as banjos made of

Charles Neville, one of the legendary Neville Brothers, performs at Jazz Fest.

DANCING THE CALENDA

*T*o dance the calenda, the Negroes have two drums made with hollow pieces of wood, all in one piece. One of the ends is left opened and the other end is covered with the skin of a goat or a sheep. The shortest of these drums is called the "bamboula" because most of the time the drum is made of a very large bambou tree. A Negro is seated on each drum upon which he beats the skin with his fingers and wrist. One Negro keeps the time slowly like a basso drum while the other keeps time rapidly with fingers and wrist. To this is added the sound of many gourds half filled with small stones or grains of corn. These are shaken by beating them with the hands by means of a handle that crosses them. When the orchestra is increased or completed the banza is added to these drums and the gourds. The banza is a coarse violin made with four cords that are pinched with the fingers. The Negresses standing in a row keep time with their hands, clapping them together, and they take the chorus from a song improvised by one or two Negresses who sing with a very loud and piercing voice. Negroes have great talent to improvise music and words adapted to the music.

The dances, always a pair, a man and a girl, dances in the middle of the circle that is formed on a level piece of ground and always out of doors. This dance consists of the following: The dancer turns around, spinning on himself around his partner. He keeps his arms close to his body, wrist tightly closed, then raises alternatively the arms one after the other. In the meanwhile, the Negresses forming the circle keep time with the beating of their hands. The dancer moves her feet forward alternatively, hitting the ground sometimes with the point of the toes and sometimes with the heel. Each one has a turn to dance in the middle of the circle, and the rhythm is always perfect. They are so fond of dancing that they would keep on dancing all night, and when orders are given to stop the dancing it is always with regret that they leave their ball.

—Helen d'Aquin Allain, memoir describing
New Orleans, c. 1830s

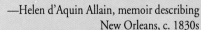

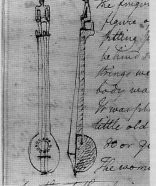

Pieces of a journal kept by Benjamin (Henry) Latrobe illustrate the instruments he saw being played at Congo Square in 1819. (The Maryland Historical Society)

cheese boxes and percussion instruments of kitchen implements.

The word "jazz" was not applied to the new sound until a good 20 years after the music had already found its way to the ears and tapping feet of New Orleanians, who referred to it with slang terms such as "gutbucket," "ragtime," or "ratty music." Ironically, it is believed that a white band was first called a "jazz" band. In 1915, Tom Brown took his white Dixieland band to Chicago and audiences requested uptempo, or "jass" music. Meanwhile, the Chicago Musician's Union angrily used "jass" as a slur against the musicians for playing that dirty New Orleans "jass music." ("Jass" was an Elizabethan English word that meant roughly "to do with enthusiasm," and later came to refer to sexual fluids.) Back in New Orleans, on June 20, 1918, the good reporters at the *Times-Picayune* referred to jazz as a "musical vice."

Chicago audiences knew a catchy word when they heard it and began calling the group "Brown's Dixieland Jass Band." By the time the next white band went north, the five-man ensemble led by **Nick LaRocca** was officially called the **Original Dixieland Jazz Band.** This group was to have a great impact on audiences in London, Chicago, and New York. In 1917 they became the first New Orleans jazz group to make successful records, some of which sold more than a million copies. The hits from their 20-year career, including "Tiger Rag," "Ostrich Walk," "Livery Stable Blues" and "Clarinet Marmalade," continue to be mainstays for both black and white traditional bands.

Buddy Bolden (1878-1931) is the man credited with throwing all of the city's musical ingredients into a big pot and turning out a feast with a uniquely New Orleans flavor. With his fiery cornet, he and his band added pepper and spice to the "legitimate" music of the day. They played music that was raunchy and gut-bucket, born of poverty and passion. An example was Bolden's theme song, "Funky Butt Blues." No recordings exist of his music, but accounts from those who heard him play say that he was the greatest cornet player who ever lived. He was also thrown out of his own band on occasion when he drank away all of the band's profits. His career was cut short when he went wild at a Labor Day Parade in 1907, and was committed to the East Louisiana Mental Hospital, where he spent the last 24 years of his life, rotting away with venereal disease.

After Buddy Bolden left town, **Freddie Keppard** (bandleader of the Original Creole Orchestra) became the "king" of the New Orleans cornetists. Keppard and his O.C.O. spread the sounds of New Orleans on vaudeville tours between 1914 and 1918. Asked to make a jazz recording, Keppard reportedly refused saying, "Why should I put my stuff down on a record for other people to steal?"

■ STORYVILLE SOUND

While legend has it that New Orleans jazz was born in the brothels of the infamous Storyville district, the truth is that the music was most often played in saloons nearby, or to accompany social activity. Buddy Bolden himself played in Lincoln Park and the streets of the city more often than in Storyville. Outdoor musical processions, a concept practiced by Bolden, Jelly Roll Morton, Freddie Keppard, King Oliver, and Louis Armstrong, created wide audiences for jazz. Nonetheless, the popular brothels of Storyville were a venue for this music, and steady gigs—usually for pianists—meant steady income and the opportunity to grab the attention of the upper-class patrons.

Meanwhile, ragtime was setting feet to tapping in low-life juke joints. Made popular by Missourian **Scott Joplin** and characterized by highly syncopated melodic lines played against a 2/4 bass, ragtime was to have great influence in the New Orleans jazz scene. In New Orleans, ragtime aquired a heavy dose of Latin rhythms.

Jazz pianist **Jelly Roll Morton** (Ferdinand Joseph La Mothe, 1890–1941) insisted that he, and only he, had created jazz. While that might not have been exactly accurate, most agree that at the very least, Jelly Roll was the first notable jazz composer and arranger. As a Creole of color, he tended to feel that he was superior intellectually to many musicians. He was quite a dandy, and had a diamond embedded in his front tooth to add flash to his smile. He led a colorful life as well—he was a ladies' man, and an expert pool hustler. Possessed with a terrific fear of the power of voodoo, he was known to throw away a good suit of clothes and completely re-outfit himself if he thought someone had thrown voodoo powder on him. Morton's autobiography, *Mr. Jelly Roll,* based on Alan Lomax's 1938 interviews, was published in 1950. Jelly Roll died in 1941 in California.

The ragtime pianists, such as **Steve Lewis, Spencer Williams,** and **Manuel Manetta,** were known as the Storyville "professors." This mock title went to talented musicians who served as mentors to the younger ones.

While performing in bordellos such as Hilma Burt's Mirror Mansion and Lulu White's Mahogany Hall, Spencer Williams, the ward and a blood-relative of Lulu White, began playing music as a young child and went on to write such jazz standards as "Basin Street Blues," "I Ain't Gonna Give Nobody None O' My Jelly Roll," and the "Mahogany Hall Stomp." In 1925, Williams migrated to Paris where he wrote music for Josephine Baker.

Jelly Roll Morton playing piano in a Storyville bordello. (Hogan Jazz Archive, Tulane University Library)

During the same period "spasm bands" were filling the back alleys, train stations, and markets with their hot music. These bands began with street urchins playing on improvised instruments—comb and paper, cigar box guitars, barrel basses, bottles and jugs—for whatever coins passersby were willing to throw. These grew into more established ensembles, among them **"Stalebread" Lacoume's Razzie Dazzie Spasm Band.** The popularity of these hot dance bands bolstered the city's mania for dancing in Storyville, Treme, and Seventh Ward dance halls, at places such as the Economy and the San Jacinto. Dance halls sprang up in many neighborhoods, rich and poor, particularly in the years between the Spanish American War in 1898 and the Great Depression in 1929.

■ MAJOR PLAYERS

Several other great stars were to emerge in the early years of the 20th century. **Edward "Kid" Ory** was a Creole of color who grew up upriver from New Orleans at San Francisco Plantation (a home owned by a white family also named Ory). Here, he and some of the other teenagers formed a spasm band, the Woodland Band. By the time that Ory found an audience in New Orleans, the group had become a woodwind, horn, and percussion ensemble in which Ory played the valve trombone. After this ensemble split up, he began leading bands at Economy Hall and the prestigious, whites-only New Orleans Country Club, as well as spots in Lincoln Park and Storyville.

In 1919, Ory left New Orleans for a Creole-of-color community in California. There he organized the Sunshine Band, which in 1921 became the first black New Orleans jazz band to record in Southern California. After stints playing with King Oliver, Louis Armstrong, and Jelly Roll Morton in New York and Chicago, he retired from music in the early 1930s. Ory later returned to perform for an even wider audience in the '40s as the grand old man of jazz, continuing to play professionally until his death in 1973.

Joe "King" Oliver, one of the immortal cornetists and bandleaders of the early years of jazz, took what he perfected in New Orleans and spread it around the world. After migrating from rural Louisiana, he began playing in New Orleans in 1904, with the Onward Brass Band. By 1910, Oliver had begun to perform in Storyville and with Kid Ory at Pete Lala's. After the closing of the Storyville district during World War I, Oliver left for Chicago, sending for Louis Armstrong as his second cornetist. It was here in 1919 that his nickname "Bad Eye" (an accident blinded him) was replaced with the moniker "King." During the 1920s King Oliver and his two bands, the Creole Jazz Band (1920–24) and the Dixie Syncopaters (1925–30), enjoyed great popularity and recorded over 30 records. Those who knew him remember him as being "cocky, cute, and meaner than a nine-balled tomcat." By the 1930s, Oliver was losing his teeth and finding himself increasingly unable to play the cornet. More and more frequently he asked Armstrong to replace him. When Oliver died in Savannah in 1938, he was destitute, and the world of jazz had passed him by.

Another star of these years was **Sidney Bechet** (1897–1959), a master of the clarinet and soprano sax, known for his particular "bending" of notes. Bechet began playing clarinet at age six, and by 1914 he had already worked with many of the city's greats. After working with Clarence Williams and King Oliver, he moved to Chicago, and later to New York. Bechet ended up in Paris and continued to play the New Orleans style of jazz, ultimately becoming something of a legendary figure in Paris. To savor the Bechet style today, his student Jacques Gauthe regularly

King Oliver's Creole Jazz Band, from left: Honore Dutrey on trombone; Baby Dodds on drums; Louis Armstrong on slide trumpet; and behind Armstrong, King Oliver on cornet. Armstrong's wife, Lil Hardin, is on piano; Bill Johnson plays banjo; and Johnny Dodds on clarinet. (William Ranson, Hogan Jazz Archive, Tulane University Library)

performs at Jazz Meridien, 614 Canal Street.

The name **Louis Armstrong** is virtually synonymous with New Orleans jazz. Born on August 4, 1901 (he claimed July 4, 1900), Armstrong got his earliest musical training when he was on the streets and a ward of the Jones Colored Waifs' Home. He began playing professionally with Kid Ory in Lincoln Park and later with King Oliver. By 1918, Armstrong was playing on river boats, and in 1922 he left New Orleans to join King Oliver's band in Chicago. He spent the next 40 years performing around the globe, but rarely in the city that was his home. The sponsorship of the State Department enabled Armstrong and his All Stars to tour the world as a "goodwill ambassador" from the 1940s to the '60s. He died in 1971.

■ MARCHING BANDS AND SOCIAL CLUBS

The tradition of brass band street parades goes back well over a century to the first jazz funerals, held by jazz musicians when one of their brethren died. In the jazz

Opening night in August of 1923 of the Pythian Temple Roof Garden, an elite Creole-of-color nightclub. (Hogan Jazz Archive, Tulane University Library)

funeral parade, the band follows the coffin, behind which is the "second-line" made up of family, friends, and mourners. On the way to the grave the mood is somber, the bands often playing "Flee as a Bird," a slow dirge with muffled drum. On the walk home, jubilation and rejoicing overtake the crowd as they celebrate the departed's joyful entry into heaven, often to the tune of the up-tempo jazz "Oh, Didn't He Ramble." Today, these marching jazz bands are made up primarily of brass, reeds, and percussion. They can be hired to play at both funerals and parades, and still often donate their services for fellow musicians. Contemporary practitioners include **Duke Dejan's Olympia, The Onward, The Original Tuxedo,** and **The Dirty Dozen.** Today a new form is emerging with groups such as **Coolbone** melding traditional brass band sounds with modern hip-hop.

The early brass-band parading tradition expanded after the founding of the African-American benevolent societies known as "social aid and pleasure clubs" or "SA&PCs." In the 1880s, these clubs began hiring brass bands to play at their social functions. By the turn of the century, some of the clubs decided to hold an annual second-line parade strictly for the fun of incorporating a brass jazz band into the day street celebrations. Their names bespeak their spirit of pleasure, such as **The Money Wasters** and the **Calliope High Steppers.** In the uptown area,

The Young Olympian Soul Rebels play at Jazz Fest.

clubs include **The Fun Lovers** (a women's club), **Kool & Gang,** and **The Avenue Steppers. The Young Men's Olympia Social Aid & Pleasure Club** was founded in 1884 and is the oldest SA&PC in New Orleans. It is a non-profit organization whose purpose is two-fold: performing civic work, including acting as a funeral society within the African-American community; and mounting an annual parade. Their annual parade, advertised by word of mouth, is generally held on the fourth Sunday in September, though club members also parade at the Jazz Fest.

The Scene Boosters, another of the uptown groups, were chartered in the summer of 1973 as a combination of SA&PC and marching club. Their annual parade is the first Sunday in November; they're also regulars at the Jazz Fest. The most prestigious of the downtown clubs is the Jolly Bunch, organized in 1941. Members alternate their annual parade between uptown and downtown routes. They can be seen in the Zulu parade at Carnival, and each January the club celebrates its anniversary with the Majestic Brass Band or the Pin Stripe, parading from church to church. Another of the downtown groups is **The Louis Armstrong Golden**

Trumpets, which was founded in the Seventh Ward in 1974 by Freida Germaine, a member of the Ladies Auxiliary of the Jolly Bunch. Their parade is distinguished by the use of the basket, the fan, and the umbrella to signify the first division, second division, and preppy division, respectively.

The social clubs assume all the expense of the parade, including hiring the bands. Bands can cost well over $1,000, and the police escorts and parade permits cost over $1,500. The total expense for a parade can be $5,000; obviously, this is difficult for those groups

At the Sudan Club parade.
(Michael P. Smith)

who have but several handfuls of members and want to continue to mount parades annually for the thousands of second-liners that participate.

■ OTHER JAZZ SPOTS

Beyond Congo Square and Storyville were many other venues for New Orleans' jazz musicians. Musicians sometimes congregated in the clubs and cottages in the Treme area, including Perseverance Hall, still standing at 1644 North Villere as the Holy Aid Comfort Spiritual Church. Another early jazz site was located in Faubourg Marigny, the Francis Amis Hall, an exclusive Creole-of-color Social Aid and Pleasure Club. These halls became popular with the freed slaves who had migrated into New Orleans during and after Reconstruction. In the early years of the twentieth century, Buddy Bolden, Kid Ory, and King Oliver entertained local residents in Lincoln and Oakland parks. The racially mixed Oakland Park was later sold at auction and redeveloped as the New Orleans Country Club, an elite whites-only club. (It's sad to note that while whites could "hang out" with black musicians and learn from them in their clubs, the reverse was not true.)

The old gym (now the ROTC building on Freret Street) at Tulane University introduced jazz to the Uptown/Garden District students of both Tulane and its sister school, Sophie Newcomb, as early as 1917 at their "script" dances. Here the kids could boogie to the music of King Oliver, Johnny Wiggs, Papa Celestin, and Kid Ory. Many parents were horrified at this revolutionary form of wild dancing, preferring their children listen to Guy Lombardo or other orchestras at hotels. But by the '30s, jazz was embedded in popular culture and constantly played on the radio.

New Orleanians also went to nightclubs in the Milneburg and Spanish Fort areas, a series of "camps" constructed in the late 19th century on pilings over the waters of Lake Ponchartrain. Here New Orleanians could go to nightclubs and listen to Dixieland, "Sweet" Emma Barrett, and A. J. Piron's Society Orchestra. Piron is remembered for promoting jazz as a socially acceptable form of music with the polite society of both races. He even played at debutante balls.

Later on, it was the gambling circuit that supported some New Orleans musicians—among them Louis Armstrong, who visited New Orleans to entertain the patrons of the Suburban Gardens casino in 1931. If Armstrong played to packed houses, they were white only, causing a great deal of resentment within his own black community. In July of 1935, he returned to New Orleans again, this time playing for black audiences at the Golden Dragon.

In the city, the era of ragtime-inspired jazz lasted until the end of World War I, when it evolved into the uninhibited dance crazes of the Roaring Twenties and the Swing Era of the '30s. With the advent of the swing bands in the rest of the country, the national popularity of the classical jazz of New Orleans began to fade. In the 1940s jazz shaded into be-bop and mixed with the funk and blues of urban blacks to become rhythm and blues.

New Orleans enters the last decade of the twentieth century, having played host to the soul of jazz for over a hundred years. New Orleans now nurtures music as a living, breathing link with the past. For many native sons, this musical heritage is a foundation on which to build new styles. Artists who emerged during the 1980s tip their hats to traditional styles of composition and performance. The fame of such musicians as Terence Blanchard, Donald Harrison, and the Marsalis family —Ellis, Wynton, and Branford—fostered a resurgence of interest in New Orleans jazz and, as a result, in venues where traditional jazz and Dixieland can still be

(above) Wynton Marsalis and Danny Barker play at Jazz Fest. Preservation Hall (right) is New Orleans' most famous venue for traditional New Orleans jazz .(both photos, Syndey Byrd).

BECHET ON JAZZ

*P*eople come up to me and they ask me, "Are you going to play Tin Roof Blues?" They ask me, "What's be-bop?" or what do I think of some record Louis Armstrong put out. But if I was to answer that, I'd have to go back a long way. That's why I have to tell a lot more than people would expect.

They come to tell me they like this record or that, and they ask me what I'm trying to do by my music. They ask me what's going to happen to Jazz? Where's it going? One night a man came to see me when I was playing in Paris; I'd known his son in New York. He came in with this party, and after the band had finished playing I got to talking with him. He started to tell me it meant a lot to him to hear me play; he'd had an experience he'd never had before. I told him I played like I always played. That's really all I can say.

But he was in a kind of feeling he wanted to talk. . . . "This music is your music," he said.

But, you know, no music is my music. It's everybody's who can feel it. You're here . . . well, if there's music, you feel it—then it's yours too. You got to be in the sun to feel the sun. It's that way with music too.

—Sidney Bechet, *Treat It Gentle*, 1960

Music in the sun: the Kid Thomas Band opens a gas station in 1961.
(Hogan Jazz Archive, Tulane University Library)

heard. The great living museum for the city's early jazz is **Preservation Hall** at 726 St. Peter, and another superb venue is the **Palm Court Cafe** at 1204 Decatur Street. Donna's, at 800 North Rampart, and Funky Butt, at 714 North Rampart, offer bodacious blasts of brass.

■ BOURBON STREET

There is no other seven-block stretch in America more evocative of excess, the erotic and exotic, and traditional jazz and R&B than Bourbon Street. One might guess the street was named for the Kentucky whiskey rather than an 18th-century royal family. Between the world wars a rather sedate residential street in the French Quarter turned into a raucous strip designed to titillate tourists and tempt them into parting with their money. Although the architectural treasures are upstaged by the neon and fluorescent lights, and there's a scent of old oyster shells and beer in the air, Bourbon Street's bustle and flamboyance are quintessential New Orleans.

The musicians who hold down the regular gigs on the strip are all remarkable professionals and masters of their art form. They have played each song a thousand times but can still pump it out with enthusiasm. Even after one club closes down for the morning, the musicians will drift down the street to jam with a band at another club.

Early evening for traditional jazz on Bourbon Street is often a more ethereal experience than sharing the music with prowling late-night tourists. The **Can Can Cafe,** 300 Bourbon Street in the Royal Sonesta Hotel, is the home of the brilliant **Silver Leaf Jazz Band,** noted for their expert presentation of jazz classics. **Fritzel's,** 733 Bourbon, is a favorite of Quarterites, especially in May for **Fritzel's Jazz Fest,** when jazz bands from around the world perform.

Best bets for Bourbon Street blues are the **Old Absinthe Bar,** 400 Bourbon Street, and **Funky Pirate,** 727 Bourbon Street, where old-school shouter. Big Al Carson belts the blues.

■ MARDI GRAS INDIAN TRIBE MUSIC

If there is a long-simmered roux at the base of the gumbo of New Orleans jazz and R&B, it is the warrior chants of the **Mardi Gras Indians.** Beginning in the 1880s, these semi-organized "gangs" melded the old call-and-response chants of their

Birthday party for Norman Bell, second chief of the Wild Tchoupitoulas. (Michael P. Smith)

African heritage with diverse percussion instruments—cowbells, whistles, conga drums—thus beginning the traditional music of the Indian tribes. The chants also included voodoo terms from the Caribbean and even some North American Indian words and intonations. Handmade percussion instruments are still beaten in rapid back-beat time to arouse dancers to a fever pitch of excitement.

Tribes speak to each other through rhythms, chants, and dance. Traditionally, rival tribes greet each other with a war dance. In earlier days, if a warrior couldn't dance a rival to the ground, he would knock him down, and the rest of the elaborately clad tribe would join in. The waving of handkerchiefs and the chant "Hecky Pocky Way" (the modern version of a 19th-century Mardi Gras Indian phrase) were originally just a smidgen more inflammatory than giving a rude hand gesture. Today, when tribes move through the streets, their meetings consist of dancing, formal costume display, tribal gestures, and shared "Indian" pride. (See "CARNIVAL" for further information.) Their influence can be heard in the music of everyone from Jelly Roll Morton to Sugarboy Crawford, Professor Longhair to Dr. John. The Indians' music directly touched the Neville Brothers,

(opposite) Big Chief Larry Bannock of the Goldenstar Hunters. (Syndey Byrd)

as it was their uncle, George Landry, Big Chief Jolly, the founder of the Wild Tchoupitoulas, who first called the family together to make an album.

The raucous sound of the Mardi Gras Indians seems to voice the untamed, emotional charge of New Orleans itself. The closer to Carnival, the wilder the music. Musician Charles Neville explains, "You just sing the bad spirits of the week on their way before you have to go back to work Monday. The Big Chief could hit that tambourine so loud it sounded like a pistol shot." Today's tribes are becoming more organized, with official posters and a museum under development near Armstrong Park.

■ RHYTHM AND BLUES

During the '40s, music played on the now ubiquitous radio drew a wider and wider audience and brought the taste for big-city, Harlem-generated be-bop to New Orleans. The term "rhythm and blues" is said to have been coined in *Variety* as a category for its hit charts. Of course, in the back streets of New Orleans, the local

Professor Longhair (above) plays his birthday cake in 1977 (right), three years before his death. (Michael P. Smith)

musicians put a slightly different spin on what they heard. They added soul and jazz, and began to hammer out rhythm and blues. The Dew Drop Inn (at South La Salle and Washington Avenue) was noted as the club where this fusion took place. Originally opened in 1938 as a lunch stand and barber shop, it featured blues players Gatemouth Brown and Big Joe Turner, the jazz orchestras of Lionel Hampton and Duke Ellington, and local entertainers such as Irma Thomas, Allen Toussaint, Charles Neville, and Guitar Slim. (Although the Dew Drop no longer exists, each year the Jazz & Heritage Festival produces a "Dew Drop Inn Revisited" concert to showcase many of the musicians who performed there.)

In 1949, a former tap dancer and blues pianist named Henry Roeland Byrd took the professional name of **Professor Longhair,** "Fess," and created a musical tornado with his unique blend of mambo, rhumba, calypso, jazz, Mardi Gras Indian music, and the blues. Until his death in 1980, the Professor's style had a profound influence on most of the younger R&B performers that were recording. Fats Domino hit the national scene in 1950 with a rocking and rolling piano style for such chart toppers as "Blueberry Hill" and "Walkin' to New Orleans." One of the musicians most influenced by Fess was a white pianist named Mac Rebenneck.

The Dixie Cups take their audience to the "Chapel of Love" in 1977 (above) while Aaron Neville tells it like it is at an early Jazz Fest event. (Michael P. Smith)

In 1968 Rebenneck hit it big as **"Dr. John,"** a name taken from the famous voodoo priest of the 19th century.

In the 1960s, Allen Toussaint, a Creole of color from a musical family, had the foresight to gather and nurture the talents of many popular local talents: Aaron Neville ("Tell It Like It Is"), Ernie K-Doe ("Mother in Law"), the Dixie Cups ("Chapel of Love"), Lee Dorsey ("Working in a Coal Mine"), and Irma Thomas ("It's Rainin'"). By 1966, when the ground-breaking Meters hit the stage with their fusion of indigenous funk and jazz, the New Orleans audience responded enthusiastically.

In the 1970s, the Warehouse, a psychedelic brick dungeon that sat wharfside on Tchoupitoulas Street, served as a venue for white rock from England and the West Coast, while local music often seemed to be relegated to a few clubs and fraternity parties. Then in 1977, Aaron Neville joined his brothers to form the legendary **Neville Brothers** and began performing at the Nitecap on Louisiana Avenue.

The 1980s saw a renaissance of New Orleans music. Two former students from the New Orleans Center for the Creative Arts, inspired by the early sound of jazz, managed to win Grammy Awards while they were still in their twenties. These

(above) Dr. John, named after one of voodoo's most famous 19th-century priests, plays at Tipitina's. (opposite) Cajun music master Ambrose Thibodeaux at the first Jazz Fest, in 1970. (both photos, Michael P. Smith)

were Wynton Marsalis, son of a noted jazz pianist and educator, trumpet player Terence Blanchard (also noted for his movie scores, including Spike Lee's *Malcolm X)* and Harry Connick, Jr., whose father is a local district attorney *and* a cabaret singer. Other famed NOCCA graduates include grammy nominees Donald Harrison and Marlon Jordan. The queen of New Orleans R&B, Irma Thomas, occasionally performs at her own club, The Lion's Den, at 2655 Gravier.

■ CAJUN AND ZYDECO

The motifs and themes of Cajun, swamp pop, and zydeco share the same ingredients—Acadian folk, the accordion, homespun percussion instruments, and the French language. Acadian folk stems from the 18th-century French ballads that the first Acadian settlers brought with them when they were ousted by the British from Nova Scotia and eastern Canada. A generation later, German farmers, encouraged by the French to come grow wheat in Louisiana, brought the accordion. The Acadian dance party, *"Fais Do-Do,"* literally means "Make Sleep," though it is really a joyful social event. Unlike jazz, with its sometimes mournful feeling, Cajun music is usually upbeat.

The Cajun music of the white Acadians is still characterized by the fiddle and hand-held triangle. Its danceable tempo favors the timing of a waltz or two-step. The typifying "chanka-chanka" sound is a blend of European and African rhythms synthesized in the 1920s and '30s by Amadée Ardoin. In the late '20s, Ardoin was the first black accordion player to be recorded. Stylistically, Cajun music holds hands with American country and bluegrass music. In the 1970s, a new generation of Acadian musicians began to rejuvenate the old music, among them Michael Doucet and his band Beausoleil, who've continued to build on the traditional Cajun sound. Other such groups include: Bruce Daigreport, Eddie LeJeune & The Morse Playboys, and D. L. Menard. The legendary Cajun fiddler Dewey Balfa led his family band at the Newport Festival.

Zydeco combines African blues and R&B components with traditional Cajun dance music. Its name is an elision of the old dance tune "Les Haricots N'est Pas Sale," which loosely translated means "The Snap Beans Aren't Salty." In Cajun French, *les haricots* sounds like "lay-zy-de-co." Saxophones, "piano" accordions,

Cajun music star Waylon Thibodeaux. (Syndey Byrd)

and the rub-board—a corrugated metal vest that is played against the chest—are paired with electric guitars and pulsating rhythm to give the music its irresistibly danceable style.

The king of zydeco was the late Clifton Chenier of Opelousas, who won the Grammy in 1983 for Best Ethnic/Folk Recording. Some of those artists who continue the tradition are his son **C. J. Chenier, Buckwheat Zydeco,** Grammy-winning **Queen Ida Guillory** and her **Bon Temps Band, Willis Prudhomme & Zydeco Express, Rockin' Dopsie, Jr.,** and **Sunpie and the Sunspots.**

"Swamp boogie" or "swamp pop" is rock and roll with a Cajun/country accent. The style goes back to the post-World War II era when songs written by Cajun white boys hit the charts. These chart-toppers included Bobby Charles's "See Ya Later Alligator" and Phil Phillips' "Sea of Love." Look for great Zydeco at **Mid-City Lanes Rock 'n' Bowl,** 4133 South Carrollton Avenue. The Zydeco shoot-outs where performers vie for the title King of Zydeco is a crowd pleaser.

(above) Duke Ellington and Mahalia Jackson at Jazz Fest in 1970.
(opposite) Howlin' Wolf, the legendary blues performer, plays at a New Orleans club in 1973.
(both photos, Michael P. Smith)

Newsman Ed Bradley makes a guest appearance with the Neville Brothers at Jazz Fest. (Syndey Byrd)

■ NEW ORLEANS JAZZ & HERITAGE FESTIVAL

The last weekend in April and the first one in May showcase over 7,000 musicians, cooks, and craftsmen in a 10-day event, held in the infield of a racetrack. Performers include internationally known jazz artists, gospel choirs, Cajun and zydeco bands, R&B bands, and many others. The food offerings are impressive and tasty, and the crowd can be as entertaining as the musicians. Early January is a good time to book airline tickets, and mid-February is when the rush begins for hotel and restaurant reservations. Book tickets early by calling Ticketmaster at (800) 488-5252 or (504) 522-5555; write P. O. Box 53407, New Orleans, LA, 70153.

Once in the city for "Jazz Fest," you'll find parking to be a nightmare; it's best to stay in a guest house in the back of the French Quarter or on Esplanade, then rent a bike or take a taxi to the fairgrounds. Having the proper equipment is also a must. Don't leave home without a pair of good rubber boots that won't come off even in squishy mud, a rain poncho, plenty of sunscreen, a hat, a long-sleeve cotton shirt for sun protection, and comfortable running shoes. Nighttime concerts, held in air-conditioned venues throughout the city, require much less equipment. Tickets for these evening events sell quickly, so order ahead.

(top) Irma Thomas performs at Jazz Fest.
(bottom) Michael Doucet of Beausoleil. (both photos, Syndey Byrd)

■ MUSIC CLUBS

Following is a listing of New Orleans clubs featuring live music. Call ahead for hours, since in New Orleans there are no official closing times. Get up-to-the-minute information from the monthly music newspaper *Off Beat.* For current listings, use e-mail: offbeat@neworleans.neosoft.com. Other good sources are the Friday "Lagniappe" section of the *Times-Picayune,* the weekly paper *Gambit,* or listening to WWOZ at 90.7 FM. A favorite way to hear jazz in New Orleans is to catch "jazz brunch" at a local restaurant; see page 255 for listings.

*(S) Safer area, although caution is always advised.

Traditional New Orleans Jazz

Can Can Cafe. Royal Sonesta Hotel, 300 Bourbon St.; (504) 586-0300. Home of the Silver Leaf Jazz Band, noted for their expert presentation of traditional jazz classics. *(S)

Creole Queen. Aquarium of the Americas dock and Canal St. dock; (504) 529-4567/(800) 233 BOAT. Jazz buffet cruises on the Missisipi.

Donna's Bar & Grill. 800 N. Rampart; (504) 596-6914. Brass bands and barbecue every night from 8:00 P.M.

Fritzel's European Jazz Club. 733 Bourbon St.; (504) 561-0432. Popular with French Quarterite jazz aficionados.

Funky Butt at Congo Square. 714 N. Rampart; (504) 558-0872. Superb brass music.

Jazz Meridien. Hotel Meridien, 614 Canal St.; (504) 525-6500. Jacques Gaute's sound is as close to Sidney Bechet's as can be found. *(S)

Kemp's. 2720 La Salle between Washington & Fourth; (504) 891-2738. A funky neighborhood, but terrific brass.

Molly's at the Market. 1107 Decatur St., (504) 525-5169. Traditional Irish pub with jazz a few nights a week during "season," i.e., January to May.

Palm Court Jazz Cafe. 1204 Decatur St.; (504) 525-0200. Best place in town to hear traditional jazz in comfort.

Pete Fountain's. Hilton Hotel, 2 Poydras; (504) 523-4374. The club's namesake performs Tuesdays only. *(S)

Preservation Hall. 726 St. Peter St.; (504) 522-2841. No food or drink, no A.C., but a museum for the "real thing."

Snug Harbor. 626 Frenchmen St.; (504) 949-0696. An intimate setting. Look for Ellis Marsalis or Charmaine Neville.

Vaughan's Lounge. 800 Lesseps at Dauphine St.; (504) 947-5562. Take a cab to this hot spot, especially Thursdays, when Kermit Ruggin and his Barbecue Swingers play.

Piano Bars

Bombay Club. 830 Conti St.; (504) 586-0972. Sophistication and martinis reign.

Carousel Revolving Bar. Monteleone Hotel, 214 Royal St.; (504) 523-3341. A versatile chanteuse serenades.*(S)

Dos Jefes Uptown Cigar Bar. 5535 Tchoupitoulas; (504) 891-8500. Cadillac Red lights a spark.

Lafitte's Blacksmith Shop. 941 Bourbon St.; (504) 523-0066. A clinker of a piano doesn't dampen the gusto of the patrons.

Margaritaville Cafe. 1104 Decatur St.; (504) 592-2552. Eddie Bo is the best R&B/jazz pianist in town.

Pat O'Brien's. 718 St. Peter St.; (504) 525-4823. Hurricanes only add to the enthusiasm.

Polo Lounge. Windsor Court Hotel, 300 Gravier; (504) 523-6000. A noted jazz professor performs the classics in a comfortable palatial estate-like setting.

Rock/Blues/R&B

Benny's. 938 Valence St. at Camp; (504) 897-9690. Everything from heavy metal to great brass.

Café Brasil. 2100 Chartres St. at Frenchmen; (504) 947-9386. Cutting edge bands.

Carrollton Station. 8140 Willow; (504) 865-9190. Boogie bands in a small club.

Dream Palace. 534 Frenchmen St.; (504) 945-2040. Tightly packed crowds; great tunes with a salsa beat.

House of Blues. 225 Decatur St.; (504) 529-BLUE. Great music, but locally known as "House of Rules" for its heavy-duty security, and "House of Snooze" for the long wait to get in.

Howlin' Wolf. 848 S. Peters St.; (504) 523-2551. Features bouncers the size of Buicks and a mini mosh pit. This locally owned club rocks.

Jimmy's Music Club & Patio Bar. 8200 Willow; (504) 861-8200. A mixed bag of great music in the University area.

Lion's Den. 2655 Gravier; (504) 822-4693. Irma Thomas usually performs on weekends to a standing-room-only crowd.

Maple Leaf Bar. 8316 Oak St.; (504) 866-9359. An intimate uptown club with everything from zydeco to brass.

Margaritaville Cafe. 1104 Decatur St.; (504) 592-2552. Jimmy Buffett's club. Tightly packed tables and no dance floor.

Mid-City Lanes Rock 'n' Bowl. 4133 S. Carrollton Ave.; (504) 482-3133. The best dancing in town, but lines can be long, so go early.

Old Absinthe House. 400 Bourbon St.; (504) 525-8108. Gut-bucket blues.

Rendon Inn. 4501 Eve St.; (504) 822-9858. College and 20-something crowd.

Rivershack. 3449 River Rd.; (504) 835-6933. Honky-tonk ambiance, tacky ashtrays, and terrific music on weekends.

Tipitina's. 501 Napoleon Ave.; (504) 895-8477/897-3943. Also, 310 Howard Ave.; same phone. An eclectic mix of music ranging from ska to cajun.

Cajun/Zydeco

Michaul's. 840 St. Charles Ave.; (504) 522-5517.*(S)

Mulate's. 201 Julia St.; (504) 522-1492.*(S)

Patout's Cajun Cabin. 501 Bourbon St.; (504) 529-4256.

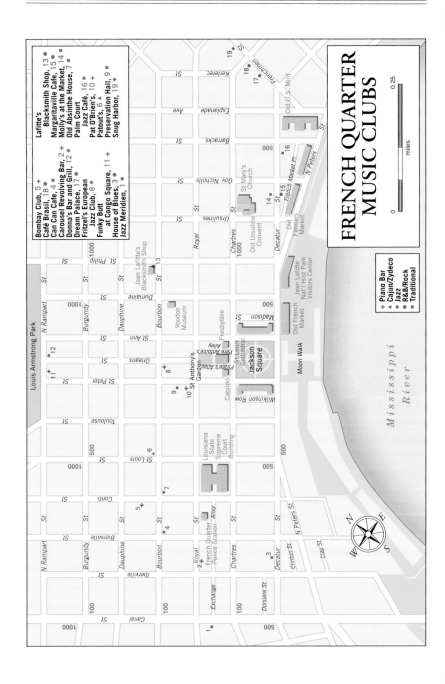

FRENCH QUARTER MUSIC CLUBS

Bombay Club, 5 ♦
Café Brasil, 18 ♦
Can Can Cafe, 4 ♦
Carousel Revolving Bar, 2 ♦
Donna's Bar and Grill, 12 ♦
Dream Palace, 17 ♦
Fritzel's European
  Jazz Club, 8 ♦
Funky Butt
  at Congo Square, 11 ♦
House of Blues, 3 ♦
Jazz Meridien, 1 ♦

Lafitte's
  Blacksmith Shop, 13 ♦
Margaritaville Cafe, 15 ♦
Molly's at the Market, 14 ■
Old Absinthe House, 7 ■
Palm Court
  Jazz Café, 16 ■
Pat O'Brien's, 10 ♦
Patout's, 6 ▲
Preservation Hall, 9 ■
Snug Harbor, 19 ♦

Legend:
♦ Piano Bar
▲ Cajun/Zydeco
♦ Jazz
● R&B/Rock
■ Traditional

0   0.25
miles

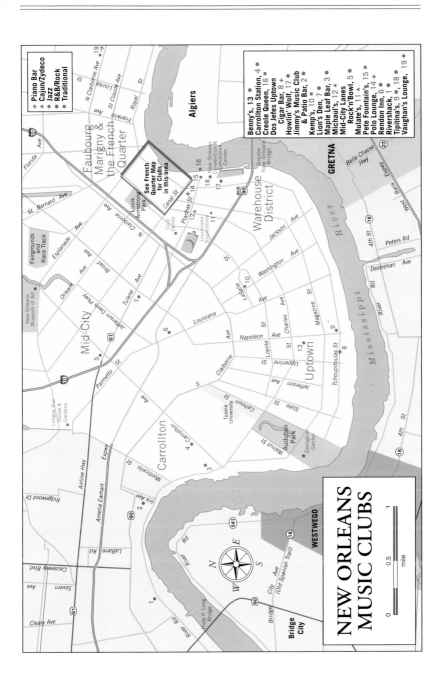

NEW ORLEANS MUSIC CLUBS

Legend:
- + Piano Bar
- ▲ Cajun/Zydeco
- ● Jazz
- ◆ R&B/Rock
- ■ Traditional

Benny's, 13 ●
Carrollton Station, 4 ■
Creole Queen, 16 ■
Dos Jefes Uptown ●
Cigar Bar, 8 +
Howlin' Wolf, 17 ◆
Jimmy's Music Club & Patio Bar, 2 ◆
Kemp's, 10 ■
Lion's Den, 7 ●
Maple Leaf Bar, 3 ●
Michaul's, 12 ▲
Mid-City Lanes Rock'n'Bowl, 5 ●
Mulate's, 11 ▲
Pete Fountain's, 15 ●
Polo Lounge, 14 +
Rendon Inn, 6 ●
Rivershack, 1 ◆
Tipitina's, 9, 18 ●
Vaughan's Lounge, 19 ◆

SPIRITUAL CHURCHES

The Spiritual churches of New Orleans comprise a singular African-American religion which combines elaborate rituals, eclectic beliefs, and highly emotional services. Like other New World religions such as Santería, the Spiritual churches are syncretic, containing elements of Catholicism, Pentecostalism, and voodoo. Although members practice Christian rituals such as Holy Communion and baptism, they also observe unique rites including the "helping hand service" and the "candle drill." Worshippers honor Catholic saints with fervor, but also seek guidance from the American Indian warriors Blackhawk and Sitting Bull. The beliefs, practices, and structures of the church's individual congregations can vary widely. What distinguishes them are prophecy and healing, the two "gifts of the spirits" when worshippers may be filled with the Holy Spirit, as in Pentecostal churches, or "entertain" spirits, as in voodoo and other forms of spiritualism.

The beginnings of New Orleans' Spiritual churches remain something of a mystery. Today's Spiritual practitioners often credit Chicago Spiritual church organizer Mother Leafy Chase with bringing her faith to New Orleans on a 1920 visit, yet the church's beliefs—rooted in popular Catholicism, voodoo, and, to a certain degree, in 1850s American Spiritualism—well predate this woman's arrival. The churches more likely represent a religious movement that developed from the intersection of various belief systems during the latter nineteenth century, and became organized in the 1920s. Earliest records show that women filled the church leadership during the 1920s, suggesting that the Spiritual church was first organized as a women's movement. In the mid-1930s, in an effort to legitimize the religion, men assumed the most important leadership positions. Because membership then as now consisted largely of working-class women, this produced a certain unresolved male-female tension between hierarchy and church members which continues to this day. Nonetheless, members and leaders alike interact informally and familiarly, and many important church leaders are women.

Perhaps because of its diverse origins, the church fosters spiritual individuality, encouraging its members to have a personal relationship with the sacred. As Archbishop Lydia Gilford of the Infant Jesus of Prague Spiritual Church of Christ comments, ". . . So that's what I've been doing: trying to help the small individual, doing what God is telling me to do, and giving the individuals belief in themselves

. . . He says, 'Where you find two or three assembled, there will be God in the midst.' That means you don't have to have a big crowd to serve God. You've got three: God, you, and me in every church. You see, we feel the presence. That's what I like about it . . . "

—Julia Dillon

Archbishop Lydia Gilford of the Infant Jesus of Prague Church. (Michael P. Smith)

TASTE OF NEW ORLEANS

NEW ORLEANS CULINARY STYLE, which has been tickling palates for 200 years, was created with a secret recipe that is five parts tradition and one part instinct, marinated in generations of cultural isolation from the rest of the United States, and seasoned with the innate Latin desire to eat well. As the saying goes: "There are two times of day in Louisiana—mealtime and in between."

■ CAST-IRON MELTING POT

The local culinary traditions of Creole cooking, the sophisticated urban cuisine containing such jewels as trout meunière, and Cajun cooking, its country cousin known for its stew-like etouffées, did not evolve directly from French cooking. As internationally known chef Kevin Graham explains it, "The confusing part is that the Creoles felt no qualms about appropriating French names and techniques and then running off with them in another direction. The first time I ordered shallots I got green onions! And the local court bouillon is really an Italian or Spanish fish stew in a red sauce."

Bernard Guste, a direct descendent of Antoine's original proprietor, sees Louisiana's food as being truly Creole; i.e., of Old World parentage in New World surroundings. "Our Oysters Rockefeller is the perfect example of a Creole dish. It was invented in the New World by my ancestor who was applying the classical techniques he learned in France. Cajun cuisine is more of a one-pot, eat-to-survive kind of food that gets a lot of its sizzle from German salt meats and sausages."

Creole and Cajun cuisines have constantly evolved. In each bowl of gumbo served in Louisiana today, there is French roux, African okra, American Indian filé, Spanish peppers, Cajun sausage, and oysters supplied by Yugoslav fishermen, served over Chinese-cultivated Louisiana rice.

Paul Prudhomme, arguably one of the 20th century's most influential chefs, is fascinated with dishes *with some age on them*: "What I learned is that if a recipe survives from one generation to the next, it serves a need. Some dishes build a fire in your body, and they are the ones worth remembering."

Classic Louisiana food labels from the Sharon Dinkins Collection.

History shows that had it not been for the kindness of the Indians, New Orleans' earliest settlers would have starved to death long before they had an opportunity to invent a cuisine. The Indians introduced the French to a variety of breads and mushy cereals made from corn; various kinds of squash, including the chayote (or "mirliton") and cashaw, which are still popular in Louisiana today; and dried beans. The French sweet tooth was satisfied with syrups made from persimmons, and piqued with chokecherries which were used to flavor smoked meats. Stews were thickened with powdered sassafras, today called filé powder.

Despite the abundance of these Indian foods, the colonists were still Frenchmen to the core and yearned for the flavors they had known at home. In France during this period thousands of new recipes were created and volumes written on the subject of food, and it was fashionable for every nobleman to have not only his own accomplished chef, but also a sauce named for him. Of course, settlers who classified as noblemen were few and far between. The majority of settlers were peasants, convicts, and prostitutes unaccustomed to a particularly luscious diet. Before coming to Louisiana, they had been eating the same thing as their ancestors —boiled, grainy, weevil-laden flour mush mixed with animal blood, carrots, turnips, and even topsoil. Bread was literally the highlight of their diet, and in Louisiana, far from home, that was what was missing. Unfortunately the area around New Orleans was too wet to grow wheat.

It was the Ursuline Sisters, the daughters of French aristocratic and middle-class families, who brought to Louisiana the knowledge of the latest French culinary skills. One of their order, Sister Xavier Herbert, was the first woman pharmacist in the New World. A condition of the contract between the Company of the Indies (the French company which first financed settlement of Louisiana) and the Ursulines was that Sister Xavier would plant an herb garden. The Ursulines taught settlers the benefits of using bay leaf in stews and soups to prevent souring and in flour to prevent weevils; dill for soothing sleep; oregano to reduce swelling; parsley to remove the smell of garlic; shallots for strength; and sage "to put fever to flight."

The letter of the young nun Sister St. Stanislaus, written between 1727 and 1728 to her family in France, provides a glimpse of the diet of the average colonist. She says it consisted of rice cooked in milk, and *sagamite,* a mixture of ground Indian corn boiled in water with butter or bacon fat (the forerunner of grits, no doubt).

GUMBO FILÉ

A gumbo can be a gumbo fevé, filé, or calalou.

Gumbo filé: The filé is a greenish powder usually prepard by the Indians, the degenerated and poor descendants of those proud Chactas Indians praised by Chateaubriand. To make the filé gumbo it is necessary to make a good stew with chicken, ham and oysters. The stew is strongly seasoned with a good quantity of water, and before serving, that aromatic powder is poured in it like a thin rain, and instantly it begins to "filé" (get stringy). That soupe should be eaten like the two others with boiled rice and seasoned with strong pepper.

—Helen d'Aquin Allain, memoir of life in New Orleans, c. 1830s.

Indian woman selling sassafras leaves, from which filé powder is made, in a New Orleans market during the 1890s. (Historic New Orleans Collection)

A Creole of color wearing a tignon, a required head-covering during the slave era that evolved into a fashionable headdress. (Historic New Orleans Collection)

"We [the Sisters] live on wild beef, deer, swans, geese and wild turkeys, rabbits, chickens, ducks, teals, pheasants, partridges, quail and other fowl and game of different kinds. The rivers are teeming with enormous fish unknown in France."

While the Ursulines were teaching the rudiments of French cuisine, the African slaves were on the culinary frontlines, trying to create edible fare from what was available to them. Noted chef Leah Chase, whose restaurant Dooky Chase is the black counterpart of Antoine's, says, "There isn't one famous Creole dish that didn't pass through the hands of a black chef or cook before it came to be written down." These black cooks came from an ancient and sophisticated African culinary tradition. Documents indicate that their African ancestors had traded with the Arab spice merchants since the 11th century. By the 16th century West African farmers were cultivating peanuts, eggplant, corn, yams, garlic, and onions, which they had assimilated into their traditional diet of rice, beans, leafy vegetables, and okra. They prepared their food with various slow cooking methods or roasting. The popular Lenten Creole soup, gumbo z'herbes, came from a West African dish. In some parts of Africa and in Louisiana's Creole society, tradition has it that a new friend will be made for each green used in the soup.

In New Orleans, as in France, having a good cook was crucial to one's social status, and also as in France, a Creole lady did not venture far from the kitchen while the meal was being prepared. Male and female slave cooks were taught to read and write in order to better adapt French recipes to the Louisiana kitchen. An Anglican bishop was once visiting in a proper Creole household in the 1850s. As he sat at the breakfast table, he became fascinated by the loud chants of the servants in the kitchen as they belted out everything from French cane-cutting tunes to Anglican hymns. He puzzled over why these French-speaking Catholics would know one of his hymns. The lady of the house explained that her cook timed her creations, from coffee to breakfast cake to boiled eggs, by the time it took to sing various songs.

Black cooks took the French peasant's thickener, the roux (from the French *roux beurre,* literally "reddish brown butter") and transformed it into a dark, redolent base for many local specialties such as etouffée, gumbo, Creole sauce, grillades, and turtle soup. (Famed French master chef Escoffier scoffed that this type of "peasant" roux was indigestible.) To the roux a cook would add tough pork or fowl too old to lay eggs, a few herbs, lots of onions and garlic, and cook it all day in a cast-iron pot into a tasty, rich stew. Even today a jar of roux made by a master cook is considered a nicer gift than a box of store-bought chocolates.

Creole cuisine might have remained a slightly countrified reproduction of 18th-century French cuisine had not the Spanish come to Louisiana. When the first Spanish arrived, they brought with them a bag of tricks they had learned from the Mayans, Aztecs, and Incas. In the 15th century, Columbus had brought yams, kidney beans, maize, red pepper, and allspice back to Europe, and later explorers brought back the tomato (known as the "wolf peach," the "apple of the moors," or the "love apple") from Mexico. (While the Italians, Spanish, and Africans adored the tomato, the French and English suspected it might be poison. The French didn't begin to use it until the 1850s, when the Empress Eugénie introduced it at Napoleon III's table.) The Spaniards then reintroduced the pepper and the tomato back to the New World in Louisiana, and began the practice of adding green pepper to sauces and meat dishes in part to slow spoiling. The tomato, when coupled with a roux, became an integral component in Shrimp Creole; the rich gravy for grillades; and the base for court bouillon (pronounced "coo-bo-yon"), a thick seafood stew similar to bouillabaisse. The Spanish paella, a rice and shellfish dish, became the Creole dish jambalaya when *jambon,* or ham, was added to it.

Political turmoil throughout the world brought refugees rich and poor to Louisiana, adding more flavor to Creole culinary style. Aristocrats fleeing the French Revolution brought the newest innovations of 18th-century haute cuisine. Planters and free people of color from the West Indies and Santo Domingo introduced fish dishes with Spanish flavors. Sicilians added their talent for rich red gravies and dishes utilizing garlic and bread crumbs, such as stuffed artichokes and eggplant, inspiring the Louisiana dish, stuffed Indian mirliton (also known as a "vegetable pear").

The dishes that evolved from these early experiments are enjoyed to this day. From breakfast, with its calas (rice cakes) or pain perdu (French toast) served with cane syrup, to the after-dinner treats of café brulot and pecan pralines, the inhabitants of New Orleans happily eat a diet uniquely their own. For generations, red beans and rice seasoned with Spanish chaurice or Cajun boudin sausage have been eaten on Monday—wash or market day. Meatless gumbo z'herbes is eaten for Lent; bread pudding with whiskey sauce or pain perdu utilizes every last crumb of French bread; and what would the Christmas turkey be without oyster dressing, or breakfast without chicory café au lait?

Creole cooking was spared from becoming another outgrowth of the aristocratic gastronomy of Europe as a result of the Civil War, which drastically changed the

Fresh produce at the French Market, where Creole cooks have been shopping since the early 1700s.

household economy of the Creoles. Suddenly, the French-speaking Creoles had to take a back seat to the Americans and the carpetbaggers who arrived in the city during Reconstruction. As the Creoles' economic position foundered, they still found pleasure in social dining. They became the "red-beans-and-rice-aristocracy" —well-educated gentry who were "too poor to paint and too proud to white-wash." No matter, the Creoles still loved to eat and entertain. When they couldn't afford the finest meats, they would make a fine gumbo from fresh vegetables and a little leftover chicken or seafood. When the price of ice exceeded their means, they would crush glass and sew it into cheesecloth bags which were floated in pitchers of water to give the tinkle of ice. No matter, guests never suspected their hosts of skimping, because everything was prepared with such care and love that it was always satisfying and delicious.

It is this tradition of hospitality and pride that has fostered and preserved Creole cuisine. Ironically, tourism, which rejuvenated the city's economy in the 1950s, '60s, and early '70s, came close to destroying the flavors that were innately Creole. During this period most Americans were still gastronomic *ingénues*. Local hotel restaurants and popular large eateries were forced to create an Americanized version of the "exotic" local cuisine. Chicory was taken out of the coffee; filé powder was rarely used; murky morsels of crab and oysters were banished from the gumbo; and freshly ground black pepper replaced cayenne pepper in every dish. Creole home cooking and household resourcefulness retreated, staying alive only in homes and in the city's family restaurants.

In the 1970s nouvelle cuisine came and went in local restaurants, without making so much as a ripple on the roux-based sauces of Creole and Cajun home-cooking. By the late 1980s, foodies were hungry for spunky flavors, and suddenly Creole and Cajun cuisines were yanked out of the culinary closet—New Orleans cooking was native American, fervent, ethnic, inexpensive, relatively easy, and far more vital than the sleek, elegant culinary style of the past decade. Today, chefs experiment with eclectic variations on the theme. Finally, after more than 200 years, Creole food achieved culinary respectability—and the rest is just history.

There is a Creole proverb, *"Jardin loin, gombo gaté."* It means that when the garden is far, the gumbo is spoiled. Two of the four top agricultural money-makers in Louisiana are edible crops—rice and sugarcane. There are over a hundred alligator farms in southern Louisiana. Add to this the fact that Louisiana is the world's number one producer of crawfish, and that catfish ranks just behind crawfish as the state's top aquaculture product. Now note that the number one vegetable crop is sweet potatoes. Louisiana's Creole tomatoes and Ponchatoula strawberries are about the best varieties in the world. That will give you an idea of the bases for this cuisine's best dishes.

To eat a meal in New Orleans today is to dive head first into tradition, flavor, and cholesterol. It is a city where food is fried to perfection in lard, where French-fried potato po-boys still appear on some menus, and where sugar, liquor, and coffee —the region's three favorite indulgences—can be obtained in one glorious after dinner concoction: café brulot. About the only nod to healthy eating comes when a local cleanses his palate with iceberg lettuce swimming in rémoulade sauce, or runs a lap or two around Audubon Park between a double order of Café du Monde beignets and a slab of Camellia Grill pecan pie.

■ ANTOINE'S: CLASSIC CREOLE RESTAURANT

Today, more than 150 years since its founding, Antoine's is America's oldest restaurant under single-family ownership. One of the main reasons for its longevity is the power of the New Orleans palate. In the rest of America, a dish may become famous for its flavor; in New Orleans it only achieves greatness when it has fervor. New Orleanians cherish those dishes that prod the subconscious, bringing back memories of savory feasts. Antoine's is a living culinary museum. Devoted third- and fourth-generation patrons not only eat at their great grandparents' favorite table, but also enjoy the same Creole dishes created centuries ago in New Orleans. Not long ago, the late Helen Hayes requested that Bernard Guste, the great grandson of the founder, reconstruct the dinner that his grandfather, Jules Alciatore, had created for the actress in 1918. A bit of research produced the recipe for the orange brûlot that brought tears of pleasure to Mrs. Hayes's eyes.

Cecil B. DeMille once exclaimed, "Many a chef has created a dish, but only God could have cooked that fish." Supposedly he was referring to Antoine's *Pompano en Papillote* which had been created to honor a visiting French balloonist: the chef prepared the fish in a paper bag that was fashioned to resemble the fellow's magnificent balloon.

Antoine's menu has changed little since the 1840s. It is still written in French, and the dishes still reflect the preferences of the mid-19th-century palate for sweet sauces and heavier food. The staff still dims the lights in the restaurant when either *Café Brulot Diabolique* or *Crêpes Suzettes* are served, so that patrons can see the

Bernard Guste (right), owner of Antoine's restaurant and great grandson of the founder, stands with Samuel le Blanc, who is retiring after 50 years of service. (Photo courtesy of Antoine's Restaurant)

azure flames of the ignited brandy. The private library at Antoine's contains over 400 cookbooks as well as books on wine and other related subjects; some of the volumes are over 250 years old, with one dating back to 1659.

In the back Dining Room Annex, five American Presidents—Hoover, Coolidge, Taft, and both Roosevelts (Carter, Nixon, Reagan, Ford and Clinton have also eaten at Antoine's, but not while they were in office)—and two British Princesses—Princess Margaret and Princess Anne—have dined, as well as numerous celebrities whose photos grace the walls. The mirrored front room of Antoine's is considered to be a social no-man's land by many locals, but since it is also the "No Smoking" area, some prefer enjoying its mirrors and gilt to sitting in the darker back room, rubbing elbows with the elite amid clouds of tobacco smoke.

ALLIGATOR RIPPLES

*D*o you know why that alligator kept on attacking the man who was working on the plumbing under his house in Metairie—that alligator who had that guy by the leg and wouldn't let go—? 'Cause the man was crouched down under that peer-and-beam house and he just couldn't stand up. Peer-and-beam houses in New Orleans—at least most of them—are just high enough off the ground for you to crawl under and play, or do some plumbing or electric work or something like that. I expect that when the gator sees you crouched low to the ground, stooping on a log, or all curled up in a ball, he can't see you've got two long legs and maybe are five to six feet tall. He's looking down on you—not straight up. He's lookin' at the silhouette of dinner and, for sure, if he's hungry, he's gonna check you out—like the one that had that man by the leg and wouldn't let go.

continues

PHOTO BY MICHAEL P. SMITH

One day my daughter Josephine (who was about seven when this happened) and I went for a walk to go fishing for brim and sacalait down the old road by Half Moon Lake. We walked about a mile with worms, poles, and buckets way in the back where nobody usually goes. There's a good bank to fish from there. We fished, moving around the bank and around the far corner of the lake for maybe an hour or so, and caught a few blue gills perch and kept them alive in a bucket of water. Josie liked watching them swim. During the spawn they get so colorful—blue, orange, and green . . . look like tropical fish.

After a while, Josie and I got tired of moving around and the fishing got slow, so I sat crouched down on the ground with my back against this fallen-down tree on the bank of the lake. I laid my pole on the ground next to me where I could reach it if I got a bite. Josie sat and rested on the top of the log on the side of me. She looked like a little fur ball with her long hair shining in the sun behind her.

All the while we were fishing we were watching other things—like a big blue heron, white egrets, mosquito hawks, and regular hawks (the bird kind), and some alligators in the lake far away. The alligators were treading water still as stumps— they were almost on the other side of the lake. After 10 minutes or so of sitting down we noticed at least four alligators now in the middle of the lake closer to us. (It seems like an alligator can move in any direction with very little effort and make absolutely no disturbance in its surroundings.) I've seen a 12-foot alligator—which must weigh 700 pounds—treading water with head and back almost fully exposed on the surface of the water—then completely submerge itself and disappear without making the slightest ripple in smooth-as-glass water.

Josie and I counted the gators again. There were now five and getting nearer. In a matter of minutes we were counting eight alligators and the closest one was 20 to 30 feet from us. Josie asked me, "Daddy, how close will they get?" At first I didn't want to frighten her, but I decided she'd better know that to those alligators the way we were crouched we looked like their favorite appetizer and main dish—dinner for eight.

They treaded water even closer and Josie suggested that we stand up and show them how tall we were. Right away the gators eased off and we decided it was time to go back to the camp and get a bite to eat.

—Story told by Bernard Guste, owner of Antoine's restaurant, 1993

■ CREOLE AND CAJUN CULINARY LEGACIES

Cajun specialties are indicated with a ↻

Andouille. ↻ ("Ahn-doo-we") A fat, sassy country sausage containing hog stomach, or "chitterlings." Often used in jambalaya and gumbo, and as an accompaniment to red beans and rice.

Beer. Local beer brands are another point of honor. Many people won't consider serving boiled crawfish without a Dixie longneck, while others swear by Turbo Dog, Voodoo, or Abita Amber Beer.

Beignet. ("Been-yay") Diamond-shaped, raised doughnuts without the hole which are doused in powdered sugar.

Bisque. ↻ ("Bisk") A rich, spicy roux-based soup with crawfish, oysters, or shrimp.

Boudin. ↻ ("Boo-dan") A spicy Cajun sausage. *Boudin blanc* is the pork-and-rice-dressing sausage available in the cooler months; *boudin rouge* is the blood sausage made in Cajun country.

Bread Pudding. French bread soaked in a custard and baked.

Café au Lait. ("Cafay-oh-lay") Chicory coffee served with steamed milk. The average American drinks 1.5 cups of coffee a day; New Orleanians consume 3.2 cups a day. What sets New Orleans coffee apart from that of the rest is the addition of chicory, which produces a rich cup of coffee with the same consistency but only half the caffeine of full-bodied crude. Chicory is the easily grown relative of the dandelion whose young leaves are known as endive. The root resembles that of the dandelion and when dried, roasted, and ground, produces a deep brown, syrupy beverage with an almost peppery tang that doesn't taste at all like coffee. Café au lait (literally coffee with milk) is served as Creoles like it 24 hours a day, seven days a week at Café du Monde, between Jackson Square and the river.

Kaldi's Coffee Museum and Coffeehouse is an excellent place to learn about the evolution of coffee. Located at 914 Decatur Street in the French Quarter, the old bank building is dominated by a two-story mural of Kaldi, the legendary North African goatherd who first touted the rejuvenating effects of coffee.

Café Brulot. Combines coffee, sugar and liquor. Served flaming.

Calas. Fried, sweet, rice cakes.

Court Bouillon. ("Coo-bo-yon") A fish stew in an authoritative red sauce.

Crawfish. (never "cray-fish") These little spicy toy lobsters are best eaten spread out on newspaper on a picnic table. Sometimes called "mudbugs."

Crème Caramel. A custard similar to flan.

Dirty Rice. No, this is not the *nom de plume* that local author Anne Rice uses when she publishes erotica. It is a rice dish made with liver and spices, and is similar to a rice dressing.

Eggs Sardou. Artichoke hearts, poached eggs, spinach, hollandaise sauce. (At Brennan's they sell 750,000 poached eggs a year due to the popularity of this and their other brunch egg dishes, such as Eggs Benedict.)

Etouffée. ℰ℧ ("Ay-too-fay") A thick tomato-based sauce usually containing either shrimp or crawfish.

French Bread. Many of the finest restaurants in town continue to be as persnickety about the staff of life as the early French settlers. Those crusty small loaves of hot French bread, called "gigitts," come from Angelo Gendusa's at 1801 North Rampart.

Filé. The mature green leaves of the sassafras tree, which contain a mucilaginous substance, are dried and powdered to produce this aromatic thickening agent. In the days when flour was more scarce than truffles, this substance became essential in turning a weak stock into a hearty soup. Filé must only be added to gumbo after the soup has been removed from the heat, and stirred in a few minutes before serving. If the soup should boil with filé, it becomes stringy and inedible.

Garlic. The Creole cook believes what Balzac said about garlic, "even the chef should be rubbed with it." Local folk wisdom has always known that garlic can prevent both heart and vampire attacks, as well as cure digestive disorders.

Grillades. ("Gree-yodds") A roux-based beef-and-tomato gravy with thin slices of beef or veal.

Gumbo. A murky roux-based spicy soup that can contain a variety of shellfish, okra, poultry, and/or sausage, depending on the mood of the cook.

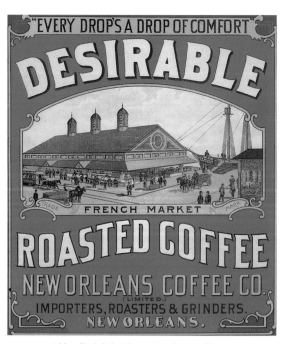

Old coffee label. (Sharon Dinkins Collection)

Crawfish are an important ingredient in many Cajun and Creole dishes.

Hurricane. During such events as the Sugar Bowl, Mardi Gras, and the Super Bowl, the French Quarter takes on a particularly cloying, fruity smell generated by the thousands of these rosy rum punches. They are served in souvenir glasses that will later be filled with Mardi Gras beads, decorating dorm rooms from San Diego to New Rochelle. The beverage has all the punch of a blow on the head with a baseball bat, with a similar day-after result.

Hush Puppies. A seasoned, fried, cornmeal ball used to accompany fried seafood.

Jambalaya. ✌ ("Jam-bul-eye-a") A rice-based dish similar to paella, but heavier on the local sausage and poultry.

Mint Julep. The French totally ignored mint as an herb. The Spanish (who got the herb from the Arabs) are thought to have brought the passion for mint tea to the sultry South. The name of the plant comes from a Greek myth that would do a Tennessee Williams's julep-guzzlin' heroine proud. It seems that Pluto became enamored with a wood nymph named Menthe, which greatly perplexed his beloved Persephone, the Goddess of Spring. Persephone knew that murdering her rival would push Menthe right back into Pluto's arms in the underworld. Thus, she transformed Menthe into a lowly plant doomed to be trampled underfoot. The fragrance of Menthe's spirit rose to haunt each time the plant was trod upon.

Mirliton. ("Mill-a-ton") A pear-shaped vegetable known also as chayote, similar in taste to zucchini. It is generally served stuffed with bread crumbs and seafood.

Muffuletta. A round stormdrain-sized Italian sandwich stuffed with Italian meats and cheeses and liberally doused with garlicky olive salad. Try Progress Grocery, Central Grocery, or The Napoleon House. Bayou Ridge makes a luscious muffuletta pizza.

Okra. Most New Orleanians aren't born liking okra. Next to the first raw oyster, eating that first slimy piece of okra is a sort of culinary rite of passage for Louisiana children. Okra is a mucilaginous pod that grows on a tall, ornamental tropical annual of the hibiscus family, a cousin of the cotton plant. Legend has it that okra was brought to the New World by slaves who hid the seeds in their hair and ears. During the warm months when okra is in season, it replaces Indian filé powder as the thickening agent in gumbo. Okra was originally known as "kingcombo;" hence, "gumbo."

Oysters. There are about 50 oyster bars in New Orleans. In the 1930s U.S. Senator Huey P. Long included in his anti-Roosevelt-sponsored-legislation filibuster the recipe for fried oysters. Long concluded, "There is no telling how many lives have been lost by not knowing how to fry oysters, but serving them as an undigestible food. Many times we hear of some man who was supposed to have had an acute attack of indigestion or cerebral hemorrhage or heart failure, and the chances are the only thing that was the matter was that he had swallowed some improperly cooked oysters." Of course, New Orleanians like cooked oyster dishes too, such as fried oysters and Oysters Rockefeller.

Pain Perdu. ("Pan pair-do") This Creole version of French toast is made with French bread.

Pepper. There is an old Creole proverb, "Misery makes the monkey eat red pepper," which perhaps holds a clue as to why the use of hot peppers gained such a foothold in this region of the country. The Cajuns were economically, culturally, and geographically cut off from the more cosmopolitan areas. From the Spanish period onward, each household, no matter how poor, could easily grow one or two varieties of hot peppers. The flavors of food (be it anything from old raccoon meat to "mud bugs," or crawfish) were greatly enhanced by the addition of a little salt and a dose of red pepper. Pepper-eating (both pickled and raw varieties) remains a popular south Louisiana barroom sport.

If the Spanish influence on southern Louisiana cuisine was ever in danger of fading, the trend was reversed in the mid-19th century when hundreds of Louisiana boys went off to fight the war

CULINARY TIMELINE

1699 Sieur de Bienville and Sieur d'Iberville eat their first meal in Louisiana. They are said to have dined on buffalo.

1751 First sugarcane is introduced by Jesuits from Santo Domingo.

1791 First recorded restaurant in New Orleans, Café des Emigrés, becomes a popular meeting place for exiles from uprisings in the Indies.

1800s Creole businessmen begin conducting much of their business in the local "exchanges" or coffeehouses.

1820 The owner-chef of the Tremoulet Hotel in the French Quarter invents meunière sauce.

1827 Antoine Alciatore brings the secret recipe for Pommes de Terre Soufflée to the Western Hemisphere.

1840 Antoine's restaurant opens at 50 St. Louis Street.

1868 McIlhenny Company begins production of Tabasco sauce.

1860s Café du Monde founded.

1880 Commander's Palace opens.

1881 La Louisiana restaurant is opened by a member of Antoine Alciatore's family.

1899 Jules Alciatore invents "Oysters à la Rockefeller." Since that day over 18 million Oysters Rockefeller have been served at Antoine's.

1907 Dixie beer makes its debut.

1908 Eggs Sardou, the city's first famous brunch dish, is created by Jules Alciatore at Antoine's, and named for his guest, the French playwright Victorien Sardou.

1918 Arnaud's Restaurant is founded by "Count" Arnaud Cazenave.

1920s Huey P. "Kingfish" Long's favorite drink, the Ramos Gin Fizz, is invented at the Stag Saloon on Gravier Street.

1937 Pat O'Brien's "Hurricane" is invented when the bar owner overbuys rum and a case of hurricane-shade-shaped glasses.

1941 Edgar and Emily Chase establish the famed eatery Dooky Chase.

1955 The Brennan family moves their Bourbon Street restaurant to its permanent location at 417 Royal.

with Mexico and returned home with a renewed passion for the pepper. One such man brought the McIlhenny family of Avery Island some special Mexican pepper seeds. The result? Tabasco sauce, which sells over 50 million bottles annually all over the world. Other hot sauce brands include Cajun Chef, Crystal, Louisiana Red, and Louisiana Gold —one of the hottest on the market.

Po-Boys. A sandwich served on French bread. To be served "dressed" means with mayo, lettuce, and tomato. Common fillings include ham, fried oysters, meatballs, or roast beef.

Pommes de Terre Soufflée. Puffed, twice-fried potatoes.

Pralines. ("Praw-leens") A sugar-and-pecan candy so sweet it will make your fillings itch.

Ramos Gin Fizz. Gin, orange water, lime juice, lemon juice, cream, egg white, powdered sugar, and ice. Huey Long's favorite cocktail.

Red Beans and Rice. The late Louis Armstrong used to sign all of his letters "red beans and ricely yours." The dish of beans and rice couldn't be simpler, but in the hands of a good cook they can become a gloriously satisfying blend of

Leah Chase, owner of Dooky Chase Restaurant, prepares one of her famous meals. (Syndey Byrd)

the flavors of smoked pork, onions, garlic, and hot sauce.

Rémoulade Sauce. ("Rum-a-laad") The spicy, mustard-based, Creole cocktail sauce to perk up seafood.

Roman Candy. One of the fixtures of the Uptown neighborhood is the Roman Candy Man. The mule-drawn white-and-red-painted wagon is now the base of operations for the founder's grandson, Sam Cortese to sell the toffee-like confection. Two places where he can be found are on St. Charles Avenue between Audubon Park and Tulane University, and near Spanish Plaza at the foot of Canal Street by the River, close to the Aquarium.

Hot sauces are the spice of life in New Orleans.

Root Beer. The Root Beer Institute of America reports that New Orleanians drink twice as much as other Americans. Until the last generation, there were 18 brands for sale in local stores and eateries. Nowadays Barq's is the brew of choice.

Sauce Piquante. ("Pee-cont") The local spicy version of an Italian red gravy.

Sazerac. Bourbon and bitters. Reputed to be the first cocktail.

Shrimp Creole. Shrimp mixed with a lusty red sauce with onions, garlic, and bell pepper.

Snow Ball. This ice and flavored syrup concoction makes the weather bearable. Some people like to buy one the size of a large bucket of popcorn, take it home, douse it with rum, and suck on it all day.

Tasso. A red-pepper-seasoned version of smoked ham.

Trout Meunière. A pan-fried filet of trout served under a rich butter sauce.

Turtle Soup. A New Orleans tradition, actually often made with alligator.

Restaurants

■ NEW ORLEANS RESTAURANTS

Don't be fooled into thinking that any regular mortal can eat three meals a day in New Orleans and live to tell the tale. Take it from one who knows: plan one pull-out-all-the-stops meal a day, take one long walk, an even longer nap, and then buy a local cookbook so that you can create the dishes you missed in your own kitchen.

Note: Because the restaurant business is ever-changing, please call the restaurants to check on days and hours before embarking on your food odyssey.

Attire: In some of the nicer restaurants, shorts are not considered acceptable despite outrageous degrees of humidity. Call to see if coat and tie are required.

———— ?€ ————

Prices = *Per person, excluding drinks and tip:*
$ = under $10; $$ = $10–20; $$$ = $20–30; $$$$ = over $30

———— ?€ ————

The Cajun Restaurant Myth: The countrified, hearty cuisine of the Cajuns is a mainstay in most New Orleans homes and restaurants. A pure Cajun restaurant in the city, however, is viewed more as a hook for tourists than an ethnic dining experience. So when Cajun food is what you have a hankerin' for, go to a Creole restaurant (Antoine's, for example, has one of the best Cajun-style crawfish bisques around) and ask your waiter to recommend Cajun dishes on the menu.

Acme Oyster House. *Seafood.*
  724 Iberville St.; (504) 522-5973
The oyster shuckers here move quickly, the oysters are fat and salty, and the place has the ambiance of a typical, slightly unkempt, local oyster house. **$$**

Antoine's. *Traditional Creole.* 713 St. Louis St.; (504) 581-4422
Owned by the same family for five generations, Antoine's offers over 130 dishes on its vintage turn-of-the-century French menu. Best dishes include pommes de terre soufflée, and a combination of oyster dishes —Rockefeller, Foch, and Bienville—followed by a crème caramel make for one of the finest lunches or dinners in town. **$$$$**

Arnaud's. *Traditional Creole.* 813 Bienville St.; (504) 523-5433
Jackets are required in this large (six public dining rooms, 12 private) French Quarter institution. (See "Sizzling Musical Brunches," p. 255.) **$$$$**

Bacco. *Italian/Creole/Bistro.*
  310 Chartres St.; (504) 522-2426
Wood-fired pizzas and seafood; jazz brunch on Sundays. **$$$**

Bangkok Cuisine. *Thai.* 4137 S. Carrollton; (504) 482-3606
Consistently good Thai cuisine. **$$**

Barrow's. *Seafood.* 2714 Mistletoe (just off Earhart Blvd. in the Uptown area); (504) 482-9427

For close to 50 years this family-owned restaurant has been the spot for cornmeal-battered fried catfish. It's so good that it's all they have. **$$**

Bayona. *Bistro.* 430 Dauphine St.; (504) 525-4455

Chef Susan Spicer has combined her talent and elegant style to create a terrific menu for her own intimate restaurant. From garlic soup to a black beans and shrimp appetizer, her culinary style is clever, not overbearing. **$$$**

Bella Luna. *Bistro.* 914 N. Peters; (504) 529-1583

Languish in the visual splendor of one of the grandest vistas of the Mississippi and indulge in an elegant array of fresh pastas and seafood creations in this chef-owned restaurant. **$$$**

Blue Bird Cafe. *Breakfast.* 7801 Panola; (504) 865-7577

Funky, hippie-chipper service, great eggs, grits, and pancakes. **$**

Bombay Club. *Late Night.* 830 Conti; (504) 586-0972

A watering hole of the cafe society with a penchant for martinis and escargot en croute. **$$$**

Bottom of the Cup. *Coffeehouse.* 732 Royal St.; (504) 523-1204/ 616 Conti; (504) 524-1997

Tarot cards, and crystal balls add a few drops of "insider" info to the sipping.

Bouchon Wine Bistro. *Wine/snacks.* 4900 Prytania St.; (504) 895-WINE

A custom oak bar and large glass windows provide a sleek backdrop for the largest selection of wines by the glass in the city, delectable tapas, desserts, and coffees. **$$**

Bozo's. *Seafood.* 3117 21st St. (at Causeway Blvd.); (504) 831-8666

Fabulous boiled and fried seafood. Everything is cooked to order. **$**

Brennan's. *Breakfast.* 417 Royal St.; (504) 525-9711

Brunch at Brennan's is one of those landmark meals to have at least once. Most famous for their poached egg dishes, Brennan's claim to sell 750,000 poached eggs a year. Eggs Sardou and Bananas Foster make a tasty way to fritter away the day. **$$$$**

Cafe Atchafalaya. *Soul Food.* 901 Louisiana Ave.; (504) 891-5271

On the fringe of the Irish Channel, this is a nothing-but-plain-food, formica top neighborhood restaurant. It is the brainchild of a feisty lady from the Mississippi Delta who is as unpretentious as they come. Her daily specials are written on a board on the wall. The vegetable plate is great, but don't expect healthy, California-style veggies. Pluses: the wide range of seafood, the beef brisket, the homemade cobblers, or the ice cream. **$**

Café du Monde. *Coffeehouse/Late Night.* 813 Decatur in the French Market; (504) 525-4544

Good Creole café au lait and beignets without much opportunity to form a meaningful relationship with fellow coffee sippers. Open 24 hours, seven days a week. **$**

Cafe Pontchartrain. *Breakfast.* 2031 St. Charles Ave.; (504) 524-0581

Eggs Sardou, fresh O.J., and other breakfast fare (including biscuits and blueberry muffins) are served with gracious ease. **$$**

Restaurants

Cafe Sbisa. (See "Sizzling Music Brunches, p. 255.)

Camellia Grill. *Late Night.* 626 S. Carrollton; (504) 866-9573

The lights are bright enough to elicit a confession and there is often a wait for one of the 29 stools, but the food is worth it. Omelets (especially the potato and onion with chili and cheese on top), hamburgers, pecan waffles, and pecan pie are all close to the best in the world. The beverage of choice is the mocha freeze. Avoid the coffee, unless you happen to like the coffee in Kansas. Clientele includes university types, ball-goers, and after-rounds physicians. $$

Casamento's Restaurant. *Seafood.* 4300 Magazine; (504) 895-9761

Closed June through August. Best fried and raw oysters in the city. The tile-lined walls are immaculate. $

Central Grocery. *Sweets and Snacks.* 923 Decatur St.; (504) 523-1620

This tiny Italian market will give any food lover a lot to think about with aisles of olive oil and other imports. Famous for muffulettas—huge sandwiches filled with ham, salami, mozzarella, and marinated, chopped green olives—that can be ordered in quarters and halves.

Clancy's. *Traditional Creole.* 6100 Annunciation; (504) 895-1111

Located in a former bar, seasoned waiters and dishes like smoked soft-shell crab give this eatery its old New Orleans feel. $$-$$$

Columns Hotel. *Breakfast.* 3811 St. Charles Ave.; (504) 899-9308

The informal atmosphere of dining on an amply columned front porch is just what the doctor ordered after one too many elaborate meals. (See "Sizzling Musical Brunches," p. 255.) $$

Commander's Palace. *Eclectic Creole/ Breakfast.* 1403 Washington Ave.; (504) 899-8221

Excellent food and service keep this restaurant's 12 dining rooms and cocktail courtyard full seven days a week. Luncheon specials are always delicious and well-priced. Fish Grieg, oysters Rockefeller soup, turtle soup, and crab dishes shouldn't be missed. For dessert, crème brûlée, lemon crêpes, and bread pudding soufflé are tops. On a nice day, request a table on the patio or in the upstairs room that overlooks it. (See "Sizzling Musical Brunches," p. 255.) $$$$

Coop's Place. *Late Night.* 1109 Decatur St.; (504) 525-9053

A back-of-the-Quarter neighborhood bar and pool hall with great omelettes and Cajun specialties. $

Court of Two Sisters. (See "Sizzling Music Brunches, p. 255.)

Crescent City Steak House. *Steak.* 1001 N. Broad; (504) 821-3271

The 1940s atmosphere and old-style steakhouse booths are the ideal backdrop for butter broiled beef. $$$

Croissant D'Or. *Sweets and Snacks.* 617 Ursulines St.; (504) 524-4663

Sweets and sandwiches can be found in this delightful pastry shop, as well as soups, salads, and espresso drinks. A cheery courtyard with a bubbly fountain accommodates both locals and tourists on a sunny day. $

Di Piazza's. *Italian.* 337 Dauphine; (504) 525-3353

Smoked duck rigatoni, *osso bucco,* and creative fish specials make this cozy trattoria a local favorite. $$

Domilise's. *Sweets and Snacks.* 5240 Annunciation St.; (504) 899-9126

French bread stuffed to bursting with fried seafood in this neighborhood institution for close to 80 years. $

Donna's. *Late Night.* 800 N. Rampart; (504) 596-6914

Try a slab of baby back ribs and grand beans as the live brass bands boogie in the background. $$

Dooky Chase. *Traditional Creole/Late Night.* 2301 Orleans Ave.; (504) 821-2294

Elegant black Creole food. The crabmeat Farci, shrimp Clemenceau, fried catfish, sweet potatoes, and bread pudding are all exceptional. Service can become slow as the hour grows late. $$

Dunbar's. *Soul Food.* 4927 Freret St.; (504) 899-0734

Guests who nestle into the red-tufted banquettes are in for a hard time, having to decide between some of the best fried chicken in the city, knock-your-socks-off mustard greens, fantastic red beans and rice, and bell peppers stuffed with shrimp and meat. Soul food breakfast from 7:00 A.M. $-$$

Emeril's. *Bistro.* 800 Tchoupitoulas St.; (504) 528-9393

Chef Lagasse wows diners with his own food laboratory in the Warehouse District using scratch ingredients such as herbs, cheeses, and fresh produce culled from his network of farmers. Go with a few friends and order six appetizers, then finish off with Creole cream cheese cake. $$$

Feelings. *Traditional Creole.* 2600 Chartres St.; (504) 945-2222

Away from the bustle of the Quarter, this venue has been noted for more than 20 years for its updated renditions of creole favorites like Chicken Clemenceau. $$

Felix's Restaurant and Oyster Bar. *Seafood.* 739 Iberville St.; (504) 522-4440

A top-of-the-line seafood house. The oyster shuckers are characters worthy of starring roles on a sit-com, and the cooked oyster and crab dishes are home-style. $$

Fiorella's Cafe. *Breakfast.* 45 French Market Pl.; (504) 528-9566

French Quarter ladies use the front door and French Market truckers use the back, on the market side, where the hours are earlier. Either way, the food and atmosphere are as real as it gets. $

Franky & Johnny's. *Seafood.* 321 Arabella; (504) 899-9146

Good timin', good drinkin', and good ol' neighborhood-style seafood. The turtle soup and crawfish dishes are terrific. $

Gabrielle's. *Traditional Creole/Bistro.* 3201 Esplanade; (504) 948-6233

Plump soft shell crab, homemade sausages, festive sauces, and friendly service reign in this unpretentious chef-owned bistro at the edge of the French Quarter. Reservations recommended. $$

Restaurants

Restaurants

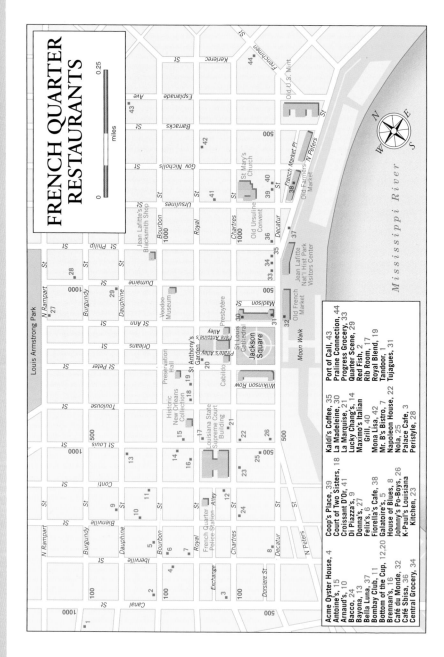

FRENCH QUARTER RESTAURANTS

miles

0   0.25

Acme Oyster House, 4
Antoine's, 15
Arnaud's, 10
Bacco, 24
Bayona, 13
Bella Luna, 37
Bombay Club, 11
Bottom of the Cup, 12,20
Brennan's, 16
Café du Monde, 32
Café Sbisa, 36
Central Grocery, 34

Coop's Place, 39
Court of Two Sisters, 18
Croissant D'Or, 41
Di Piazza's, 9
Donna's, 27
Felix's, 6
Fiorella's Cafe, 38
Galatoire's, 5
House of Blues, 8
Johnny's Po-Boys, 26
K-Paul's Louisiana Kitchen, 23

Kaldi's Coffee, 35
La Madeleine, 30
La Marquise, 21
Lucky Chang's, 14
Maximo's Italian Grill, 40
Mona Lisa, 42
Mr. B's Bistro, 7
Napoleon House, 22
Nola, 25
Palace Cafe, 3
Peristyle, 28

Port of Call, 43
Praline Connection, 44
Progress Grocery, 33
Quarter Scene, 29
Red Fish, 2
Rib Room, 17
Royal Blend, 19
Tandoor, 1
Tujagues, 31

Mississippi River

Restaurants

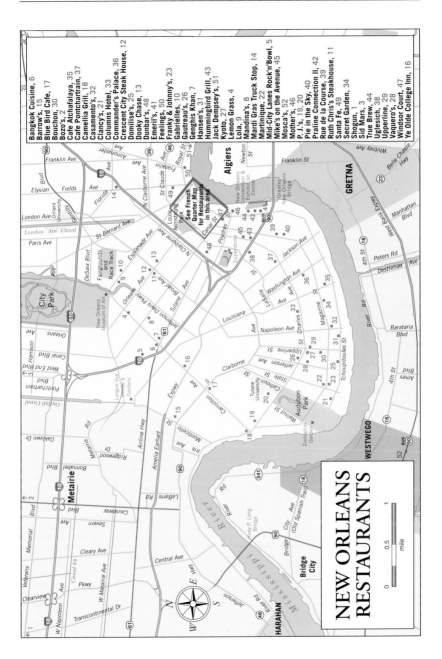

Bangkok Cuisine, 6
Barrow's, 15
Blue Bird Cafe, 17
Bouchon, 30
Bozo's, 2
Cafe Atchafalaya, 35
Cafe Pontchartrain, 37
Camellia Grill, 18
Casamento's, 32
Clancy's, 21
Columns Hotel, 33
Commander's Palace, 36
Crescent City Steak House, 12
Domilise's, 25
Dooky Chase, 13
Dunbar's, 48
Emeril's, 41
Feelings, 50
Franky & Johnny's, 23
Gabrielles, 10
Gautreau's, 26
Genghis Khan, 7
Hansen's, 31
Hummingbird Grill, 43
Jack Dempsey's, 51
Kyoto, 27
Lemon Grass, 4
Lola, 9
Mandina's, 8
Mardi Gras Truck Stop, 14
Martinique, 22
Mid-City Lanes Rock'n'Bowl, 5
Mike's on the Avenue, 45
Mosca's, 52
Mother's, 46
P. J.'s, 19, 20
Pie in the Sky, 40
Praline Connection II, 42
Rue de la Course, 39
Ruth Chris's Steakhouse, 11
Santa Fe, 49
Secret Garden, 34
Shogun, 1
Sid Mars, 3
True Brew, 44
Uglesich, 38
Upperline, 29
Vaquero's, 28
Windsor Court, 47
Ye Olde College Inn, 16

NEW ORLEANS
RESTAURANTS

Restaurants

Galatoire's. *Traditional Creole.*
209 Bourbon St.; (504) 525-2021
Oysters en brochette, the Godchaux salad (not on the 6-page menu), trout almandine or with crabmeat, and the crabmeat Yvonne are some of the finest seafood dishes to be found. Best time to go is between 1:30 and 4:00 P.M. on a Saturday or Sunday. $$$

Gautreau's. *Bistro/Eclectic Creole.*
1728 Soniat St.; (504) 899-7397
American-Creole cuisine at its finest. Don't miss the corn crabmeat soup and the crawfish and crab cakes. $$$

Genghis Khan. *Korean.* 4053 Tulane; (504) 482-4044
Korean food, often accompanied by live classical music. $$

Hansen's Sno-Bliz. *Sweets and Snacks.*
4801 Tchoupitoulas St.; (504) 891-9788
Famous for "snowballs": shaved ice doused with flavored syrups ranging in size from small cups to garbage-can party size. Perfect for beating the heat. $

House of Blues. *Late Night.* 225 Decatur St.; (504) 529-BLUE
Enjoy jazz and R&B as well as an extensive menu of dolled-up soul food. (See "Sizzling Musical Brunches," p. 255.) $$

Hummingbird Grill. *Late Night.*
804 St. Charles Ave.; (504) 561-9229
In spite of the fact that the "Hummer" is a favorite dingy hang-out for the downtrodden, cops, and patrons with imaginary

Portia's Restaurant No. 2 in 1972. (Michael P. Smith)

Restaurants

friends, the food is home-style and yummy. The breakfasts, the thick slabs of corn-bread, and the hamburgers are all good. $

Jack Dempsey's. *Seafood.* 738 Poland Ave. Ninth Ward; (504) 943-9914
An old-timey, just-plain-folks place where fried seafood literally drips off the plate and the juke box is rockin' with oldies. $$

Johnny's Po-Boys. *Sweets and Snacks.* 511 St. Louis St.; (504) 524-8129
A good, honest po-boy is actually a rare find in the French Quarter, but Johnny's makes up for this disappointment. Choose from New Orleans classics such as roast beef and gravy, fried oysters, shrimp, or ham, sandwiched between crusty French bread. $

K-Paul's Louisiana Kitchen. *Soul Food.* 416 Chartres St.; (504) 524-7394
K-Paul's chef, Paul Prudhomme, has made Cajun cuisine famous beyond its Louisiana borders. Among the many favorites are blackened fish, creative gumbos, sweet potato–pecan pie, and jalapeño-laced mar-tinis served in canning jars. K-Paul's na-tional recognition has made the restaurant extremely popular with tourists. Newly re-vamped, the dining room now accepts reservations. $$$

Kaldi's Coffee Museum and Coffeehouse. *Coffeehouse.* 941 Decatur St.; (504) 586-8989
A vibrant atmosphere fueled by a rich as-sortment of music. On a hot day the Italian cream sodas and the iced coffees are mighty refreshing. $

Kyoto. *Japanese.* 4920 Prytania; (504) 891-3644
Lush chairs and a sleek dining room; an interesting repertoire of sushi and Japanese cooking. $$

La Madeleine. *Sweets and Snacks.* 547 St. Ann St.; (504) 568-9950/ 601 S. Carrollton Ave.; (504) 861-8661
This ever-popular French cafe/bakery chain offers quality baguettes and brioches from its wood-burning oven. A selection of tarts, eclairs, and other temptations can serve as finales to a lunch from their kitchen. The lines are long, but move quickly. $

La Marquise. *Sweets and Snacks.* 625 Chartres St.; (504) 524-0420
Intimate and tiny; good coffee, croissants, and pastries. $

Lemon Grass Cafe. *Vietnamese.* 216 N. Carrollton Ave.; (504) 488-8335
Cozy elegance and continental flavored Vietnamese dining. Reservations recom-mended. $$

Lola's. *Spanish.* 3312 Esplanade; (504) 488-6946
A jumping hole-in-the-wall featuring Span-ish/Louisiana-style seafood paella. $$

Lucky Chang's. *Asian.* 720 St. Louis St.; (504) 529-2045
Asian/Creole cuisine, campily served by cross dressers. $$

Mandina's. *Soul Food.* 3800 Canal St.; (504) 482-9179
This Mid-City spot is famed for its stiff drinks, seafood, Italian food, and red beans. Waiters wear white coats; the pa-trons are generally more casual. $$

Mardi Gras Truck Stop. *Late Night.* 2401
Elysian Fields Ave.; (504) 945-1000
Some of the best grillades and grits in
town; crawfish dishes are also worth a try. $

Martinique. *Caribbean.* 5908 Magazine
St.; (504) 891-8495
This chef-owned bistro features delightful
fish dishes and ambrosial homemade ice
creams. Lovely dining patio. $$$

Maximo's Italian Grill. *Late Night/Italian.*
1117 Decatur St.; (504) 586-8883
Innovative northern Italian cuisine in a
chic bistro with a Roman-style grill and
outdoor dining. $$-$$$

Mid-City Lanes Rock'n'Bowl. *Late Night.*
4133 S. Carrollton St.; (504) 482-3133
Great ribs and fried alligator. $$

Mike's on the Avenue. *Bistro.* Lafayette
Hotel, 628 St. Charles Ave.; (504) 523-
1709
In a town known for its own regional style,
Mike's has made quite a hit among those
seeking something different. Here the culinary styles of the Orient, American Southwest, France, and Italy are all borrowed, cre-
ating a clever, visually appealing fare. $$$

Mr. B's Bistro. *Bistro/Eclectic Creole.*
201 Royal St.; (504) 523-2078
This pop version of Commander's Palace,
Jr., has remained fresh and innovative since
it opened in 1979. Sample the coconut-
and beer-battered shrimp, any of the items
from the grill, or pasta jambalaya, followed
by killer chocolate cake or a custardy bread
pudding. $$$

*Uglesich's simplicity contrasts with the elegance of Galatoire's (right)—two
restaurants known for their excellent food.*

Mona Lisa. *Pizza.* 1212 Royal St.; (504) 522-6746
Some of the best pizza in the city. $

Mosca's. *Seafood.* 4137 US 90 W, Avondale; (504) 436-9942
An old, wood-framed roadhouse with a beer sign has been the culinary mothership of the Mosca family's unique Creole-Italian crab, oyster, and shrimp dishes for two generations. Food is seved family-style, dripping in garlic and olive oil. Extremely difficult to find; check your map! $$$

Mother's. *Sweets and Snacks.* 401 Poydras St.; (504) 523-9656
Since 1938 locals have been lining up for "debris" po-boys made from the roast beef and gravy scraped off the bottom of the roasting pan. $

Napoleon House. *Sweets and Snacks.* 500 Chartres St.; (504) 524-9752
Look beyond the cocktails to partake in this historic spot: the muffulettas, gumbo, and Italian ice cream are worth a try. $

Nola. *Bistro/Eclectic Creole.* 534 St. Louis St.; (504) 522-6652
A "Baby Emeril's" sizzling with conversation and lively plates of rich food. Don't be put off by the snooty maitre d'. $$$-$$$$

P. J.'s. *Coffeehouse.* 5432 Magazine St.; (504) 895-0273
7624 Maple St.; (504) 866-7031
24 McAllister St.; (504) 865-5705
Uptown housewife types and university students gather for a cup of joe. $

Palace Cafe. *Bistro.* 605 Canal St.; (504) 523-1661

The chicken with garlic mashed potatoes, and custardy bread pudding with white chocolate sauce are sinfully delicious. This is another Brennan family restaurant. (See "Sizzling Musical Brunches," p. 255.) $$$

Peristyle. *Bistro.* 1041 Dumaine St.; (504) 593-9535
Chef Anne Kearney's 56-seat restaurant is a treat, from the fresh flowers and gracious waitstaff to her delectable food. It is also no longer a local secret, since she was named as one of the nation's "Rising Stars of 1997" by the James Beard Foundation. Reservations are a must. $$$

Pie in the Sky. *Pizza.* 1818 Magazine St.; (504) 522-6291
A perfect stop while antiquing. $

Port of Call. *Late Night.* 838 Esplanade Ave.; (504) 523-0120
Hard-core '60s vintage partiers will fit right into this den of blackness. Serves fantastic charbroiled hamburgers. $$

Praline Connection. *Soul Food.* 542 Frenchmen St.; (504) 943-3934
Cool soul; white, lima, or red beans; stewed or fried chicken; and fantastic pralines. Outside the French Quarter is **Praline Connection II Gospel & Blues Hall,** 901-907 S. Peters; (504) 523-3973. Come here, lunch or dinner, for jambalaya, gumbo, and red beans and rice. Praline Connection II also hosts a jazz brunch. (See "Sizzling Musical Brunches," p. 255.) $-$$

Progress Grocery. *Sweets and Snacks.* 915 Decatur St.; (504) 525-6627

Next door and similar to Central Grocery, this spot offers gastronomic goodies like muffulettas, etc. Word has it that Progress offers a better deal with a larger selection and lower prices. $

Quarter Scene. *Late Night.* 900 Dumaine St.; (504) 522-6533
The snap and pop of deep Quarter attitude, crammed tables, and dishes named after Tennessee Williams characters. $$

Red Fish Grill. (See "Sizzling Music Brunches, p. 255.)

The Rib Room. *Steak.* Royal Orleans Hotel, 621 St. Louis St.; (504) 529-7045
The focal point of this elegant dining room is a wall of rotisseries. The rib roast is crusty and succulent, and the chocolate mousse is a must for chocoholics. $$$$

Royal Blend. *Coffeehouse.* 623 Royal St.; (504) 523-2716
Offers an exceptional selection of coffee drinks in a courtyard setting. $

Rue de la Course. *Coffeehouse.* 1500 Magazine; (504) 529-1455
An ideal spot to park grumpy husbands while antiquing. $

Ruth's Chris Steakhouse. *Steak.* 711 N. Broad St.; (504) 486-0810 Metairie: 3633 Veterans Blvd.; (504) 888-3600
When only a well-aged, prime slab of beef will do, Chris's, that testosterone-affirmative home-away-from-the-car-phone for politicos and sports fans, serves the best steak to be found east of Fort Worth. Peppermint

stick ice cream is the perfect complement for such gustatory decadence. $$$$

Sante Fe. *Tex-Mex.* 801 Frenchmen St.; (504) 944-6854
Southwestern and Tex-Mex style cuisine. $$

Secret Garden Tea Room. *Tea room.* 3626 Magazine St.; (504) 895-2913
A stop at this 32-seat classic tea room for locally blended teas, quiche, soups, salads, and desserts in a casual garden room atmosphere is an ideal recess from shopping, six days a week. $

Shogun. *Japanese/Steak.* 2325 Veterans Hwy., Metairie; (504) 833-7477
Friendly service and a fabulous sushi bar, Kaiseki, Sukiyaki, and Hibachi griddle table. $$

Sid Mars. *Seafood.* 1824 Orpheum, Bucktown near the lakefront; (504) 831-9541
A meal of boiled crabs on the screen porch at this small fishing enclave is a trip back to a calmer era. $-$$

Tandoor. *Indian.* 115 University Pl.; (504) 529-9909
Indian food, with well-prepared Tandoori roasted meat dishes. $$

True Brew. *Coffeehouse.* 200 Julia St.; (504) 524-8441
This coffeehouse/theater attracts an artsy, Warehouse District crowd. $

Tujague's *Traditional Creole.* 823 Decatur St.; (504) 525-8676
The second oldest restaurant in New Orleans with the city's oldest standing bar

Restaurants

originally was conceived to serve the working class. Today it's noted for a Wednesday lunch special: veggie soup and a hunk of brisket with mashed potatoes. Other days, shrimp rémoulade and the garlicky chicken bone femme are worth a visit. $$

Uglesich Restaurant & Bar. *Seafood.* 1238 Baronne; (504) 523-8571
Fried seafood po-boys, plate lunches, real French fries, onion rings, and raw oysters all add to the already pithy ambiance of a hopping, Old World neighborhood eatery. $

Upperline. *Bistro.* 1431 Upperline St.; (504) 891-9822
Nestled Uptown is this charming cozy bistro, whose culinary style begins with local products and is elevated with Latin, Anglo-Indian, and classic French cooking techniques. All of the crispy duck dishes are perfection, though the one with ginger peach sauce edges out the others. $$$

Vaqueros. *Mexican/Southwest.* 4938 Prytania; (504) 891-6441
Authentic Mexican and Southwestern cuisine with a Creole accent in a family-style cantina. $$

Windsor Court. *Tea room.* 300 Gravier St.; (504) 523-6000
Overstuffed chairs, live classical music, and an elegant English tea service make an afternoon in Le Salon a memorable experience. $$

Ye Olde College Inn. *Sweets and Snacks.* 3016 S. Carrollton Ave.; (504) 866-3683
A sprawling family-style resaurant serving up a plethora of po-boys since 1933. $$

Camellia Grill, known for its pecan pie.

■ NEW ORLEANS RESTAURANTS BY CUISINE

Bistro
Bacco $$$
Bayona $$$
Bella Luna $$$
Bouchon Wine Bistro $$
Emeril's $$$
Gabrielle's $$
Gautreau's $$$
Mike's on the Avenue $$$
Mr. B's Bistro $$$
Nola $$$-$$$$
Palace Cafe $$$
Peristyle $$$
Upperline $$$

Breakfast
Blue Bird Cafe $
Brennan's $$$$
Cafe Pontchartrain $$

Columns Hotel $$
Commander's Palace $$$$
Dunbar's $
Fiorella's Cafe $

Coffee/Tea
Bottom of the Cup $
Café du Monde $
Kaldi's Coffee Museum $
P. J.'s $
Royal Blend $
Rue de la Course $
Secret Garden Tea Room *(Tea room)* $
True Brew $
Windsor Court *(Tea room)* $

Creole (Eclectic)
Bacco $$$
Commander's Palace $$$-$$$$
Gabrielle's $$

Live music and bowling mix to the beat at Mid-City Bowling Lanes.

Restaurants

Creole (Eclectic) cont'd
Gautreau's $$$
Mr. B's $$$
Nola $$$-$$$$

Creole (Traditional)
Antoine's $$$$
Arnaud's $$$$
Brennan's $$$$
Clancy's $$-$$$
Dooky Chase $$
Feelings $$
Galatoire's $$$
Tujague's $$

Foreign Fare
Bacco *Italian* $$$
Bangkok Cuisine *Thai* $$
Di Piazza's *Italian* $$
Genghis Khan *Korean* $$
Kyoto *Japanese* $$
Lemon Grass Cafe *Vietnamese* $$
Lola's *Spanish* $$
Lucky Chang's *Asian/Creole* $$
Maximo's Italian Grill *Italian* $$-$$$
Mona Lisa *Pizza* $
Pie in the Sky *Pizza* $
Sante Fe *Tex-Mex* $$
Shogun *Japanese/Steak* $$
Tandoor *Indian* $$
Vaqueros *Mexican/Southwest* $$

Late Night
Bombay Club $$$
Cafe du Monde $
Camellia Grill $$
Coop's Place $
Donna's $$
Dooky Chase $$
House of Blues $$
Hummingbird Grill $
Mardi Gras Truck Stop $

Late Night cont'd
Maximo's Italian Grill $$-$$$
Mid-City Lanes Rock'n'Bowl $
Port of Call $$
Quarter Scene $$

Seafood
Acme Oyster House $$
Barrow's $$
Bozo's $
Casamento's Restaurant $
Felix's Restaurant and Oyster Bar $$
Franky & Johnny's $
Jack Dempsey's $$
Mosca's $$$
Sid Mars $-$$
Uglesich $

Soul Food
Cafe Atchafalaya $
Dunbar's $-$$
K-Paul's Louisiana Kitchen $$$
Mandina's $$
Praline Connection $-$$

Steak
Crescent City Steak House $$$
The Rib Room $$$$
Ruth's Chris Steakhouse $$$$

Sweets and Snacks
Bouchon Wine Bistro $$
Central Grocery $
Croissant D'Or $
Domilise's $
Hansen's Sno-Bliz $
Johnny's Po-Boys $
La Madeleine $
La Marquise $
Mother's $
Napoleon House $
Progress Grocery $
Ye Olde College Inn $$

Restaurants

SIZZLING MUSICAL BRUNCHES

The ideal way to fritter away a weekend afternoon in New Orleans is to combine the city's two favorite pastimes: listening to music and eating. The following restaurants are guaranteed to provide a delightful brunch as well as outstanding music.

Price = brunch for one, excluding tip and drinks:
$ = under $10; $$ = $10-20; $$$ = $20-30; $$$$ = over $30

Arnaud's. 813 Bienville St.; (504) 523-5433 $$$$
Shrimp Arnaud in a tart rémoulade sauce, crème brûlée, cinnamony bread pudding, and flaming café brûlot served to the strains of traditional jazz on Sundays. Reservations a must.

Cafe Sbisa. 1011 Decatur St.; (504) 522-5565 $$$
Sunday jazz brunch and an assortment of seafood delights are served up in this turn-of-the-century dining room.

Columns Hotel. 3811 St. Charles Ave.; (504) 899-9308 $$
Complimentary champagne and live jazz accompany a small but pleasant selection of entrees on Sundays. Reservations preferred.

Commander's Palace. 1403 Washington Ave.; (504) 899-8221 $$$$
Traditional jazz weekends in this sprawling Victorian mansion, where excellent service and eggs de la Salle with crabcakes and trout with pecans make for a delightful only-in-New Orleans experience. Reservations required.

Court of Two Sisters. 613 Royal St.; (504) 522-7261 $$$
Brunch seven days a week and the city's largest courtyard. Reservations preferred.

House of Blues. 225 Decatur St.; (504) 529-BLUE $$$
An extensive buffet and non-stop mimosas accompany arm-waving, Lord-praisin' gospel on Sundays. Reservations required.

Palace Cafe. 605 Canal St.; (504) 523-1661 $$$
The roast chicken with garlic mashed potatoes and the custardy bread pudding with white chocolate sauce taste even better with a dose of the blues on Sundays.

Praline Connection II. 901-907 S. Peters St.; (504) 523-3973 $ - $$
A down-home version of the upscale Sunday brunches with a healthy splash of gospel. Feed your stomach *and* your soul.

Red Fish Grill. 115 Bourbon St.; (504) 598-1200 $$ - $$$
A steel drum band serenades on 55-gallon steel drums as patrons dine in the casual atmosphere on smoked salmon Benedict and oysters Rockefeller omelettes.

Climate

PRACTICAL INFORMATION

Note: Compass American Guides makes every effort to ensure the accuracy of its information; however, as conditions and prices change frequently, we recommend that readers also contact local chambers of commerce for the most up-to-date information.

■ AREA CODES

All phone numbers listed in this book, unless otherwise noted, are in the 504 area code. Some cities in the New Orleans area, including Baton Rouge, also use the same area code, and 504 must be dialed when calling from New Orleans. The Lafayette area (Cajun country) has a 318 area code, and all of Mississippi has 601.

■ METRIC CONVERSIONS

degrees C = (degrees F − 32) $\times$ $5/9$
meters = feet $\times$ .3
kilometers = miles $\times$ .62
kilograms = pounds $\times$ .45

■ CLIMATE

In the semi-tropical city of New Orleans, there are about 57 days a year when the temperature rises over 90 degrees F. Average temperatures do not take into account that the humidity is about 76 percent, which makes the air as thick as a

Climate

Month	Temperature		Rainfall	Month	Temperature		Rainfall
	High	Low	(in inches)		High	Low	(in inches)
January	62	47	4.7	July	90	76	6.4
February	65	50	5.6	August	90	76	5.9
March	71	55	5.2	September	86	73	5.5
April	77	61	4.7	October	79	64	2.8
May	83	68	4.4	November	70	55	4.4
June	88	74	5.4	December	64	48	5.5

NEW ORLEANS CLIMATE

steambath in midsummer. Local weather forecasters report the "heat index," which factors in humidity; for example, when it is 90 degrees, the heat index may be 104 degrees.

In the summer most of the public buildings are over air-conditioned. This is undoubtedly why locals are as likely to contract pneumonia in August as they are in January. But some of us actually enjoy the summer heat. We tote fans with us, drink lots of iced tea, eat snowballs, and hold ice on our wrists to cool our blood. When we can, we eat our biggest meal after dark and take naps in the hottest part of the day.

Most of the time, New Orleanians don't turn off their air conditioning until the temperature dips below 68 degrees. At 50 degrees "cold front frenzy" sets in. Of course, raised houses designed to afford maximum cross-ventilation do tend to get a bit brisk inside.

For a daily weather recording, call (504) 828-4000.

Most desirable months: March to May; October to mid-December.

Rainiest months: July to August. With 60.6 inches of annual rain, New Orleans is the rainiest city in the United States.

Driest months: October to November.

Humidity: Mornings often have 100% humidity that wanes toward midday, and rises in the early evening.

Hurricane season: June to November.

Unlike earthquakes, hurricanes do plenty of sword-rattling before they ever come into the Gulf, so there is no excuse for ever being caught off guard. Just be

Map of Southeast Louisiana

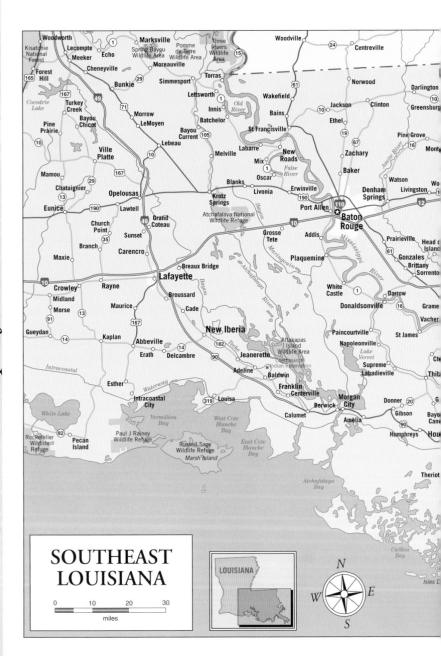

SOUTHEAST
LOUISIANA

0   10   20   30
miles

LOUISIANA

N
W   E
S

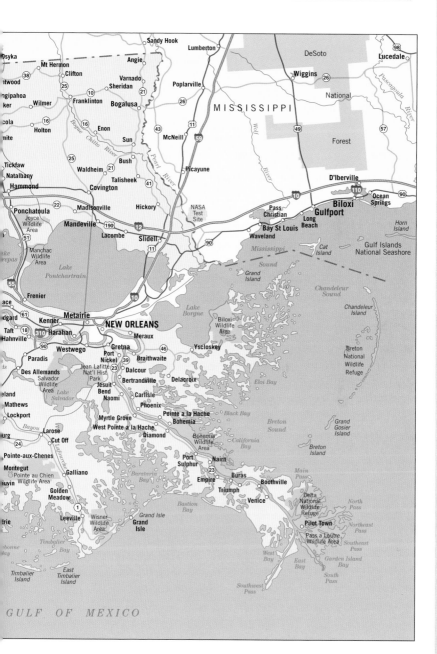

GULF OF MEXICO

warned—New Orleans is located at the heart of the hurricane target area. It's important to remember that the city is below sea level, is surrounded by water, and is a popular target for hurricanes and tropical storms. If a tropical storm is headed into the Gulf, postpone your trip. Even with a tropical storm the city can lose telephone service and power (which means no air conditioning).

■ GETTING AROUND

When navigating the streets of New Orleans, think of Canal Street as the great dividing line. At 171 feet wide, it is the widest main thoroughfare and one of the longest streets in the United States. Historically the border between the Creoles and the Americans, today it marks the division between the Central Business District (CBD) and the French Quarter. Where streets cross Canal, those to the north are prefixed "North," likewise those to the south are prefixed "South." Addresses on these streets begin with 100 at Canal and move out to the north and south.

■ AIRPORT TRANSPORTATION

New Orleans International Airport is in Kenner, about 14 miles northwest of the downtown area. The least expensive way to get to town from the airport is by **Airport Express** ($2.00) which picks up/lets off on the second level on the far right as you exit, and lets off/picks up at Elk and Tulane near the Public Library. Call (504) 737-9611 for information. The 11-passenger **Airport Shuttle** ($10.00) departs every 15 minutes for all major hotels and B&Bs in the downtown and French Quarter neighborhoods, and for the universities. A ticket booth is inside the airport. Call (504) 522-3500 for information. Taxis and limos are also available.

■ TRAIN SERVICE

Several Amtrak passenger trains leave from New Orleans for Atlanta, Chicago, Los Angeles, and New York. Contact **Amtrak,** Union Passenger Terminal (Downtown), 1001 Loyola Ave.; (504) 528-1631/ (800) 872-7245.

■ BUS SERVICE

Greyhound-Trailways Bus Service. Transportation Center, Union Passenger Terminal (Downtown), 1001 Loyola Ave.; (504) 525-6075/(800) 231-2222.

■ LOCAL TRANSIT SERVICE

The city has 429 buses and 35 streetcars, including 7 riverfront cars. A one-day pass is under $5.00 (unlimited mileage); a three-day is $8.00. Regular one-way fare is $1.10 with a transfer; exact change is required. (Subject to change.)

Regional Transit Authority (RTA). (504) 248-3900. Timetables and routes available.

The Lift–Handicapped Service. (504) 827-7433. A fleet of 40 vehicles; door-to-door pick up.

■ RECOMMENDED CAR SERVICES

Limousine Livery: (800) 326-1345; Stretch Lincolns, Cadillacs, and sedans. Vintage cars also available. Most of the chauffeurs are licensed tour guides.

London Livery: (504) 586-0700/(800) 284-0660; a fleet of 21 Lincolns fully equipped with radios and phones.

Touch of Class: (800) 878-6352; 12 Lincolns.

United Cab: (504) 524-9606/(504) 522-9771.

Yellow Checker: (504) 525-3311.

■ FERRIES

Ferries offer a lovely short cruise from one side of the Mississippi to the other at Jackson Avenue/Gretna, Canal Street, and Chalmette. They are free for pedestrians and a dollar for vehicles (collected only on West Bank leg). The Jackson Avenue/Gretna ferry runs every half hour from 5:30 A.M. to 9:15 P.M.; Canal Street from 5:45 A.M. to midnight.

■ DRIVING AND PARKING

Meter maids and towing services work extremely efficiently in New Orleans. The number of drunk-driving arrests is one of the highest in the country. When it rains hard, the streets flood. If these facts aren't a deterrent from driving around, then try to stay in a hotel with valet parking. The Royal Orleans Garage on Chartres Street, the Canal Place Shopping Center on Canal Street, and the parking area behind the levee (entrance at Jax Brewery) are good, but tend to fill up fast.

(following pages) Blue Plate mayonnaise, a popular New Orleans condiment.

Accommodations

■ ACCOMMODATIONS

As in many an Old World city, New Orleans has a plethora of places to sleep, from America's top hotels and most gracious European-style guest houses to motels so seedy that the cockroaches complain. In between are the ubiquitous tourist hotels that might as well be located in Detroit or Pittsburgh, spare bedrooms owned by clever homemakers who turn a few bucks in their Sears and Robuckian specials, and some musty-smelling monoliths that haven't had a good cleaning since Eisenhower was President.

More than 45 hotels, motels, inns, and guest houses representing over 4,000 rooms can be found within the 96 blocks in the French Quarter. What follows is a list, by category, of some of the finest accommodations that the city has to offer. A few words to the wise: staying in the suburbs and commuting may be cheaper, but it will entail parking costs and the hassle of fighting traffic. By the same token, there are hotels advertised as being "close to downtown" or "10 minutes from the French Quarter." Often they are in neighborhoods in which it is unsafe to walk.

Note: Many hotels have summer specials and packages with rates lower than those the rest of the year. Also, major hotel and motel chains are well represented in New Orleans. For information call the national 800 numbers listed below, but for the best rates make your reservations at the local number; the reservations clerk is frequently authorized to quote discounted rates.

Best Western (800) 528-1234	**Hilton Inn** (800) HILTONS
Days Inn (800) 325-2525	**Holiday Inn** (800) HOLIDAY
Doubletree Hotels (800) 222-8733	**Marriott Hotels** (800) 228-9290
Fairmont Hotels (800) 527-4727	**Royal Sonesta** (800) 766-3782
Hampton Inn (800) 426-7866	**Sheraton** (800) 325-3535

Room Rates
(per person, based on double occupancy):
$ = under $90; $$ = $90-130; $$$ = $130-175; $$$$ = over $175
*(S)= Safer area, although caution is always advised.

Old World Amenities

The Windsor Court Hotel. 300 Gravier St., 70130-1035; (504) 523-6000/(800) 262-2662 *(S) $$$$

Twice ranked No. 1 by the prestigious *Conde Nast Traveler* Reader's Choice Poll and chosen as one of the top ten in the United States by *Zagat's*—no doubt for its luxurious courtliness, exceptional five-star restaurant, grand swimming pool, and health club. The nicest views are on floors 13 through 23.

THE WINDSOR COURT HOTEL

High-Rise Hotels

The Hotel Inter-Continental New Orleans. 444 St. Charles Ave., 70130; (504) 525-5566/(800) 445-6563 $$$$

Located in the heart of the city's financial district and only three blocks from the French Quarter. Offers 462 deluxe guest rooms and 20 luxury suites. Request numbers 02-08, 28-52 on each floor. The hotel is topped by a pool on the 15th floor. Special summer rates.

Le Meridien New Orleans. 614 Canal St. (across the street from the French Quarter), 70130; (504) 525-6500/(800) 543-4300 $$$-$$$$

A first-class French-owned and operated hotel. The Jazz Meridien Lounge features the best of classic jazz bands. Rooms 17-23 on each floor overlook the river. The quietest rooms per floor are 10, 11, 12, 24, and 25, which view both the river and city. The Health Club on the eighth floor is newly renovated and has an outdoor heated pool and sauna.

Hotel Monteleone. 214 Royal St., 70130; (504) 523-3341 $$$

Opened in 1886, this gracious 17-story French Quarter belle is still owned by the Monteleone family. It has been completely renovated during the last four years. Of the 600 spacious rooms, the best views of the river are in those numbered 50, 79, 81, and 82 on floors 7 and up. The beautiful Queen Anne mezzanine ballroom has a true Royal Street ambiance. Rooftop pool.

HOTEL MONTELEONE

Accommodations

The Omni Royal Orleans. 621 St. Louis St., 70140; (504) 529-5333/(800) THE-OMNI $$$-$$$$

Tops for French Quarter location and New Orleans hospitality. The 346-room hotel was built in 1960 as a replica of the palatial 19th-century St. Louis hotel. The view from the rooftop pool on the seventh floor is one of the loveliest in the city. Balconies overlooking Royal Street provide an ideal vantage point during Carnival to view the decadence below. Rooms with balconies overlooking St. Louis St. are the most expensive. Inside rooms are smaller and quieter and the nicest view is from those that overlook the Royal Garden Terrace.

THE OMNI ROYAL ORLEANS

The Pontchartrain Grand Heritage Hotel. 2031 St. Charles Ave., 70140; (504) 524-0581/ (800) 777-6193 *(S) $$$-$$$$

The 18 luxurious grand suites are the prize of this quiet 100-room hotel, though each room is individually decorated. The building dates from 1927. In the summer the grand suites rent for less than half their usual price.

The Westin Canal Place. 100 Iberville St., 70130; (504) 566-7006/ (800) 228-3000 *(S) $$$-$$$$

A 438-unit hotel that tops the tower which houses the Canal Place shopping complex. Breathtaking views of the river and the city.

Conventional Frugality

New Orleans is one of the most popular convention destinations in the country. With the convention center on the riverfront, hotels within a 10-minute radius are prized locations for the conventioneer who will mostly be using the room as a place to shower and sleep.

The Hampton Inn Downtown. 226 Carondelet St., 70130; (504) 529-9990/(800) 426-7866 $$

Located in a former Central Business District office building. The 186 rooms have sophisticated modern decor. Excercise facilities, free phone calls, continental breakfast.

The Hampton Inn Garden District. 3626 St. Charles Ave.; (504) 899-9990/ (800) 292-0653 $$-$$$

One hundred charming rooms definitely a cut above conventional chain hotels due to the European-style furnishings. Lap pool, courtyard, and petite hospitality room.

Le Pavillon Hotel. 833 Poydras St., 70112; (504) 581-3111/(800) 535-9095 $$-$$$

Called the "Belle of New Orleans" when it opened in 1907, this 226-room hotel is a well-kept secret among out-of-town attorneys. There are seven suites best described as Las Vegas–style.

Accommodations

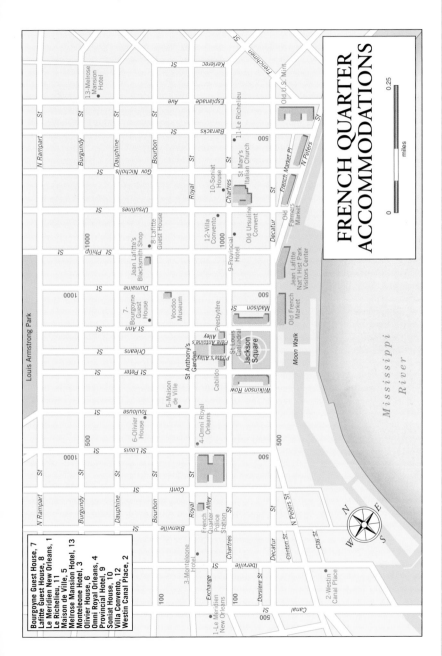

FRENCH QUARTER ACCOMMODATIONS

Bourgoyne Guest House, 7
Lafitte Guest House, 8
Le Meridien New Orleans, 1
Le Richelieu, 11
Maison de Ville, 5
Melrose Mansion Hotel, 13
Monteleone Hotel, 3
Olivier House, 6
Omni Royal Orleans, 4
Provincial Hotel, 9
Soniat House, 10
Villa Convento, 12
Westin Canal Place, 2

Accommodations

Elegantly Romantic

The Claiborne Mansion. 2111 Dauphine St.; (504) 949-7327 $$$$

A glamourous pool and patio serve the five lavish suites and two double rooms of this 1850s mansion, once belonging to the son of Governor Claiborne. The decor is sedate and elegant; the marble bathrooms grand. Facing Washington Square, it is just steps away from restaurants and three great jazz clubs.

THE HOUSE ON BAYOU ROAD

The House on Bayou Road. 2275 Bayou Rd.; (504) 945-0992/ (800) 882-2968 $$$-$$$$

A petite West Indies-style plantation (c. 1798) nestled on two acres of landscaped grounds in a picturesque historic neighborhood near Esplanade. Eight gorgeous rooms and suites (each with working fireplace); pool and Jacuzzi; and fabulous complimentary breakfasts, including a champagne mimosa brunch on weekends. Car and driver available for hire.

The Maison de Ville. 727 Toulouse St.; (504) 561-5858/(800) 634-1600 *(S) $$$-$$$$

THE MAISON DE VILLE

The hotel is concealed behind wrought iron gates and semi-tropical plants in an 18th-century French Quarter mansion. Each of its 14 rooms, two suites, and seven "Audubon Cottages" are furnished with 19th-century antiques. Rates include a continental breakfast and sherry, port, iced tea, and coffee on the patio in the evening. The outdoor pool is near the Audubon Cottages where Audubon lived in 1821 and Tennessee Williams lived while he was working on *A Streetcar Named Desire*. Parking is $15.00 a night.

Melrose Mansion Hotel. 937 Esplanade Ave., 70116; (504) 944-2255 $$$-$$$$

This luxury guest house is better on service and amenities than decor. The four suites (all with whirlpool baths) and four rooms are located in a mansion built in 1884 as a single-family residence. There's a large heated pool, stretch limo relay from the airport, and lavish Southern breakfasts, as well as an open bar and hors d'oeuvres in the evening.

THE SONIAT HOUSE

The Soniat House. 1133 Chartres St., 70116; (504) 522-0570/(800) 544-8808 $$$-$$$$
Two early 19th-century mansions containing 33 rooms (most with Jacuzzis) brim with a combination of effortless good taste, elegance, and comfort. The owners' care shows in every detail from their restoration of the Creole mansion to the crisp linen on the breakfast tray.

Local Color

B&B COURTYARDS

B&B Courtyards. 2425 Chartres St., 70117; (504) 945-9418/(800) 585-5731 $$

Located four blocks from the French Market in the historic Faubourg Marigny. Nestled behind an unassuming facade are five cozy antique-filled guest accommodations (all with private entrances), two lush courtyards, and a hot tub. The multi-national, multi-lingual owners offer a perfect balance of nuturing and privacy.

Casa de Marigny Creole Guest Cottages. 818 Frenchmen St., 70116; (504) 948-3875 $-$$-$$$-$$$$
Five cozy European-style cottages in separate 1830-1880 weekend houses, all nestled around a pool and Jacuzzi in a tropical garden. Just steps away from the jazz clubs and restaurants along Frenchmen.

THE JOSEPHINE

The Josephine. 1450 Josephine St., 70130 (one block from the Ponchartrain Hotel, near St. Charles Ave.); (504) 524-6361/(800) 779-6361 $-$$-$$$
At the fringe of the Garden District, near Jackson Ave., is an Italianate 1870s mansion with fluted Doric and Corinthian

columns. The rooms in the main house have 13-foot ceilings and are resplendent with their "Creole Baroque" decor. Room 1 at the front has a magnificent bed with ivory inlay.

The Lafitte Guest House. 1003 Bourbon St., 70116; (504) 581-2678/ (800) 331-7971 $$-$$$$
A four-story French Quarter home built in 1849, it became a guest house in the 1920s. Cole Porter celebrated his birthday here in the 1930s. The 14 rooms are furnished with Victorian antiques. Rates do not include parking. Reservations should be made at least six weeks in advance.

MCKENDRICK-BREAUX HOUSE

McKendrick-Breaux House. 1474 Magazine St.; (504) 586-1700 $$
Winner of the Mayor's "Bed & Breakfast of the Year" in 1996, this three-story Greek revival masonry townhouse was built in 1865 and lovingly restored by a young couple in the 1990s. The seven charmingly furnished guestrooms have fresh flowers, antiques, and state-of the-art plumbing. Complimentary continental breakfast. Special summer and special event rates.

Le Richelieu. 1234 Chartres St.; (504) 529-2492/ (800) 535-9653 $$
Eighty-six Victorian bedrooms in an elegant building in the back of the Quarter. Free parking.

LE RICHELIEU

Provincial Hotel. 1024 Chartres St., 70116; (504) 581-4995 $$-$$$$
This 107-room hotel is located in a series of French Quarter buildings that date from the 1800s. Parts of the complex served as a Royal Military Hospital, an icehouse, and a feedstore. With a large pool, seven patios, and a restaurant, it offers the convenience of a motel with the atmosphere of a madcap Creole bachelor's guesthouse. Excellent summer rates.

Velveteen Rabbit Ambiance

Bourgoyne Guest House. 839 Bourbon St., 70116 (In the French Quarter near the gay section); (504) 524-3621/ (504) 525-3983 $$-$$$
Located in an 1830s Creole house, this inn has been operated by a newspaper columnist since the early 1970s. There are three

studios and two suites, all with a mixture of antique and contemporary furnishings and all overlooking an ancient courtyard. Kitchen facilities and private baths in all rooms.

BOURGOYNE HOUSE

Columns Hotel. 3811 St. Charles Ave., 70115; (504) 899-9308/(800) 445-9308 $$-$$$
The large rooms are reminiscent of those romantic, funky hotels straight out of Tennessee Williams. The interior shots in the movie *Pretty Baby* were filmed here. The 19 guest rooms (nine with private baths) are

COLUMNS HOTEL

air-conditioned, and some bathrooms feature double bathtubs. Pleasant cocktail lounge. Continental breakfast and Sunday champagne brunch.

The Dusty Mansion. 2231 Gen. Pershing St., 70115; (504) 895-4576 $
Four cheerfully furnished bedrooms in a kids-friendly, laid-back, rambling family home in Uptown, six blocks from the streetcar. Off-street parking, sundeck, hot tub, and mimosas on Sundays.

Mentone Bed & Breakfast. 1437 Pauger St., 70116; (504) 943-3019. $$-$$$
A turn-of-the-century Victorian camelback located at the big toe of Bourbon St., just a block into the sedate Marigny section. Suites have private entrances, 14-foot ceilings, and luscious antiques and open onto a tropical garden. Complimentary champagne.

Olivier House. 828 Toulouse St., 70112; (504) 525-8456 $$-$$$-$$$$
Converted from an 1836 French Quarter mansion into a 42-room guest house in the 1970s. While the majority of the rooms are unpretentious, the hotel has forged a clientele of celebrity chefs, actors, and talent agents who favor the anonymity that this spot offers.

Parkview Guest House. 7004 St. Charles Ave., 70118; (504) 861-7564 $$-$$$
Built in 1884, this inn offers 15 rooms with private baths, seven with shared baths. Continental breakfast served daily. Rooms on the east side overlook the oak-lined park, have ceiling fans and brass beds; those without the view have nicer decor.

Festivals

Villa Convento. 616 Ursulines St., 70116; (504) 522-1793 $ - $$$
This four-story, 1848 Creole townhouse is located close to the old Ursuline Convent. The 25 rooms vary in price, and are furnished with reproductions of antiques. All rooms have private baths and phones.

Backpacker Specials

Loyola University. Write to Conference Coordinator, Office of Student Activities, P. O. Box 126, Loyola University, 70118, to make reservations, or call (504) 865-3737 *(S) $
Located Uptown, the school offers 300 dormitory spaces available to anyone from June 1 through August 1.

St. Charles Guest House. 1748 Prytania St., 70130; (504) 523-6556 *(S) $
Six backpacker rooms all share one bath, but there's a pool to cool off in. Near Felicity Street streetcar stop.

St. Vincent's. 1507 Magazine St.. Check in at 1415 Prytania St.; (504) 566-1515 $
This 19th-century brick orphanage has been converted into a guest house of 31 fresh, cheerfully appointed rooms with private baths and phones. A nice breakfast costs only a few dollars.

Tulane University. Office of Housing and Residence Life, Tulane University, 27 McAllister Dr., 70118; (504) 865-5724 *(S) $
Offers a great deal year-round for the public in two different facilities with suites and apartments under $50.00. Make reservations as early as possible.

YMCA Hotel. 920 St. Charles Ave., 70130; (504) 568-9622 $
Fifty institutional, spartan rooms. Each of the two floors has a female and male shower and bath facilities. Close to the streetcar; access to the Y pool and health club facilities. Try to book a month in advance.

■ FESTIVALS

For further information about individual festivals, write the Louisiana Office of Tourism, P.O. Box 94291, Baton Rouge, LA 70804-9291; (504) 342-8119. For general information packets on the state, call (800) 33-GUMBO (334-8626).

JANUARY

Battle of New Orleans Celebration. *Weekend closest to January 8* Chalmette Battlefield, St. Bernard.

FEBRUARY

Lundi Gras. Spanish Plaza by the Riverwalk, New Orleans; (504) 522-1555.

Mardi Gras. *Tuesday before lent, Mid-February to early March*
1998   February 24
1999   February 16
2000   March 7
2001   February 27

MARCH

Black Heritage Festival. *Second weekend in March* Audubon Zoo, the Riverwalk, and the Louisiana State Museum, New Orleans; (504) 827-5771.

St. Patrick's Day Parades. *On or around March 17* French Quarter, Irish Channel, Veteran's Blvd., New Orleans; (504) 525-5169.

Tennessee Williams Literary Festival. *Mid-March* Various locations, New Orleans; (504) 286-6680.

St. Joseph's Day Festivities. *On or around March 19* Piazza D'Italia, New Orleans; (504) 522-7294.

Crescent City Classic. *Mid-March to late April* New Orleans; (504) 861-8686. 10k run.

Earth Fest. *Third weekend* Audubon Zoo, New Orleans; (504) 861-2537.

Oak Alley Plantation Annual Arts & Crafts Festival. *Late March* Oak Alley Plantation, Vacherie.

Spring Fiesta. *Begins Friday night after Easter, and continues for five days* French Quarter, New Orleans; (504) 581-1367.

Piney Woods Opry. *Fourth Saturdays of March, April, and May* Abita Springs Town Hall, Abita Springs.

APRIL

Freeport-McMoran Golf Classic. *First weekend* English Turn Country Club, New Orleans; (504) 831-4653.

French Quarter Festival. *Second weekend* French Quarter, New Orleans; (504) 522-5730.

New Orleans Jazz & Heritage Festival. *Last weekend in April to first weekend in May* Fairgrounds Racetrack, New Orleans; (504) 522-4786.

MAY

Art in Bloom. *Early to mid-May* New Orleans Museum of Art, New Orleans.

Zoo-to-Do. *First Friday in May* Audubon Zoo New Orleans; (504) 565-3020. The largest single-night fundraiser in the country. Gorgeous dance under the stars among the animals at the zoo.

Greek Festival. *Weekend before Memorial Day weekend* Hellenic Cultural Center, New Orleans; (504) 282-0259.

JUNE

Great French Market Tomato Festival. *Usually the first weekend* Dutch Alley and Farmer's Market, New Orleans; (504) 522-2621.

Reggae Riddums Festival. *Second weekend* Marconi Meadows, City Park, New Orleans; (504) 367-1313/(800) 367-1317.

JULY

Go Fourth on the River. *Fourth of July* Along the riverfront, New Orleans; (504) 528-9994.

Bastille Day. *Weekend before July 15* Activities and concerts around the city.

Festivals

AUGUST

Labour Day Classic. *August 30* One mile, 5 K; (504) 482-6682.

SEPTEMBER

Honduran Independence Day Festival. *Second weekend* French Market, New Orleans.

Louisiana Swamp Festival. *Two weekends, late September and early October* Audubon Zoo and Woldenberg Riverfront Park, New Orleans; (504) 861-2537. Cajun food, music, and crafts.

OCTOBER

Oktoberfest. *All month* Deutsches Haus, 200 Galvez St., New Orleans; (504) 522-8014.

New Orleans Film & Video Festival. *Early to mid-October* Canal Place Landmark Theatre, New Orleans.

Louisiana Heritage Festival. *Last weekend* Rivertown, Kenner.

Halloween in New Orleans. *October 31* Activities include the Moonlight Witches Run, Boo-at-the-Zoo for kids; haunted houses around town; and Anne Rice's Coven Party. For information call the Visitor's Bureau at (800) 672-6124.

NOVEMBER

Settlers Day, Louisiana Nature & Science Center. *Mid-November* New Orleans.

Thanksgiving Day Race. *Thanksgiving* New Orleans. Five miles.

Bayou Classic. *Last weekend* Louisiana Superdome, New Orleans; (504) 523-5652. Annual football game between Grambling and Southern.

Celebration in the Oaks. *End of the month through early January* City Park, New Orleans; (504) 482-4888. Gorgeous Christmas lights in the park. Take a carriage tour.

DECEMBER

New Orleans Christmas. *All month* French Quarter, New Orleans; 522-5730. Candlelight caroling, madrigal dinners, historic homes dressed for Christmas.

Festival of Bonfires. *Early to mid-December* Luther Gramercy.

Countdown (to New Year's). *New Year's Eve* Jackson Square, New Orleans; (504) 566-5055.

■ GARDENS, MUSEUMS, AND ZOOS

K = *Museums that kids might enjoy*

American Aquatic Gardens. 621 Elysian Fields; (504) 944-0410
A nursery specializing in water plants such as water lilies and native grasses.

Aquarium of the Americas. One Canal St. at Woldenberg Park; (504) 861-3033 **K**
More than 7,000 different creatures swim in 60 separate displays. A 16-acre park surrounds the aquarium. The facility includes a restaurant and IMAX theatre.

Archbishop Antoine Blanc Memorial. 1100 Chartres St.; (504) 529-3040
A six-edifice museum complex, including the Old Ursuline Convent, the oldest building in the Mississippi Valley.

Arnaud's Germaine Wells Mardi Gras Museum. 813 Bienville; (504) 523-5433 **K**
Open daily. Free.

Audubon Zoological Gardens. 6500 Magazine St.; (504) 861-2537
The Leon Heymann Conservatory has both native and exotic species of plants.

Beauregard-Keyes House. 1113 Chartres St.; (504) 523-7257
Parterre and herb garden in 1830s style.

Blaine Kern's Mardi Gras World. 233 Newton; (504) 361-7821 **K**
Ride on the ferry to the historic district of Old Algiers and walk through warehouses where parade floats are made.

City Park. End of Esplanade Ave.; (504) 482-4888
A 1500-acre, oak-lined park full of traditional, native plant life. Free.

Confederate Museum. 929 Camp St.; (504) 523-4522
Louisiana's oldest museum, containing Civil War memorabilia, including uniforms, weapons, flags, and personal effects of Southern leaders.

Contemporary Arts Center. 900 Camp St.; (504) 523-1216
Local visual and performing arts.

Gallier House Museum. 1118-32 Royal St.; (504) 525-5661
Courtyard garden kept in its 1857 style.

Global Wildlife Center. 26389 LA Hwy 40, Folsom, LA; (504) 624-WILD **K**
A non-profit conservation facility home to over 900 free-ranging animals and birds from around the world. Covered wagons lead visitors over 900 acres. Accommodations available at the Safari Lodge.

Hermann-Grima House and Courtyard. 820 St. Louis St.; (504) 525-5661
Vieux Carré garden in its 1860 style.

Historic New Orleans Collection. 533 Royal St.; (504) 598-7100
A tour through the Williams Residence, a 19th-century townhouse, and the Louisiana Historic Museum and Research Center in the 1792 Merieult house provide a vivid trip into New Orleans's past.

Gardens, Museums, and Zoos

Jean Lafitte National Historic Park. Barataria Unit; (504) 589-2330
Nature trails and guided canoe trips, especially nice in the early spring when the native iris are in bloom.

Kleibert's Turtle and Alligator Farm. 1264 W. Yellow Water Rd. (near Hammond); (504) 345-3617 **K**
Veritably crawling with awesome specimens from March to November.

Longue Vue House and Gardens. 7 Bamboo Rd.; (504) 488-5488
Extensive, well-maintained formal gardens.

Louisiana Children's Museum. 420 Julia St., 2nd Floor; (504) 523-1357 **K**
From a do-it-yourself newsroom to a child-sized supermarket, the museum is geared towards stimulation for the very young. All exhibits are interactive.

Louisiana Nature and Science Center. 11000 Lake Forest Blvd. at Read Blvd. (Eastern New Orleans); (504) 246-5672 **K**
The science resource center offers a bird-feeding window, hummingbird and butterfly gardens, forest and wetland trails. Planetarium and laser show, too.

Louisiana State Museum. Jackson Square in French Quarter; (504) 568-6968
The largest museum in Louisiana, and one of the nation's finest historical museums.

Louisiana State Railroad Museum. 3rd St. and Huey P. Long Ave. (Gretna); (504) 283-8091 **K**
The historic Gretna Railroad Station houses a collection of steam engines and a research library.

Louisiana Toy Train Museum. 519 Williams Blvd. (Kenner); (504) 468-7223 **K**
Seventh heaven for train aficionados, with seven working miniature train layouts, a toy carousel, and an 1890s toy train: in all, 17,000 pieces, many of them one of a kind.

Louisiana Wildlife and Fisheries Museum and Aquarium. 303 Williams Blvd. (Kenner); (504) 468-7232 **K**
Operated by the Louisiana Nature and Science Center, the museum features a 15,000-gallon aquarium stocked with native species and many hands-on exhibits.

Mardi Gras Collection. Old U.S. Mint, 400 Esplanade Ave., (504) 568-6968
Costumes, photographs, antique invitations, favors, pins. The crown and scepter collection rivals the Tower of London's.

Mardi Gras Museum. 421 Williams Blvd., Kenner; (504) 468-4037 **K**
Carnival sights and sounds, films, costumes, and photographs.

Musee Conti Wax Museum of Louisiana Legends. 917 Conti St.; (504) 525-2605 **K**
Features displays of costumes from the Knights of Sparta ball, to a miniature recreation of the 400 block of Royal during an early parade.

National D-Day Museum. Howard and Magazine St.; (504) 527-6012
An extensive collection highlighting the major invasions of all campaigns of World War II. 50,000 sq. ft of exhibition space indoors and out, with planes, tanks, and photographs; also oral histories, theatre, films.

New Orleans Botanical Garden. Victory Ave., City Park; (504) 483-9386.
Lovely rose garden and regular series of gardening lectures.

New Orleans Historic Voodoo Museum. 724 Dumaine St.; (504) 523-7685
Tourists can glimpse voodoo as it is practiced in New Orleans. The museum includes a working altar and offers ritual tours and voodoo walking tours of the French Quarter.

New Orleans Museum of Art. 1 Collins Diboll Circle; (504) 488-2631
Of particular note is the Mathilda Geddings Gray Foundation Fabergé Collection as well as one of the finest photography collections in the South.

New Orleans Pharmacy Museum. 514 Chartres St.; (504) 565-8027
The building that houses this museum was built in 1823 for America's first licensed pharmacist.

Ogden Museum of Southern Art. 615 Howard Ave.; (504) 539-9600
A 66,000 sq. ft. collection dedicated to the evolution of the visual arts in the South. Opening in 1999.

Zemurray Gardens. Loranger, LA (near Hammond); (504) 878-6731
Numerous paths lined with a zydeco of Snow White and Peach Blow azaleas and marble statues surround a 20-acre lake. Six-week season only, March to April.

■ ART GALLERIES

■ FRENCH QUARTER

A Gallery for Fine Photography. 322 Royal St.; (504) 568-1313. Rare prints and books for sale by noted photographers.

Gallery I/O. 829 Royal St.; (504) 523-5041.

Le Boeuf Gras. 630 Chartres St.; (504) 523-BULL. Top Mardi Gras artisans.

Martin Laborde Gallery. 631 Royal St. (504) 587-7111. Flights of fantasy.

Peligro! Folk Art. 305 Decatur St.; (504) 581-1706. Self-taught Southern artists.

Photoworks. 839 Chartres St.; (504) 593-9090. Photographs by top local artist Louis Sahuc.

Rhino Contemporary Craft Co. Canal Place Shopping Ctr.; (504) 523-7945. Work by over 80 Louisiana crafts artists.

Shaun Wilkerson Furniture Design. 631 Royal St.; (504) 522-0034. Award-winning furniture.

■ MAGAZINE STREET

Academy Gallery. 5256 Magazine St.; (504) 899-8111. Realist paintings and drawings.

Angele Parlange Design. 5419 Magazine St.; (504) 897-6511. Handblown glass chandeliers, silk and taffeta shades.

Art Galleries

Art of the Americas/ Merrill B. Domas. 3634 Magazine St.; (504) 891-0103. Regional Native American weavings, pottery, and works on paper.

Cole Pratt. 3800 Magazine St.; (504) 891-6789. A spicy gumbo of regional works.

Davis Gallery. 3964 Magazine St. (504) 897-0780. Internationally known dealers in African art.

Gallery I/O. 3105 Magazine St.; (504) 899-9900. Fabulous lighting, jewelry, and decorative accessories.

Hernan Caro Gallery. 1532 Magazine St.; (504) 529-1843. Metal lamps, sconces, and furniture combined with decorative pieces.

Mario Villa Gallery. 3908 Magazine St.; (504) 895-8731. International artists as well as decorative-arts creations by local super-star designer.

■ WAREHOUSE DISTRICT

Ariodante. 535 Julia St.; (504) 524-3233. Fine contemporary crafts, especially glass.

Arthur Roger Gallery. 432 Julia St.; (504) 522-1999. Large space with works by noted local artists from Kohlmayer to Gordy.

Chris Maier. 329 Julia St.; (504) 586-9079. Custom-crafted cabinetry.

DOCS. 709 Camp St.; (504) 524-3936. Work by up-and-coming local artists.

Gallerie Simone Stern. 518 Julia St. (504) 529-1118. National and local modern artists.

Gallery of Southern Photographers. 608 Julia St.; (504) 529-9811

Heriard-Cimino Gallery. 440 Julia St.; (504) 525-7300. A collection of the quirky and the exquisite.

Marguerite Oestricher Fine Arts. 626 Julia St.; (504) 581-9253. A cutting edge gallery.

Mary Viola Walker. 834 Julia St. (504) 523-0562. Wood art furniture.

Still-Zinsel. 328 Julia St. (504) 588-9999. Photography to sculpture.

Wyndy Morehead. 603 Julia St.; (504) 568-9754. Prints, ceramics, and paintings.

Ya/Ya Gallery. 628 Baronne; (504) 529-3306. Internationally-known art by an innovative youth cooperative.

■ ANTIQUES

New Orleans has been a shopping mecca ever since the days when pirate Jean Lafitte and his brothers sold contraband out of a shop in the French Quarter. These days antique shops have been clustered in two major areas—the Chartres/Royal Street area of the French Quarter and Magazine Street in the Garden District/ Uptown Area. The Royal Street Guild, the Chartres Street Association, and the Magazine Merchants Association have free brochures which list shops, addresses, and hours and may be obtained from stores on the street. One of the most efficient means of scouring the bargains is to work with Macon Riddle and her asociates at **Let's Go Antiquing,** (504) 899-3027. They will custom design a safari for any group from 1 to 25 persons.

■ FRENCH QUARTER

Animal Art Antiques. 617 Chartres St.; (504) 529-4407. Natural prints and objects.

Antique Book Gallery. 811 Royal St.; (504) 524-6918. Rare books.

Arcadian Books and Art Prints. 714 Orleans Ave.; (504) 523-4138. Rare books.

Beckham's Book Shop. 228 Decatur St.; (504) 522-9875. Rare books and recordings.

Bevolo Gas and Electric Lights. 521 Conti; (504) 522-9485. Custom lighting.

Bienville Gallery. 629 Chartres St.; (504) 529-2300. Natural prints and objects.

Blackamoor. 324 Chartres St.; (504) 523-7786. Art pottery, porcelain, ceramics.

Centuries Old Maps & Prints. 517 St. Louis St.; (504) 568-9491. Rare books.

Crescent City Books. 204 Chartres. (504) 524-4997. Rare books.

Dauphine Street Books. 410 Dauphine St.; (504) 529-2333. Rare books and recordings.

Faulkner House Books 624 Pirate's Alley; (504) 524-2940. Rare books.

French Antique Shop Inc. 225 Royal St.; (504) 524-9861. French furniture; chandeliers and sconces.

Harper's Antiques. 610 Toulouse St.; (504) 592-1996. Fine jewelry.

J. Herman Son Galleries. 333 Royal St.; (504) 525-6326. Fine jewelry.

Keil's. 325 Royal St.; (504) 522-4552. Continental furniture.

Librairie Book Shop 823 Chartres St.; (504) 525-4837. Rare books.

Louisiana Music Factory. 210 Decatur St./ 400 Esplanade; (504) 586-1094/ 524-5507. Vintage recordings.

Lucullus. 610 Chartres St.; (504) 528-9620. Culinary antiques.

Antiques

MS Rau, Inc. 630 Royal St.; (504) 523-5660. Art glass and pottery.

Peter Patout. 920 Royal St.; (504) 522-0582. Louisiana and American furniture.

Record Ron's Stuff. 239 Chartres. St.; (504) 522-2239. Vintage recordings.

Rock 'N' Roll Records and Collectibles. 1214 Decatur St.; (504) 561-5683.

Royal Antiques, Ltd. 307-309 Royal St.; (504) 524-7033/7035. Continental furniture.

Starling Books and Crafts. 1022 Royal St. (504) 595-6777. Rare books.

Trashy Diva. 304 Decatur St.; (504) 581-4555. Vintage clothing.

Waldhorn Co., Inc. 343 Royal St.; (504) 581-6379. Fine jewelry; porcelain.

Whisnant. 222 Chartres St.; (504) 524-9766. Fine antique and ethnic jewelry; tribal and Oriental objects.

■ MAGAZINE STREET

As You Like It. 3025 Magazine St.; (504) 897-6915. Antique silver.

Bep's. 2051 Magazine St.; (504) 525-7726. Porcelain, ceramics; vintage recordings.

Blackamoor. 3433 Magazine St.; (504) 897-2711. Porcelain and ceramics.

Bragg Antiques. 3901 Magazine St.; (504) 895-7375. Textiles and pottery.

Bremermann Designs. 3943 Magazine St.; (504) 891-7763. French and Italian decorative objects.

Bush Antiques. 2109-11 Magazine St.; (504) 581-3518. Boudoir accessories, linens, lace.

Didier Inc. 3439 Magazine St.; (504) 899-7749. Early 19th-century American antiques; ornithological print

French Collectibles. 3420 Magazine St.; (504) 897-9020. French antiques.

George Herget Books. 3109 Magazine St.; (504) 891-5595. Rare books.

Jacqueline Vance. 3944 Magazine St.; (504) 891-3304. Rugs.

Jim Smiley. 2001 Magazine St.; (504) 528-9449. Textiles and vintage clothing.

Jon Antiques. 4605 Magazine St.; (504) 899-4482. Porcelain and ceramics

Mac Maison, Ltd. 3963 Magazine St.; (504) 891-2863. French and Italian decorative objects.

Mariposa Vintage Clothing. 2038 Magazine St.; (504) 523-3037.

Neal Auction Company. 4038 Magazine St.; (504) 899-5329.

New Orleans Auction Galleries Inc. 801 Magazine St.; (504) 566-1849.

Retroactive. 5418 Magazine St.; no phone. Vintage clothing.

Sixpence. 4904 Magazine St.; (504) 895-1267. English and French antiques.

Talebloo. 4130 Magazine St.; (504) 899-8114. Rugs.

Wirthmore. 3900 Magazine St.; (540) 899-8811 and 5723 Magazine St. 897-9727. French and Italian furniture and decorative objects.

■ PLANTATIONS AND FINE COUNTRY HOMES

Each neighborhood in New Orleans has its own grand scale exhibitions of architectural whimsy. One of the most unique is the pair of identical "**Steamboat Houses**" on Egania Street (in the vicinity of the Chalmette Battlefield) which sit beside the levee. They were erected in 1905 by Captain Milton Doullut, a steamboat captain, who brought his love of boats with him to dry land.

It is outside of the city that men of means dotted the landscape with their full-blown, mini-Parthenons among the bull frogs. It is a sad fact that the economy along the riverfront has changed greatly over the past 50 years. Many of the plantation houses once were part of vast plantations and now sit on postage-stamp-sized plots on commercially zoned land.

The fortunes that were made in rural Louisiana from indigo and sugar gave rise to a lifestyle bent on great monuments. By the 1840s vast plantations staffed by communities of slave labor appeared. The benefits reaped by the planters were used to build architectural monuments. Their homes were palaces inspired by classical style, sometimes ornamented with Gothic and Italianate flourishes.

Along the backroads, one sees once-great plantation houses in virtual ruins. Ashland/Belle Helène, a mansion surrounded by 30-foot-tall columns, is still fighting. The home was thought to have been designed by James Gallier, Sr. and completed in 1841 near a cypress swamp five miles north of Darrow.

To understand the working life of the plantations, it is necessary to visit the **Rural Life Museum** where the slave cabins, Cajun cottages, and sharecroppers houses have been saved from the wrecker's ball. Call (504) 765-2437.

Asphodel Village & Plantation. (504) 654-6868

Built in 1820 as a three-story Doric-columned Greek Revival residence that served as the seat of a plantation with more than 400 slaves. It was the setting for the Paul Newman and Joanne Woodward movie, *The Long Hot Summer.* It is located in Jackson, Louisiana, near Baton Rouge and is now operated as an inn, restaurant, and gift shop.

Destrehan Plantation. (504) 764-9315

Built in 1787, it is the oldest plantation home still intact in the lower Mississippi Valley. Destrehan, a sprawling West Indies mansion with eight mammoth columns across its front, is about half an hour from downtown New Orleans.

Plantations and Fine Country Homes

Plantations and Fine Country Homes

HOUMAS HOUSE

Houmas House Plantation & Gardens.
(504) 473-7841
Sitting cool and dignified near Burnside, this home was built in 1840 by the daughter of General Wade Hampton of Revolutionary War fame, and later served as the setting of *Hush, Hush, Sweet Charlotte* with Bette Davis and Olivia DeHavilland.

Laura Plantation. (504) 265-7690
Built in 1805, it is best known as the home of Br'er Rabbit. Since 1993 the Marmillion family has been painstakingly rescuing the buildings from collapse.

Madewood Plantation. (800) 375-7151
Set apart from the other River Road plantations sits a 21-room palatial Greek Revival plantation house designed by Henry Howard and constructed between 1840 and 1848. It is also operated as a bed-and-breakfast.

Magnolia Mound. (504) 343-4955
A former indigo plantation built in the 1790s in Baton Rouge. The vegetable garden and kitchen are also worth a visit.

MAGNOLIA MOUND

Myrtles Plantation. (504) 635-6277
Built in 1796, the mansion is billed as "America's Most Haunted House" and is located in St. Francisville.

Nottoway Plantation. (504) 545-2730
This "White Castle" was an Italianate/Greek Revival palace designed by Henry Howard. Built in 1859 with 64 rooms and 53,000 square feet, it holds the distinction of being the largest antebellum plantation house in the South. It serves both meals and functions as a bed-and-breakfast.

Oak Alley Plantation. (504) 265-2151
Seven and a half miles upriver from the Veteran's Memorial Bridge in Gramercy. Built in 1839 and named for the alley of 28 evenly spaced monumental live oak trees that are thought to have pre-dated the home by a hundred years, this Greek Revival home is a bit more romantic from a distance than it is up close. It was here that

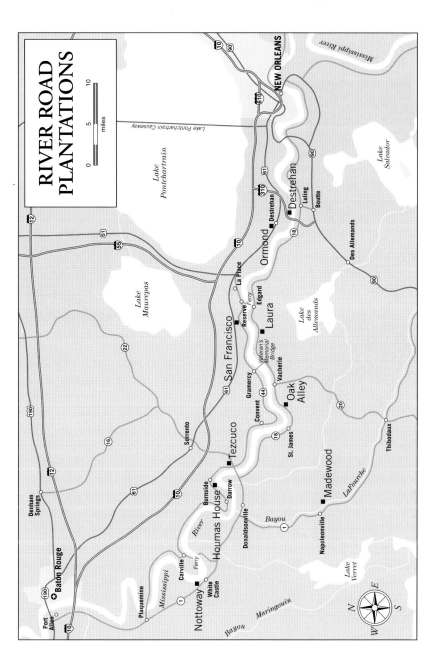

Plantations and Fine Country Homes

the first scientific cultivation of pecans in Louisiana took place. A restaurant and accommodations are located on the grounds.

OAK ALLEY

Ormond Plantation. (504) 764-8544/ (504) 764-0691

Louisiana Colonial style home built before 1790.

Parlange Plantation. A classic two-story raised cottage near New Rhodes, this home has been in the same family since it was constructed in 1750.

Rosedown Plantation. (504) 635-3332

One of the loveliest homes in St. Francisville. This 16-room antebellum mansion was built in 1835 and is surrounded by 200-year-old oaks and 28 acres of formal gardens modeled after those at Versailles.

St. Francisville. Contact the West Feliciana Historical Society at 364 Ferdinand Street by writing Box 338, St. Francisville, 70775, or call (504) 635-6330

One of the oldest and most picturesque towns in the state. Named after St. Francis of Assisi, the community was established in 1785 on land granted to the Capuchine

friars by the Spanish Crown. Other sites of interest include Grace Episcopal Church, Barrow House, Oakley, Catalpa Plantation, Afton Villa Gardens, The Cottage, and Greenwood Plantation. For further information. Attending the "Audubon Pilgrimage" the third week in March or "Christmas in the Country" in December are nice ways to capture some of the essence of the town.

SAN FRANCISCO PLANTATION

San Francisco Plantation. (504) 535-2341. This 1856 home's original name *Sans Frusquin* is French slang for "without a penny." The exuberantly painted "Steamboat Gothic" mansion was commissioned by a man who thought the Greek Revival mansions of his friends to be dull. A belvedere similar to a ship's crow's nest caps the third-floor ballroom.

Tezcuco Plantation. (504) 562-3929

The raised cottage, fronted by six square columns joined by wrought-iron railings, was completed in 1855. It is seven miles (10 km) above the Sunshine Bridge and has guest cottages and an antique shop.

■ TOURS

There are literally dozens of tours advertised in the tourist literature. To determine the best we asked various concierge and museum operators as well as the Office of Tourism for their recommendations. Because of new zoning regulations in the historic neighborhoods, the large buses cannot wind through many of the streets in the older neighborhoods. For this reason, the smaller companies' minivans are best for viewing architecture.

■ CITY TOURS

Gray Line of New Orleans. (504) 587-0709/(800) 535-7786
This tour service of New Orleans and surrounding area by coach is thorough and slightly institutional. Eight tours daily depart from behind Jax Brewery.

Helicopters Su West Airways Inc. (504) 242-4883
Pilot's eye view of the city; trips from one-half to two hours from the downtown heliport by the Superdome or the lakefront.

Limousine Livery. (504) 561-8777/(800) 326-1345
Many of the drivers are licensed tour guides and they charge no more for the service. When price is no object, the family-operated company can structure a half or full day of activities to the needs of the client. Priced by the hour, 3-hour minimum. Some cars accommodate 10 people.

Tours by Inez. (504) 486-1123
Two friendly, fun, and informative tours daily, departing from 339 Chartres, the courtyard of the Hotel de la Poste. Tours of houses and gardens on request. There is an 8-person minimum, 40 person maximum. Seven languages spoken. Tours must be booked ahead.

Tours by Isabelle. (504) 391-3544
The Combo Tour, a personalized four-hour city tour, offers an overview of all neighborhoods. Vans visit the French Quarter, the Garden District, St. Louis III cemetery, and the house and garden at Longue Vue. Both bi-lingual and disabled friendly, this is one of the best buys going for the discerning traveler.

Roots of New Orleans: A Heritage City Tour. (504) 596-6889/(888) 337-6687
Roots offers a variety of regularly scheduled and custom-designed routs of the city's plethora of fascinating African-American sites. The Sunday morning **Roots N' the Church** combines a gospel mass, brunch, and city tour; **Roots N' the Nite,** includes dinner and visits to several jazz and blues clubs; and **Roots of New Orleans City Tour** is an insightful four-hour mini-bus tour.

Tours

■ FRENCH QUARTER

Friends of the Cabildo. (504) 523-3939
The informative two-hour walking tours begin at the Friends of the Cabildo Store at 523 St. Ann on Jackson Square, and generally take place twice a day. No reservations necessary.

Jean Lafitte National Historic Park and Preserve. French Quarter Unit, 916 N. Peters St., 70116; (504) 589-2636/3840
Three 90-minute tours a day, varying depending on the time of day. First come, first serve.

Tours by Inez. (504) 486-1123
Inez and her 26 guides offer insiders' tips on everything from happy hours to cheap music. Inez gives an overview, heading visitors in the direction of their interest, nipping into private courtyards for a history lesson. Around two hours. By reservation only.

■ GARDEN DISTRICT

Hidden Treasures Tours. 1915 Chestnut; (504) 529-4507
Specially designed walking or motor tours, seven days a week. The only motor tour with a visit to a private mansion including interior walking tour. Reservations required.

Jean Lafitte National Historic Park and Preserve. Garden District Tour, 916 N. Peters St., 70116; (504) 589-2636
"Faubourg Promenade" is a one-mile, hour-and-a-half, park ranger–guided stroll through the historic area each afternoon. Reservations can be made by phone or letter up to three months in advance. The meeting place for those with reservations is the corner of First and St. Charles Ave. Free.

■ SELF-GUIDED TOURS

New Orleans Self-Guided Walking and Driving Tours. (504) 566-5068
A 1996 publication of the Greater New Orleans Tourist & Convention Commission. Free.

René Beaujolais's French Quarter Extraordinary Guide
An inexpensive, jumbo brochure for sale in many of the shops in the French Quarter, this illustrated do-it-yourself walking tour offers an overview of the important sites of the Quarter and contains an easy-to-follow double-page color map.

Your Sound Promenade. 8018 Trout Rd., 70126; (504) 243-1098
Two excellent 90-minute oral-history cassettes play like marvelous old radio. The author/historian grew up in the French Quarter in the 1930s and his reminiscences include his boyhood talks with Civil War veterans who lived in the Quarter. The tapes are filled with legends and the sounds of the city.

■ CEMETERY TOURS

Hidden Treasures. (504) 529-4507. See "Cities of the Dead," p. 136 for details.

Lakelawn Metairie Cemetery Tours. (504) 486-6331
Cassette and map for walking tour are available at the funeral home. Free. See "Cities of the Dead," p. 136 for details.

Save Our Cemeteries. (504) 525-3337
Reservations are a must. See "Cities of the Dead," p. 136 for details.

Tours by Inez. (504) 486-1123
Tours of the St. Louis and Lafayette cemeteries by reservation.

■ RIVER TOURS

John James Audubon Riverboat Zoo Cruise. Foot of Canal St.; (504) 586-8777/(800) 233-BOAT (2628)
This tiny paddlewheeler chugs back and forth between the Aquarium at Canal St. and the zoo. A fantastic way to see the river.

New Orleans Paddlewheel, Inc. *Creole Queen/Cajun Queen.* (504) 529-4567/(800) 445-4109
Live jazz buffet cruises on the Mississippi River on replicas of 19th-century paddlewheelers. Day cruises to the Chalmette Battlefield. Depart from the Aquarium of the Americas Dock and Canal St. Dock.

Steamboat Natchez. Behind Jax Brewery; (504) 586-8777/(800) 233-BOAT (2628)
Narrated bayou and harbor cruises; day jazz cruises; and dance and dinner cruises. Fridays and Saturdays only, Thanksgiving through Mardi Gras.

■ PLANTATION TOURS

Gray Line. (504) 587-0861
Eight- or four-hour guided coach tours along the river road.

Tours by Isabelle. (504) 391-3544
A personalized eight-hour trip through three antebellum mansions with lunch at Madewood in the formal dining room.

■ MILITARY SITE TOURS

Fort Pike State Commemorative Area. (504) 662-5703
Tour of the historic museum and the fort built after the War of 1812 to defend New Orleans waterways.

Jean Lafitte National Historic Park. Chalmette Unit. (504) 589-4428/4573
The site of the 1815 Battle of New Orleans. There is a 30-minute movie shown on request and four talks daily on the battlefield. Free.

Tours by Inez. (504) 486-1123
By request to the Steamboat House, Jackson Barracks, and battlefields. A half day.

■ SPECIAL INTEREST

Accent Companions for Kids/Accent on Children's Arrangements. (504) 524-1227
Far more than babysitting, these tours allow children (ages 6 to 18) to see sites and learn history and culture with specially trained adult companions. Also offer innovative events and parties for kids.

Anne Rice's Very Own New Orleans Tours. (504) 899-6450
Walking and motor tours highlighting Ms. Rice's own properties and the New Orleans sights that influenced her writing.

Architectural Tours. 604 Julia St.; (504) 581-7032
The Preservation Resource Center can arrange an in-depth tour of the historic neighborhoods with an emphasis on architecture. Forty-eight hours notice required.

Tours

Hidden Treasures of Esplanade Ridge.
(504) 529-7172
Specially designed tours for groups no larger than 12. Includes a visit to the Degas house and City Park.

Jean Lafitte National Historic Park and Preserve. Islenos Unit, 1357 Bayou Rd., St. Bernard; (504) 682-0862
The Islenos Unit is a museum dedicated to the Islenos people of St. Bernard Parish, whose ancestors settled in Louisiana during Spanish Colonial rule. Free.

Let's Go Antiquing. (504) 899-3027
Macon Riddle and her associates, antique aficionados one and all, offer half- and full-day "hunting" expeditions designed for the needs of the specific client.

Litera-Tour! 6123 Loyola St.; (504) 861-8158
A highly informative two-hour French Quarter walking tour through the city's literary history with author Carolyn Kolb.

Louisiana Superdome. Sugar Bowl Dr.; (504) 587-3885
Daily tours will thrill sports fans.

Take a Hike. (504) 861-7187
Take a hike or a jog through City Park, the Chalmette Battlefield, or some of the River Road plantations with a personal trainer.

■ **B I L I N G U A L   T O U R S**
Tours by Inez. (504) 486-1123
Chinese, French, German, Italian, Japanese, Russian, and Spanish.

Tours by Isabelle. (504) 391-3544
French and Spanish, no extra charge. All other languages, including Chinese, Dutch, German, Italian, Japanese, and Swedish, are a few dollars extra per person.

■ **S P E C I A L   E V E N T S**
Historic Homes Christmas Tours. Preservation Resource Center, (504) 581-7032
Holiday tours to seven or eight private historic homes over the first weekend in December.

March Shotgun House Month. (504) 581-7032
The Preservation Resource Center sponsors tours of several private homes in this style.

Spring Fiesta. (504) 581-1367/945-2744
In early to late April, this group sponsors tours of private homes in the French Quarter and several other historic districts.

■ **S W A M P / B A Y O U   T O U R S**
Cypress Swamp and Bayou Segnette Swamp Tours. (504) 561-8244/ (800) 633-0503
A picturesque swamp tour which focuses on the lives of the Indians, Creoles, and Americans.

Honey Island Swamp Tours. (504) 641-1769
The 250-square-mile (650-square-km) wetland area on the Pearl River is explored with ecologist Dr. Paul Wagner and native guides.

Lil Cajun Swamp Tour. (504) 689-3213/ (800) 725-3213
Two hours of wildlife and swamp offered by a proud Cajun and his pet alligator, Julie, on a 49-passenger boat.

Jean Lafitte National Historic Park.
Barataria Unit; (504) 589-2330
Nature trails and guided canoe trips, especially nice in the early spring when the native iris are in bloom.

Southern Seaplane. (504) 394-5633
Air tour of the marsh environs and the city.

Tours by Isabelle. (504) 391-3344
Cajun alligator hunters give tours in isolated cypress swamps. Or take the 8-hour swamp/plantation package tour, which includes lunch and a tour of Oak Alley Plantation.

■ RADIO STATIONS

The local airwaves of late have become rather rife with surprises as programmers, on-air personalities, formats, and owners remain in a constant state of flux.

WRBH, 88.3 FM Books and newspapers read for the print-impaired, including wonderful bedtime stories for kids and late-night erotica for grown-ups. (504) 899-1144.

WWNO, 89.9 FM University of New Orleans' broadcasting, classical music, jazz, and National Public Radio (NPR). (504) 286-7000.

WWOZ, 90.7 FM is owned by the New Orleans Jazz & Heritage Foundation and is staffed with volunteer music aficionados.

The station is alive 24 hours a day with the sounds of traditional jazz, gospel, country, and R&B as well as a variety of programs on Caribbean, African, bluegrass, and Irish music. Call (504) 568-1238 or visit their Web site: www.nojazzfest.com.

WNOE, 101.1 FM Rip-roaring country format aimed at the urban fans of Reba and Travis. (504) 529-1212.

BIG EZ 102.9 FM Classic soul hits from the '60s and '70s. (504) 593-2223.

■ VISITOR INFORMATION

Events Information. (504) 566-5055
Travelers Aid Society. (504) 525-8726
Weather Recording. (504) 828-4000
Chamber of Commerce/New Orleans and the River Region. 301 Camp St., New Orleans 70130; (504) 527-6900.
Greater New Orleans Tourist & Convention Commission. Superdome, 1520 Sugar Bowl Dr., N.O. 70112; (504) 566-5011.

Jefferson Parish Information Center. 300 Veterans Blvd., Kenner 70062; (504) 468-7527.
Kenner Office of Tourism. 2100 Third St., Unit 10, Kenner 70062; (504) 468-7527.
Louisiana State Office of Tourism. (504) 568-5661/(800) 33-GUMBO (334-8626).

Visitor Information

RECOMMENDED READING

■ FICTION

Bosworth, Sheila. *Almost Innocent.* New York: Simon & Schuster, 1984. The dark side of a proper Catholic girls' school upbringing.

Brite, Poppy Z. *Lost Souls.* New York: Bantam, 1993. *Drawing Blood.* New York: Delacorte, 1993. Hardcore local generation X color with visceral horror.

Brown, John Gregory. *Decorations in a Ruined Cemetery.* New York: Avon, 1994. A lyrical expression of a family of mixed blood confronting its secrets.

Brown, Sandra. *Fat Tuesday.* New York: Warner Books, 1997. A *NY Times* best-selling pot boiling.

Burke, James Lee. *Black Cherry Blues.* New York: Avon, 1989. Winner of the Edgar Award. *Neon Rainbow.* New York: Pocket Books, 1987. *Heaven's Prisoners.* New York: Pocket Books, 1988. *Burning Angel.* New York: Hyperion, 1995. New Iberia's charming cajun detective Dave Robichaux makes many forays into New Orleans.

Butler, Robert Olen. *A Good Scent from Strange Mountain.* New York: Henry Holt, 1992. Compelling 1992 Pulitzer Prize–winning short stories set in the local Vietnamese community.

Capote, Truman. *Music for Chameleons.* New York: Random House, 1975. A young boy's experience of New Orleans.

Chopin, Kate. *The Awakening.* Amherst, NY: Prometheus Press, 1996. A poignant tale of a 19th-century Creole wife who must come to grips with her own sexuality.

Edwards, Louis *N.* New York: Dutton, 1997. A mystery set in an African-American bookshop.

Faulkner, William. *Mosquitoes.* New York: Liveright, 1955. The swinging set of the 1920s.

Gilchrist, Ellen. *In the Land of Dreamy Dreams.* Fayetteville: University of Arkansas Press, 1985. An anthology of short stories with recurring characters. They provide one of the strongest portraits of contemporary Uptown/old-line society.

Grau, Shirley Ann. *Keepers of the House.* Baton Rouge: LSU Press, 1995. *House on Coliseum Street.* Baton Rouge: LSU Press, 1996.

Hambly, Barbara. *Freeman of Color.* New York: Bantam, 1997. A well-known sci-fi writer switches genre in this tale of murder and betrayal set against a backdrop of the Quadroon Ballroom in 1833.

Leonard, Elmore. *Bandits.* New York: Warner Books, 1988. A contemporary adventure that crosses all social lines.

Llewellyn, Michael. *Twelfth Night.* New York: Kensington, 1997. A flowery antebellum tale of repression, forbidden romance, and sexual oppression set in 1857 upper-class French Creole society.

Martin, Valerie. *A Recent Martyr.* Boston: Houghton-Mifflin, 1987. The New Orleans Catholic culture of the future.

Miller, John, and Genevieve Anderson, Ed. *New Orleans Stories.* San Francisco: Chronicle Books, 1992. A collection of comments and descriptions of the city by a few dozen of America's finest writers.

Percy, Walker. *The Moviegoer.* New York: Knopf, 1960. A suburban stockbroker uses Mardi Gras as a metaphor for finding meaning in life.

Rice, Anne. *Interview with the Vampire.* New York: Ballantine Books, 1976. *The Feast of All Saints.* New York: Simon & Schuster, 1979. A tale of some of the free people of color before the Civil War. *The Vampire Lestat.* New York: Knopf, 1976. *The Queen of the Damned.* New York: Knopf, 1988. *Witching Hour.* New York: Knopf, 1990. *Lasher.* New York: Random House, 1993. The poetry and witchcraft of four generations of one family. The story is set in the author's own Garden District mansion. *Memnoch, the Devil.* New York: Random House, 1995. Fifth and last Vampire Lestat book.

Robbins, Tom. *Jitterbug Perfume.* New York: Bantam Books, 1984.

Saxon, Lyle. *Fabulous New Orleans.* Gretna: Pelican, 1988. Mardi Gras through the eyes of a boy and other episodes involving voodoo and plagues. *LaFitte the Pirate.* Gretna: Pelican Publishing Company, 1989. A romantic folktale of the glamorous rogue.

Skinner, Robert. *Skin Deep, Blood Red.* New York: Kensington, 1997. A mixed-race detective passes for white in this noire tale of jazz joints and murder in 1936.

Smith, Julie. *New Orleans Mourning.* New York: Ivy, 1990. *Axeman's Jazz.* New York: Ivy, 1991. *Jazz Funeral.* New York: Ivy, 1993. *New Orleans Beat.* New York: Ivy, 1994. *House of Blues.* New York: Ballantine Fawcett, 1995. *Kindness of Strangers.* New York: Ivy, 1996. *Crescent City Kill.* New York: Ballantine

Fawcett, 1997. The Edgar Award-winning Smith's mystery series, featuring queen-sized female NOPD detective Skip Langdon and a cast of memorable local charaters.

Toole, John Kennedy. *A Confederacy of Dunces.* Baton Rouge: LSU Press, 1987. Winner of Pulitzer Prize. Ignatius Riley personifies the term "Big Easy."

Williams, Tennessee. *A Streetcar Named Desire.* Copyright 1947 by Tennessee Williams, reprinted by New Directions. The well-known play portraying a less-than-happy couple dealing with the wife's bizarre sister.

Wiltz, Chris. *Glass House.* Baton Rouge: Louisiana State University Press, 1994. The complexity of racial friendships and fear in the Garden District.

■ HOME & GARDEN

The eight-volume *New Orleans Architecture Series* is the definitive record of the architectural treasures of the city. Most of the books were written in the 1970s and '80s by well-known architects and preservationists. They are available through Pelican Publishing in Gretna; (504) 368-1175.

Mitchell, William R., Jr. and James R. Lockhart, photographer. *Classic New Orleans.* Savannah, GA: A Golden Coast Book, Martin-St. Martin Publishing Company, 1993. Photographs of the interior and exterior of classic New Orleans homes.

Seidenberg, Charlotte. *The New Orleans Garden.* Jackson: University of Mississippi Press, 1993. *The Wildlife Garden.* Jackson: University of Mississippi Press, 1995. Beautiful prose written by a knowledgeable naturalist.

Sexton, Richard, and Randolf Delehanty. *New Orleans: Elegance and Decadence.* San Francisco: Chronicle Books, 1993. The essence of New Orleans style told with distinctive voice and vision.

■ HISTORY

Barry, John. *Rising Tide.* New York: Simon & Schuster, 1997. Compelling reading about the catastrophic 1927 flood.

Bellocq. *Photographs from the Red Light District of New Orleans.* New York: Random House, 1996.

Chase, John Churchill. *Frenchman, Desire, Good Children.* New York: Simon & Schuster, 1997. A humorous and enlightening look at the city's history via the origins of its unique street names.

Garvey, Joan B. and Mary Lou Widmer. *Beautiful Crescent.* New Orleans: Garmer Press, 1997.

■ CHILDREN'S BOOKS

Amos, Berthe. *The Cajun Gingerbread Boy.* New York: Hyperion, 1997. A detachable cardboard gingerbread boy leads three to seven year olds on a series of local adventures in this classic.

Dartez, Cecilia Casrall. The *Jenny Giraffe* Series. Gretna: Pelican. A delightful local series for the under-eight set.

Fontenont, Mary Alice. The *Clovis the Crawfish* Series. Gretna: Pelican. The 14-book series uses Cajun folk wisdom to help a crawfish handle life's problems.

McConduit, Denise Walter. The *D.J.* Series. Gretna: Pelican. An adorable black kid leads children on a series of New Orleans festival adventures.

Rice, James. *The Cajun Night Before Christmas.* Gretna: Pelican, 1973.

■ LOUISIANA COOKING

Chase, Leah. *The Dooky Chase Cookbook.* Gretna: Pelican, 1991. Creole-of-color heritage, history, and recipes by one of the city's premier chefs.

Folse, John. *The Evolution of Cajun & Creole Cuisine.* Gonzales, Louisiana: Chef, 1989. *Plantation Celebration.* Gonzales, Louisiana: Chef, 1994. *Chef John Folse's Louisiana Sampler: Recipes from Fairs and Festivals.* Gonzales, Louisiana: Chef, 1996. *Something Old & Something New: Louisiana Cooking with a Change of Heart.* Gonzales, Louisiana: Chef, 1997. Easy-to-follow recipes that cross Creole and Cajun lines.

The Junior League of Baton Rouge. *River Road Recipes.* Baton Rouge: Junior League, 1959. Louisiana home cooking at its finest in this granddaddy of all charity cookbooks in America.

The Junior League of New Orleans. *The Plantation Cookbook.* New Orleans: B. E. Trice Publishing, Inc., 1992. A staple for local cookssince the 1970s.

Lagasse, Emeril, and Jessie Tirsch. *Emeril's New Orleans Cooking.* New York: William Morrow & Co., Inc., 1993. *Louisiana: Real and Rustic.* New York: William Morrow & Co., Inc., 1993. By the innovative chef/proprietor of the renowned warehouse district restaurant Emeril's.

Prudhomme, Enola. *Low Calorie Cajun Cooking.* New York: Hearst Books, 1991. *Low Fat Favorites.* New York: Hearst Books, 1994. Chef Paul's sister dishes up the goodies without the fat.

■ MUSIC

Armstrong, Louis. *Satchmo: My Life in New Orleans.* New York: Da Capo Press, 1986. The jazz legend's own candid story.

Bechet, Sidney. *Treat It Gentle.* New York: Da Capo Press, 1960. The fascinating autobiography of one of New Orleans's jazz greats.

Berry, Jason, Jonathan Foose, and Tad Jones. *Up From The Cradle of Jazz: New Orleans Music Since World War II.* Athens: The University of Georgia, 1986. A behind-the-scenes look at the Dew Drop Inn and the early careers of such legends as Fats Domino and the Neville Brothers.

Carter, William. *Preservation Hall: Music from the Heart.* New York: W. W. Norton, 1991. Traditional jazz revealed with interviews and compassion.

Friedlander, Lee. *The Jazz People of New Orleans.* New York: Pantheon, 1992. Photographs of the city's jazz legends and marching bands, with a personal afterword on the jazz mecca by expert Whitney Balliett.

Rose, Al. *Storyville, New Orleans.* Tuscaloosa: University of Alabama, 1967. The music and life of this district are described by a well-known authority on jazz.

Smith, Michael P. *A Joyful Noise: A Celebration of New Orleans Music.* Dallas: Taylor, 1990. Smith's black and white photographs pay homage to the music culture of the streets of New Orleans.

Smith, Michael P. and Allison Miner. *Jazz Fest Memories.* Gretna: Pelican, 1997. Affectionate memories of the early days of the fest, coupled with the color photographs of a veteran chronicler of the local musical scene.

■ SPIRITUALISM AND VOODOO

Saxon, Lyle, Edward Dreyer, and Robert Tallant. *Gumbo Ya Ya: The Folklore of Louisiana.* Gretna: Pelican, 1987. Folktales and history reveal as much about the authors as about their subjects.

Smith, Michael P. *Spirit World.* Gretna: Pelican, 1984. The rituals of the Spiritual churches are revealed in Smith's brilliant black and white images.

Tallant, Robert. *Voodoo in New Orleans.* Gretna: Pelican, 1983. *Voodoo Queen Marie Lauveau.* Gretna: Pelican, 1983.

■ GUIDEBOOKS

Access Guide. New York: Harper Collins, 1996.

Dickinson, Joy. *Haunted City: Unauthorized Guide to the Magical Magnificent New Orleans of Anne Rice.* New Orleans: Carol Publishing Group, 1995. A very good guide for lovers of Anne Rice, vampires, and the darker side of life.

Fodor's New Orleans. New York, Fodor's Travel Publications, 1997.

Fonseca, Mary. *Weekend Getaways in Louisiana.* Gretna: Pelican, 1996. Well researched, even giving advice on which hotel rooms to choose.

Fry, Macon and Julie Psner. *Cajun Country Guide.* Gretna: Pelican. 1991. A must for any visitor to the Cajun country.

Heard, Malcolm. *French Quarter Manual: An Architectural Guide to New Orleans' Vieux Carre.* Tulane School of Architecture/University of Mississippi Press, 1997. The architecture of the quarter meticulously documented by a noted local architect and passionate preservationist.

Holl, Shelley N. C. *Louisiana Dayride.* Jackson: University of Mississippi Press, 1995. The popular local columnist shares a plethora of insider tips for excursions to the city's environs.

Pitre, Glen and Michele Benoit. *Country Roads of Louisiana.* Oaks, PA: Country Roads Press, 1996. Award-winning filmmaker and native of Cut-off, LA provides 169 pages of detailed highway-by-highway road guide information for the serious road tripster.

Sternberg, Mary Ann. *Along the River Road.* Baton Rouge: LSU Press, 1996. A comprehensive, 300-page guide to the history of the River Road plantations and the communities that border the river, complete with black and white photographs and excellent driving tours.

Toledano, Roulhac. *The National Trust Guide to New Orleans.* New York: John Wiley & Sons, 1996. An architectural resource for the serious preservationist.

I   N   D   E   X

COMPASS AMERICAN GUIDES

mpass American Guides are compelling, full-color portraits of America
travelers who want to understand the soul of their destinations. In each
de, an accomplished local expert recounts history, culture, and useful
ormation in a text rife with personal anecdotes and interesting details.
endid four-color images by an area photographer bring the region or
to life.

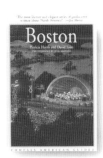

"This splendid series provides exactly the sort of historical and cultural detail about North American
destinations that curious-minded travelers need."
— *Washington Post*

Boston (1st Edition)
1-878-86776-8
$18.95 ($26.50 Can)

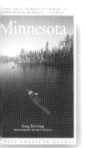

"This is a series that constantly stuns us; our whole past book reviewer
experience says no guide with photos this good
should have writing this good. But it does."
— *New York Daily News*

nesota (1st Edition)
78-86748-2
95 ($26.50 Can)

"Of the many guidebooks on the market few are as
visually stimulating, as thoroughly researched or as lively written
as the Compass American Guides series."
— *Chicago Tribune*

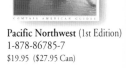

"Good to read ahead of time, then take along so
you don't miss anything."
— *San Diego Magazine*

Pacific Northwest (1st Edition)
1-878-86785-7
$19.95 ($27.95 Can)

"Compass has developed a series with beautiful color photos and a descriptive
text enlivened by literary excerpts from travel writers past and present."
— *Publishers Weekly*

ska (1st Edition)
78-86777-6
95 ($26.50 Can)

Compass American Guides are available in general and travel bookstores, or may be
ordered directly by calling (800) 733-3000. Compass American Guides are available
at special discounts for bulk purchases for sales promotions or premiums. Special
editions, including personalized covers and corporate imprints, can be created in
ge quantities for special needs. For more information, write to Special Marketing, Fodor's Travel Publica-
ns, 201 E. 50th St., New York, NY 10022; or call (800) 800-3246.

COMPASS AMERICAN GUIDES

Critics, Booksellers, and Travelers All Agree You're Lost Without a Compass

Arizona (4th Edition)
0-679-03388-2
$18.95 ($26.50 Can)

Chicago (2nd Edition)
1-878-86780-6
$18.95 ($26.50 Can)

Colorado (3rd Edition)
1-878-86781-4
$18.95 ($26.50 Can)

Hawaii (3rd Edition)
1-878-86791-1
$18.95 ($26.50 Can)

Wine Country (1st Edition)
1-878-86784-9
$18.95 ($26.50 Can)

Montana (3rd Edition)
1-878-86797-0
$18.95 ($26.50 Can)

Oregon (2nd Edition)
1-878-86788-1
$18.95 ($26.50 Can)

New Orleans (3rd Editio
0-679-03597-4
$18.95 ($26.50 Can)

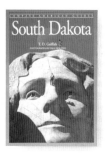

South Dakota (2nd Edition)
1-878-86747-4
$18.95 ($26,50 Can)

Southwest (2nd Edition)
0-679-00035-6
$18.95 ($26.50 Can)

Texas (2nd Edition)
1-878-86798-9
$18.95 ($26.50 Can)

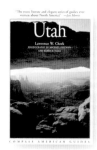

Utah (4th Edition)
0-679-00030-5
$18.95 ($26.50 Can)

Available at your local bookstore, or call (800) 733-3000 to order.

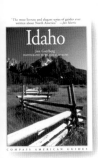

Idaho (1st Edition)
1-878-86778-4
$18.95 ($26.50 Can)

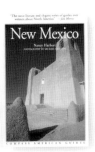

New Mexico (2nd Edition)
1-878-86783-0
$18.95 ($26.50 Can)

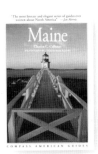

Maine (2nd Edition)
1-878-86796-2
$18.95 ($26.50 Can)

Manhattan (2nd Edition)
1-878-86794-6
$18.95 ($26.50 Can)

Las Vegas (5th Edition)
0-679-00015-1
$18.95 ($26.50 Can)

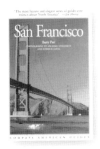

San Francisco (4th Edition)
1-878-86792-X
$18.95 ($26.50 Can)

Santa Fe (2nd Edition)
0-679-03389-0
$18.95 ($26.50 Can)

South Carolina (2nd Edition)
0-679-03599-0
$18.95 ($26.50 Can)

Virginia (2nd Edition)
1-878-86795-4
$18.95 ($26.50 Can)

Washington (1st Edition)
1-878-86758-X
$17.95 ($25.00 Can)

Wisconsin (2nd Edition)
1-878-86749-0
$18.95 ($26.50 Can)

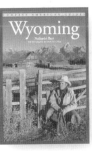

Wyoming (3rd Edition)
0-679-00034-8
$18.95 ($26.50 Can)

SYNDEY BYRD

■ ABOUT THE AUTHOR

Bethany Ewald Bultman has never ceased being an enthusiastic tourist in New Orleans, even after moving there in 1973. She first fell in love with the city as a child when she started making monthly trips from her home in Natchez, Mississippi with her parents. Her articles on food, design, travel, architecture, and ethnic culture have appeared in such publications as *Town & Country, Elle Decor, American Heritage, House Beautiful,* and *Travel & Leisure.* She served as a contributing editor for *House & Garden* 1975–1993, and has written *The Joys of Entertaining* which she co-authored with Bev Church (Abbeville Press, 18th printing, 1998), *Reflections of the South* (C&B, 2nd edition, 1997). and *Redneck Heaven* (Bantam, 1997).

■ ABOUT THE PHOTOGRAPHERS

Richard Sexton's images of architecture, interiors, and gardens have appeared in *Abitare, Home, Interiors,* the *Los Angeles Times Magazine,* the *New York Times, Southern Accents,* and *Smithsonian,* among others. He is the author and photographer of *The Cottage Book* (1989), *In the Victorian Style* (1991) and *New Orleans: Elegance and Decadence* (1993), all published by Chronicle Books. His most recent book, *Parallel Utopias,* was published by Chronicle in 1995.

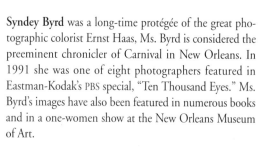

DONN YOUNG

Syndey Byrd was a long-time protégée of the great photographic colorist Ernst Haas, Ms. Byrd is considered the preeminent chronicler of Carnival in New Orleans. In 1991 she was one of eight photographers featured in Eastman-Kodak's PBS special, "Ten Thousand Eyes." Ms. Byrd's images have also been featured in numerous books and in a one-women show at the New Orleans Museum of Art.